AF706506

ENDING CUSTODIAL TORTURE

Insights, Global Practices, and Tech-Driven Approach to Accountability in Law Enforcement

DR. RAVI SHANKAR AYYANAR IPS

STARDOM BOOKS

www.StardomBooks.com

STARDOM BOOKS
112 Bordeaux Ct.
Coppell, TX 75019, USA

Copyright © 2026 by DR. RAVI SHANKAR AYYANAR IPS

All rights reserved. No part of this book may be reproduced or used in any manner without written permission of the copyright owner except for the use of quotations in a book review

FIRST EDITION MAY 2026

STARDOM BOOKS, LLC.
112 Bordeaux Ct. Coppell, TX 75019, USA

www.stardombooks.com

Stardom Books
United States and India

The author and publishers have made all reasonable efforts to contact copyright holders for permission and apologize for any omissions or errors in the form of credits given. Corrections may be made to future editions.

ENDING CUSTODIAL TORTURE
Insights, Global Practices, and Tech-Driven Approach to Accountability in Law Enforcement

DR. RAVI SHANKAR AYYANAR IPS

P. 352
cm. : 13.97 X 21.59

Category: LAW088000 Law : Trial Practice
LAW111000 Law : Judicial Power

ISBN: 978-1-957456-91-1

DEDICATION

To the Voiceless who never returned Home.
To the Families who continue to seek justice despite unending silence.
To the brave Advocates, Lawyers, Journalists, and Human Rights Defenders, who stand against injustice, often at great personal cost.
May this work serve as a reminder that every life matters and that dignity must never be surrendered even in custody.
This book stands as a call for reform, accountability, and the unyielding protection of Human Life within the framework of Justice.
And to my own family – my wife, Dr. Sumita, MCh, Professor of Plastic Surgery, whose unwavering support gave me strength and our Twin sons, Dr. Mehul & Praful, whose innocence inspires my fight for a more humane world.
Dedicated to my Late father who inculcated in me discipline, devotion to service and excellence in whatever I do.

ACKNOWLEDGMENTS

This book is an outcome of my doctoral research on custodial deaths, a subject that is as sensitive as it is significant to the rule of law, human rights, and the functioning of criminal justice institutions. The journey from a PhD thesis to a book has been both intellectually demanding and emotionally engaging, and it would not have been possible without the support and encouragement of many individuals and institutions.

I express my deepest gratitude to my research supervisor Prof. Brahmanandam, PhD (Retd.), Dean and Head of the Department of Commerce and Business Management at Nagarjuna University for his invaluable guidance, critical insights, and constant encouragement throughout the course of my doctoral work also Prof.R. Siva Rama Prasad, Dean, Faculty of Commerce & Management, Chairman, Board of Studies of Commerce and Management Studies. I also thank Prof. C. Beena, former Head of the Department of Psychology at Osmania University, and Dr. Prakash Katakam, Professor at Indira College of Pharmacy, Nanded, for their support and valuable inputs on Psychological Variables included in the study. My special gratitude goes to Mr. G. Shubhakar, K. Raghu, Additional Superintendent of Police (Retired), and Sk. Raheem, who helped by typing the manuscript and encouraged me throughout to ensure the successful completion of this work.

I thank my wife, Dr. Sumita Shankar, and my sons, Dr Mehul and Praful, for their moral support and for contributing to the success of my thesis. Their encouragement sustained me through moments of intellectual fatigue and emotional strain.

Above all, this work is dedicated to the principles of justice, dignity, and constitutional accountability. If this book contributes in any measure to informed discourse, institutional introspection, or policy improvement on custodial practices and human rights, the effort invested in this research will be truly worthwhile.

CONTENTS

ABSTRACT

Custodial deaths remain a serious issue for everyone. According to Article 5 of the Universal Declaration of Human Rights, no one should face torture or cruel, inhuman, or degrading treatment in detention. Numerous incidents show police officers abusing their authority and risking people's lives. This article emphasizes that nobody should be subjected to such treatment or punishment while in custody. Additionally, officers have reported that stress from their duties can harm their health.

Physiological stress response systems track cardiovascular and hormonal reactions during critical incident scenarios. Digital transformation has radically changed how we organize and monitor our daily lives. However, poor security system monitoring can lead to illegal activities, physical abuse, and suicidal behaviors. New technologies, methods, and ideas have significantly transformed the field of law enforcement. Adopting emerging technologies, such as the Internet of Things (IoT), artificial intelligence, facial recognition, and innovative lockup layouts, can enhance the monitoring, mapping, and management of detention facilities.

The author investigates custodial deaths in Andhra Pradesh, India, examining various factors such as physiological, psychological, legal, and organizational influences on police officers' behavior and psychological profiles during custody.

This led to the development of the "Vulnerability Index" and "Custody Quotient." The "Vulnerability Index" assesses police officers, while the "Custody Quotient" evaluates police station capacity to ensure smooth detention and prevent custodial deaths.

The study also proposes technological solutions to improve lockup monitoring through structural and environmental enhancements.

In this study, a non-probability, convenience sampling method was employed, focusing on purposeful and criterion-based cases to explore and understand the issue. The key findings reveal that 60% of the accused (sample) are aged 35 to 44, while 40% are aged 20 to 35. Characteristics of the accused officers, including physical issues like peptic ulcers, psychological factors such as anxiety and cognitive styles, and other concerns like family problems, appear to have influenced custodial deaths. The study highlights a hostile and unsupportive environment in police stations where these deaths occurred. Such an environment contributed to dissatisfaction and low productivity among officers, leading to deviant work behaviors.

There is a lack of compliance with the DK Basu guidelines during arrests. The vulnerability indices ranged from 0.246 to 0.495, showing that all accused police officers fell into the red zone and might not be suitable to handle custody and investigation of detainees moving forward. The highest value observed is 1.00, representing 100% compliance. Thus, the proposed "Vulnerability Index" helps determine whether a police officer can effectively manage detainee custody and prevent custodial deaths. Likewise, the "Custody Quotient" for each police station—a comprehensive measure considering lockup facilities, personnel, training, psychological profile, organizational vulnerability, and medical factors—should be evaluated by courts before assigning custody or arrest powers to a police station for investigations.

Proposed emerging technologies include IoT, which aims to enable real-time monitoring of prisons, lock-ups, and prisoner transport vehicles. Software applications like B-Safe, Fight Back, I-Follow, Red Alert (RA), and DISHA are designed to prevent illegal arrests, detention, and HR violations by providing precise details of arrest times and locations, along with witness confirmation.

The suggested model lock-up features aim to reduce illicit, aggressive, and suicidal behaviors among accused or suspects, enhance police conduct toward detainees, and support law enforcement efforts.

"This book will help law enforcement better understand how to address challenges, enhance the investigative process, and foster stronger communication throughout the justice system. Additionally, this report highlights strategies that encourage collective problem-solving and positive reforms within the justice system, rather than focusing on assigning blame."

INTRODUCTION

"To deny people their human rights is to challenge the very humanity."

— Nelson Mandela,

South African civil rights activist

Background

The author is an IPS officer with extensive experience in police management. He has served in the police department for over 34 years in various capacities, including with the United Nations, where he was involved in addressing war crimes. He is also a medical doctor possessing an MBBS degree from JIPMER Pondicherry. He has a Master's Degree in Police Management (MDPM) from Osmania University. Based on his professional experience, he has chosen the proposed study on Police Management, focusing on the managerial and behavioral aspects of custodial deaths, related problems, and their remedies.

We Indians are aware that Demon Narakasura was born to Bhudevi (Goddess Earth and Lord Varaha Swamy (incarnation of God Vishnu), and he kept custody of 16,000 women. Lord Krishna fought a war with him, and all of them were released from the custody of Demon Narakasura.

According to Hindu mythology, Devaki, Kamsa's sister, was married to Vasudeva. Following a prophecy that their eighth child would kill him, the tyrant Kamsa imprisoned them, and in the custody of Kamsa, they gave birth to Lord Krishna, who was later shifted to where Nanda and Yashoda brought him up.

In both cases, the custody is as per the whims and fancies of the kings. Nowadays, it will not be like the above.

Many human rights organizations are involved and seek to have the custody declared illegal and for all of them to be released, etc.

When we look at Policing, it dates back to ancient times.

Before 1750 BC, law enforcement was called "kin policing," where tribes or clans handled their own discipline. There was no neutral third party, so these actions often turned into violent, long-running "blood feuds" between families or people.

Around the same time, the Code of *Hammurabi* was established, documenting 282 rules for social conduct and their corresponding punishments. This set of laws laid the early groundwork for legal justice. By 1000 BC, *Mosaic Law* introduced a more predictable and rational legal framework where the ruling class was not the source of the law. Together, these two systems built the foundation for the modern policing structures we use today.

Peisistratus ruled Athens from 605 to 527 BC and is often credited with creating formal policing. As Greek cities grew, he replaced family feuds with a public model. This switch ended kin policing and led to the formation of Athens' first police force, often called the first secret service.

Augustus Caesar, the first Roman Emperor, established the urban cohorts of his Praetorian Guard to maintain order in the city. As crime grew worse, he also founded the Vigils, a firefighting and crime-prevention group. These vigils could protect citizens and make arrests.

Policing in Ancient Rome

In 6 CE, Emperor Augustus started the **Vigiles Urbani**, Rome's first public security and firefighting team. At first, they were freed slaves. They patrolled at night to handle minor crimes, but serious offenders were referred to the stronger **Urban Cohorts** or the **Praetorian Guard**.

The **Urban Cohorts** were a strong, armed group that kept order and controlled riots. The Praetorian Guard mostly protected the emperor but sometimes assisted with major policing duties.

Roman soldiers were also sent to fight bandits and protect the interests of the ruling class. Like other ancient societies, the Romans used prisons such as the **Carcer** as short-term holding places. They mainly held people until their trial or execution, not for long-term punishment or rehabilitation. From 6 AD through the 12th century, Rome maintained a public police force that patrolled the city around the clock. Following the fall of the Roman Empire, monarchs became the primary law enforcement authorities. Between the 12th and 18th centuries in England, kings appointed sheriffs who were assisted by constables in the service of legal documents. During this time, the *posse comitatus* allowed boys as young as fifteen to volunteer to hunt for felons; however, this reliance on young, untrained volunteers led to widespread issues with intoxication and corruption. This system ultimately favored the wealthy, who could afford private security, while leaving the poor without adequate protection. In ancient times, the modern concept of **"Police custody"** did not exist. Law enforcement was instead decentralized, harsh, and heavily influenced by a person's social standing. Rather than a standard punishment, imprisonment served primarily as a temporary means of holding individuals until their trial or final sentencing.

Facets of Custody management

Common characteristics of ancient law enforcement

In ancient times, justice was usually local. People had to handle their own legal problems. Sometimes, communities formed groups to help keep their area safe and orderly. Prisons were just holding places for people waiting for trial, torture, or execution. Only the rich or the political might stay longer, sometimes with their own helpers. How someone was treated by the law depended a lot on their social class.

In **ancient India**, the caste system meant that higher-caste Brahmans often received lighter sentences for the same crimes as lower-caste Shudras. (Manusmriti) Similarly, **ancient Mesopotamia** employed a layered social hierarchy that provided varying levels of legal protection based on an individual's rank.

Punishments were meant to be **harsh and public**, focusing on pain and shame. Visible penalties like branding, mutilation, and flogging were common. Prisoners were often put in stocks or pillories, where the community ridiculed them.

Policing in Ancient India

During the Vedic period, policing was handled by village councils. In the Mauryan period, a central system guided by Kautilya's Arthashastra was used. This setup had specialized officials who oversaw various aspects of law enforcement and public order. Ancient Indian law had tough punishments, like cutting body parts or execution, and sometimes used trials by fire or water. Prisons were built near busy roads so the public could see inmates suffer and be warned against crime.

Ancient Egypt

During the New Kingdom, the **Medjay, the first Nubian scouts, served as elite guards of** tombs and temples and conducted criminal investigations. A central system grew, with state officials as investigators under the **vizier**, who had the power to order arrests and torture. The government focused on its own crimes, but private citizens still had to start their own cases.

The English law enforcement system reached the North American colonies, where governors appointed sheriffs for each colony. In this system, sheriffs focused less on daily policing and more on tasks like collecting taxes, overseeing elections, and managing buildings. Constables—chosen by the community—handled direct duties like serving warrants and moving prisoners. Local grand juries of men investigated crimes reported by victims. General patrol work went to the 'watch,' a group of male volunteers responsible for stopping fires and preventing crime.

A Chronological History of Policing and Justice

Ancient Origins and Kin Policing (Pre-1750 BC)

Before 1750 BC, law enforcement was rooted in "kin policing," where tribes or clans managed their own internal discipline. Without a neutral third party to intervene, these efforts frequently devolved into violent, long-running "blood feuds" between families. Justice was a decentralized responsibility, relying on "self-help," in which victims and their families were expected to pursue their own legal recourse.

The Rise of Written Law (c. 1750 BC – 1000 BC)

The Code of Hammurabi established 282 specific rules for social conduct and their corresponding punishments, laying the groundwork for formal legal justice. By 1000 BC, Mosaic Law introduced a more predictable, rational framework where the law existed independently of the ruling class. Together, these systems formed the foundation for modern policing.

Ancient Egypt's Specialized Forces (New Kingdom)

In Egypt, the Medjay—originally Nubian desert scouts—evolved into an elite security force that guarded royal tombs and conducted criminal investigations. This era saw a shift toward a centralized system where state officials acted as investigators under the vizier's authority. While the state aggressively pursued crimes against the government, private citizens were generally responsible for initiating their own legal proceedings for personal matters.

Classical Greece and the Father of Policing (605–527 BC)

Peisistratus, the ruler of Athens, is often called the "father of formal policing." As Greek city-states expanded, he replaced family blood feuds with a "public" municipal model. This shift ended the era of kin policing and led to the creation of Athens' first police corps, which functioned much like the original secret service.

Ancient India and the Mauryan Empire (c. 322–185 BC)

While policing began with local village councils during the Vedic period, the Mauryan Empire developed a highly centralized system based on Kautilya's *Arthashastra.* This framework employed specialized officials to oversee public order. However, justice remained harsh; ancient Indian law utilized mutilation and "ordeals by fire or water" to determine guilt, often using public prisons near major roads to shame inmates.

The Roman Empire's Layered Security (27 BC – 12th Century AD)

Emperor Augustus created a sophisticated, multi-tiered system:

- **The Vigiles:** Rome's first public security and firefighting unit, patrolling at night to handle minor crimes.
- **The Urban Cohorts:** A heavily armed, quasi-military unit tasked with riot control.
- **The Praetorian Guard:** The emperor's personal security, which occasionally handled high-level political policing.
- **The Carcer:** Like most ancient civilizations, Roman prisons were only temporary holding pens for those awaiting trial or execution, not for long-term rehabilitation.

The English Middle Ages and the Colonial Transition (12th–18th Century)

Following the fall of Rome, English monarchs appointed sheriffs and constables to maintain order. This system relied on the *posse comitatus*—volunteers as young as fifteen—which often led to corruption and ineffective protection for the poor.

This model was eventually exported to the North American colonies. In the colonies, sheriffs focused on administrative duties, such as tax collection, while elected constables handled warrants. Daily patrol work was left to the "watch," a group of local male volunteers responsible for deterring both crime and fire.

The Universal Role of Social Status

Throughout these eras, an individual's social class dictated their treatment. From the Mesopotamian hierarchy to the Indian caste system—where Brahmans received more lenient sentences than

Shudras—legal protection and the severity of physical punishments (such as branding or flogging) were almost always determined by rank. The discourse of development has undergone a paradigm shift in the past few decades. Human development has become a central debate in contemporary developmental thinking. As the *first Human Development Report* (1990)[1] has argued, "human beings are the real wealth of a nation, and the basic objective of development is to create an enabling environment for enhancing their achievements, freedoms, and capabilities, including self-respect and human rights." In recent years, the issue of governance has moved to the forefront of the agenda for sustained human development. Instances from many countries show that while good governance can help secure human well-being and sustained development, it is equally important to recognize that poor governance could well erode individual capabilities, as well as institutional and community capacities to meet even the basic needs of sustenance for large segments of the population.[2]

It has now been fully realized that poverty is not merely the result of a bad economy; it is also due to poor governance. Being voiceless and powerless makes access to justice extremely difficult for the poor and disadvantaged people, making them easy prey to the state and its agencies, like the police and the elite class, by denying them access.

Contextualizing Custodial Violence

Custodial violence and abuse of police power have emerged as a significant issue of human rights concern and are one of the root obstacles to democracy and the development of human well-being

1. Human Development Report,1990
2. National Human Development Report 2001

in contemporary societies. Torture-caused custodial violence has devastating effects on physical and mental health, as well as the social functioning of individuals, their children, families, communities, and society at large. The victims remain in perpetual fear and horror whenever they remember their custodial agony, hatred, and trauma. They are probably never able to lead a normal life in many parts of the world.

However, the practice of custodial violence in developing countries like India is very complex. A large number of cases of police brutality take place not because of individual aberrations but because of systemic compulsions. The practice is more widespread and has gone unchecked since the British days, due to the tacit support of senior police officials, bureaucrats, politicians, and the judiciary. This practice also enjoys the support of a large section of the public in the mistaken belief that it is necessary to maintain law and order effectively.

In order to extract confessions, torture was so endemic in India that the colonial rulers, when enacting criminal laws for the country, decided to make all confessions to police officers inadmissible as evidence in the court of law. After Independence, the constitutional and statutory provisions safeguarded the life and liberty of any individual in custody, including rights against self-incrimination. Incidents of custodial crimes have become a disturbing factor in society.

In recent years, custodial crimes have drawn the attention of the public, the media, the legislature, the judiciary, and even the National Human Rights Commission (NHRC). Nevertheless, judicial activism, widespread media coverage, initiatives taken by the NHRC, and civil society intervention have shown concern for combating torture and upholding human dignity.

However, custodial crimes have not only increased in manifold dimensions but also become a part of the police practice of interrogation these days.

Studies indicate that generally, the victims of custodial crimes are poor, women, children, and disadvantaged people; those who belong to the weaker and vulnerable sections of society. The poor and socially excluded groups and people with little or no political or financial power are unable to protect their interests. Affluent members are not generally subjected to torture, as the police are afraid of their resourcefulness. The members of the weaker or poorer sections of society are arrested informally and kept in police custody for days together without any entry of such arrests in the police records. During the informal detention, they are subjected to torture, which sometimes results in death.

In the event of death in custody, in many cases, the body of the deceased is disposed of stealthily or thrown into a public place, making up a case of suicide or accident. Records are manipulated to protect the police personnel. The relatives or friends of the victims are unable to seek the protection of the law on account of their poverty, ignorance, and illiteracy. Even if voluntary organizations take up their cases or file public interest litigations, no effective or speedy remedy is available to them, leaving the erring officers to go scot-free.

The Supreme Court and High Courts, in their several landmark judgments, upheld that police personnel do indulge in custodial crimes. Through creative interpretation, the higher judiciary has evolved mechanisms for protecting torture victims' rights and their entitlements to compensation. In the leading cases of *Nilabati Behera vs. State of Orissa* and *D.K. Basu vs. State of West Bengal,* the Apex Court held that the claim of sovereign immunity arising out of the state discharging sovereign functions is no defense against acts of violation of constitutionally guaranteed fundamental human rights.

The court further held that "there is a great responsibility on the police authority to ensure that the citizen in its custody is not deprived of his right to life. By the very nature of things, his liberty is circumscribed by the very fact of his confinement. Therefore, his interest in the limited liberty left to him is rather precious. The wrongdoer is accountable, and the state is responsible if a person in police custody is deprived of his life except in accordance with procedures established by law. In this landmark case, the court has judiciously evolved a right to compensation in the context of established unconstitutional deprivation of personal liberty.

Time and again, the higher judiciary has taken a serious view of custodial crimes and issued guidelines as preventive measures. It has also evolved custodial jurisprudence to address the menace of custodial crimes.

The NHRC, since its establishment in 1993, has given new dimensions to exposing custodial crimes in police custody. While dealing with custodial violence cases, the NHRC has adopted a methodology of mandatory reporting of custodial abuse, investigatory or fact-finding of such abuse, compensation to the victims or next of kin against state impunity, and individual accountability of the responsible police personnel. On several occasions, the Commission has criticized law enforcement personnel, medical professionals, public officials, and other persons involved in custody, interrogation of any individual subjected to any form of arrest, detention, or imprisonment, and dehumanizing methods of torture, and treatment of victims of torture, and recommended measures to inculcate a culture of human rights in police custody.

However, the phenomenon of custodial crimes is still ongoing in police custody. According to the NHRC, over the years, most complaints received have pertained to the state of Uttar Pradesh (UP). In its report (2005-06), the Commission commented that the trend continues despite the state of UP having its own state human rights commission.

Human rights NGOs in India have played a significant role through public interest litigation and other initiatives in promoting and protecting human rights, including securing custodial justice. Among them, the People's Union for Civil Liberty (PUCL), the People's Union for Democratic Rights (PUDR), the South Asian Human Rights Documentation Center (SAHRDC), Asian Center for Human Rights (ACHR), Penal Reform and Justice Administration (PRAJA), Common Wealth Human Rights Initiatives (CHRI), the People's Watch, Amnesty International, and Human Rights Watch are worth mentioning. These organizations have done commendable work through fact findings, lobbying, advocacy, research, and documentation of custodial crimes and highlighted torture cases before the courts and human rights commissions, with significant administrative hurdles.

A significant development in the last few years is that some voluntary organizations have come forward to rehabilitate victims of custodial violence and torture in different states. The voluntary organizations include Centre for Care of Torture Victims, Kolkata (West Bengal), Centre for Organization, Research and Education, Manipur (North East), Subodhaya Centre for Rehabilitation of Victims of Torture and Violence (SOSRAC), Delhi, Tibetan Torture Survivors Programme, Dharmashala (Himachal Pradesh),

Torture Prevention Centre India Trust, Cochin(Kerala), Vaan Muhil, Tirunelveli (Tamil Nadu) and Vasavya Mahila Mandali Rehabilitation Centre for Torture, Vijayawada (Andhra Pradesh). These centers analyze multiple problems of victims of custodial torture and provide support services to such victims, which include legal, economic, social, psychological, psychiatric, physiotherapy, and medical aid to the victims and their next-of-kin.

Despite various efforts initiated by the government, non-government organizations, and media to combat custodial crimes, including torture in police custody, torture is endemic in India. This fact is acknowledged by the authorities and widely documented. Police forces are poorly trained in investigation methods and the absolute prohibition of torture and cruel, inhuman, or degrading treatment. Most cases of torture by state officials occur in police custody, and governmental and non-governmental studies widely acknowledge that the police operate in a system that facilitates torture and ill-treatment.

Torture is systematically used in the criminal justice system as an investigative tool. In the increasingly dysfunctional criminal justice system, torture in custody constitutes a vicious circle of deficient interrogation, falsified investigation results, and distrust of the criminal justice system. It appears that there exists a particular perception in India that torture is acceptable under extreme circumstances and for "hardened criminals" and "terrorists."

The overload within the criminal justice system also contributes to public tolerance towards violence as a means of justice. The consequence is a lack of investigation into allegations of torture, let alone of "mere beatings," and impunity for the perpetrators. Corruption within the police also provides a basis for extortion and threats.

It is reported that members of the medical profession refuse to examine torture victims or document injuries, often out of fear and threats. As a result, the number of custodial deaths is alarmingly high. The Supreme Court and High Courts of India, as well as the NHRC, have handed down many recommendations to achieve better prevention against torture and to provide redressal measures for victims. However, it has not led to the eradication of the phenomena of custodial crimes, including torture in police custody.[3]

Conceptual Aspects Of Custodial Torture

Custodial Torture: Definition and Indian Context

Torture, in the standard dictionary, refers to the act and practice of inflicting severe pain on someone as a form of punishment or to compel them to do or say something.

Custodial torture is a form of torture that generally happens when a person is alleged to have committed any crime and is under the custody of law enforcement officials. The Supreme Court has held that Custodial torture is a naked violation of human dignity and degradation, which destroys human personality to a considerable extent.

Custodial torture is a punishable offense under the existing laws, but due to various reasons, the accused do not get convicted. Specific modifications in the law are required, and more critical is the appropriate implementation of existing and newly enacted laws.

3. International Commission of Jurists 2003

Definitions of Custodial Crime

A custodial crime means "To take a person in custody to limit his freedom." Taking advantage of such a situation, the custodian may attempt to commit a crime against the person under custody. Individuals are placed in police custody for various reasons, including arrest, police remand, or unauthorized detention. The most prevalent crimes in police custody are the assault of various types, like rape and murder[4]

According to Custodial Crimes (Prevention, Protection and Compensation),Bill, 2006, Custodial Crime means "an offence caused against any arrested person ora person in custody when that person was in the custody of a police officer or a public servant who has power under any law to arrest and detain a person in custody, by the police officer or the public servant concerned having the custody of that person during that period."

The Supreme Court of India, in the landmark judgment of SAHELI-A Women Resource Center v. Police Commissioner of Delhi (A.I.R. 1990 SC 513), interpreted that "Custodial Crime" is a crime that occurs while a person's liberty is restricted in some ways, either directly or indirectly, by the police. It precisely broadens the meaning of custodial commission of crimes so that it is irrelevant whether or not the injury, torture, or assault occurs within the premises of a police station or police post(chowki); instead, what really matters is the control of the police over victims.

According to the United Nations Special Rapporteur on torture (2008),"Custodial Violence against women very often includes rape and other forms of sexual violence such as threats of rape, touching private parts of a woman, being stripped naked, invasive

---

4. Crime in India1997 published by National Crime Records Bureau

body searches, insults and humiliations that are sexual in nature, etc.

Concept of Police Custody:

Custodial crimes proceed with arrest and detention in police custody. Custody, in its strict sense, means care, safety, and guardianship. The term 'police custody' denotes surveillance or restriction on the movement of the person arrested or detained fully or partially. The police custody commences when a person is arrested. The arrest may be legal or illegal; it may be formal or informal; it may be by words or action. Every arrest amounts to custody, but vice versa is not true. Arrest and custody are not the same in all circumstances. Arrest is a formal mode of taking a person into custody, but a person may also be in custody in other ways.

Whatever the origin or category of custody, it has a necessary consequence: depriving the person arrested or detained of their liberty. A detainee's movement, actions, and even thoughts are under the exclusive control of the custodian. Thus, the personality of a detainee becomes subordinate to the person under whom she/he is placed. This situation of mastery and domination over body and mind generates various types of abuses in the custody of police, called custodial commission of crimes in police custody (Law Commission of India 1985;1994).

Concept Of Police Custody

Unlike ancient detention, which was arbitrary, hierarchy-driven, and often used violence to force confessions, modern police custody is strictly governed by **legal rights** and **due process**.

Today, there is a clear distinction between **custody** (the physical state of being held) and **remand** (the judicial order that puts someone in prison). Custody is split into two types: **police custody** for active investigation and **judicial custody** (jail) while awaiting trial.

Once judicial custody concludes, the accused is either **released on bail** (if eligible) or remains detained until their **trial**. While the court can extend this detention, police require a magistrate's **permission** for further interrogation and are strictly prohibited from using physical harm. The investigation continues until completion, at which point the case officially proceeds to trial.

In judicial custody, an individual is held in prison under a **court's authority** rather than police control. Daily life is governed by a strict **prison manual**, with security supervised by a **judicial magistrate**.

While conditions can be challenging, this state is temporary; detainees are still awaiting **trial** and maintain the right to apply for **bail.**

The core concept of **custody** involves detaining an individual for **protective care**. This principle allows authorities to arrest suspects primarily to ensure **public safety** and protect the community from potential harm.

Police Custody

When police receive a crime report or complaint, an officer arrests the suspect to prevent further illegal activity. This process of bringing the individual to a police station for detention is known as police custody.

This refers to holding a suspect in a police station lock-up for the purpose of detention and interrogation by the investigating officer. By law, this period of custody is strictly limited and cannot exceed 24 hours without further judicial authorization.

When police take a person into custody, **Section 58** of the **Bharatiya Nagarik Suraksha Sanhita (BNSS), 2023** (which replaced the old Section 57 of the Cr.P.C.) requires that the accused be produced before a Magistrate within **24 hours** of their arrest. This 24-hour limit excludes the time necessary for the journey from the place of arrest to the Magistrate's Court. This mandatory procedure acts as a vital safeguard against arbitrary detention, ensuring that any custody beyond the first day is authorized by a judicial authority rather than just the police.

Judicial Custody

In **judicial custody**, an accused person is under the direct legal control of a **Magistrate**. Unlike police custody, where a suspect is held in a police station lockup for active interrogation, individuals in judicial custody are lodged in **jail**.

The key procedural points for judicial custody under the current legal framework are:

Previously governed by Section 167 of the Cr.P.C., this process is now regulated by **Section 187 of the Bharatiya Nagarik Suraksha Sanhita (BNSS), 2023**.

Magistrate's Authority: The Judicial Magistrate has the power to authorize and extend the period of detention from time to time as required for the case.

Interrogation Limits: Once an accused is in judicial custody, police officers cannot interrogate them at will. They must first obtain the Magistrate's explicit permission to conduct any further questioning.

Flexible Remand: Under the new **BNSS** rules, the initial 15 days of police custody no longer have to be continuous; they can now be spread out across the first 40 or 60 days of the total investigation period.

Under the current Indian legal system—governed by the **Bharatiya Nagarik Suraksha Sanhita (BNSS), 2023**, which replaced the CrPC in July 2024—the differences between police and judicial custody are as follows:

Basis of Difference	Police Custody	Judicial Custody
Physical Control	The accused is under the direct physical control of the **police**.	The accused is under the legal custody of the **Magistrate**.
Location	Lodged in a **lock-up** at the police station.	Lodged in a **jail** (prison).
Beginning	Starts immediately upon **arrest** by a police officer.	Starts when a **Magistrate orders** it, typically after the initial 24-hour arrest period.
Procedure & Review	The accused must appear before a Magistrate within **24 hours** of arrest.	The accused is kept in jail until **bail** is granted or the trial concludes.
Interrogation	Police can interrogate the suspect **directly** for investigation.	Police need **explicit court permission** to interrogate the suspect in jail.
Duration(BNSS)	**Total of 15 days**, which can now be split into parts across the first 40 or 60 days of investigation.	**Up to 60 or 90 days** depending on the severity of the crime (90 days for crimes punishable by death, life, or 10+ years).

Table 1.1 Judicial versus police custody

The First "15-Day" Rule in BNSS for Police custody

Under the previous law (CrPC), police custody was generally restricted to the first 15 days of arrest. Under **Section 187 of the BNSS**, the 15-day police custody limit remains, but it can now be spread out in parts across a wider "window" of time:

For serious offenses (punishable by 10+ years, life, or death), these 15 days of police custody may be served at any time within the first **60 days** of detention.

For other offenses, these 15 days can be taken within the first **40 days**.

In criminal law, **custody** occurs when law enforcement restricts an individual's freedom through arrest, detention, or confinement. Because detainees are entirely dependent on the state, officers have a legal **duty of care** to ensure their health and safety.

Article 21 of the Indian Constitution is the cornerstone of fundamental rights, ensuring that **"No person shall be deprived of his life or personal liberty except according to procedure established by law"**

Protection Against Custodial Violence: The court ruled that any custodial torture or maltreatment in police lockups violates the right to live with human dignity under Article 21.

Rights of Prisoners: Even a convict or an undertrial does not lose their fundamental rights. Any physical or mental restraint that exceeds the court's punishment or prison discipline is unconstitutional.

Initially, the Supreme Court took a narrow view of Article 21 (e.g., *A.K. Gopalan case*). However, starting with **Maneka Gandhi v. Union of India (1978)**, the court shifted to a "substantive" approach, requiring that any "procedure established by law" must also be **fair, just, and reasonable**.

The Supreme Court's observation in **D.K. Basu v. State of West Bengal (1997)**—describing custodial death as one of the "worst crimes in a civilized society"—serves as the foundation for modern Indian "custody jurisprudence".

This judgment addressed the systemic issue in which the "protectors" of the law become "perpetrators," often under the shield of authority within the four walls of a police station.

Free Legal Aid: In this case and others like *M.H. Hoskot v. State of Maharashtra*, the court established that the state must provide free legal aid to indigent prisoners to ensure a fair procedure.

Right to Compensation: Later judgments, such as *Nilabati Behera v. State of Orissa*, solidified the right to monetary compensation for victims of custodial violence as a remedy under Article 21.

Current Status of D.K. Basu Guidelines and Implementation

Legislative Integration: Most D.K. Basu guidelines were formally codified into the Code of Criminal Procedure (CrPC) through the 2008 Amendment (Sections 41B, 41C, and 41D) and remain central under the Bharatiya Nagarik Suraksha Sanhita, 2023.

Recent Judicial Reinforcement:

- In **March 2024**, the Supreme Court expressed concern that it is still "forced to restate" these principles, directing all probe agencies to strictly follow arrest norms.
- In **February 2025**, the Court reiterated that informing an arrestee of the **grounds of arrest** is a mandatory constitutional requirement under Article 22(1) and not a mere formality.

- **Continuing Challenges**: Despite these safeguards, the National Human Rights Commission (NHRC) reported **2,739 custodial deaths** in 2024 (155 in police custody), highlighting a persistent gap between judicial guidelines and ground reality.

These landmark judgments define the Indian judiciary's zero-tolerance policy toward extra-judicial killings, establishing that those who are sworn to protect the law must be held to a higher standard of accountability.

1. Death Penalty for Staged Encounters

In **Prakash Kadam v. State of Gujarat (2011)**, the Supreme Court issued a stern warning that policemen involved in fake encounters should face the **death sentence**, categorizing such acts as the "rarest of rare cases".

- **"Contract Killers" in Uniform**: The court observed that if police officers act as "contract killers" for private interests, they behave like predators rather than protectors.
- **The "Nuremberg" Principle**: The Court rejected the defense of "following superior orders," stating that a policeman has a legal duty to refuse an illegal order to perform a fake encounter. Those who do not refuse "should know that the gallows await them".
- **Matsyanyaya (Law of the Jungle)**: Justice Markandey Katju warned that allowing such lawlessness leads to *Matsyanyaya*, where the "big fish devour the small," eventually resulting in the total collapse of the rule of law.

2. The Right to Truth and Accountability

In **Extra Judicial Execution Victim Families' Association (EEVFAM) v. Union of India (2013/2016)**, the Court addressed over 1,500 alleged fake encounters in Manipur, reinforcing that the state cannot use security concerns to bypass constitutional rights.

- **Duty to Investigate**: The Court ruled that every allegation of excessive or retaliatory force by security personnel must be thoroughly investigated, regardless of whether the victim was a "militant" or a civilian.
- **Beyond Compensation**: It established that the next of kin have a "Right to Know the Truth". Mere monetary compensation is not a substitute for criminal accountability and the prosecution of offenders.
- **AFSPA and Accountability**: The judgment clarified that even under the Armed Forces (Special Powers) Act (AFSPA), security forces do not enjoy absolute immunity and must operate within the boundaries of Article 21.
- **Binding Nature of NHRC Orders**: In **January 2025**, the Delhi High Court (in *Kiran Singh v. NHRC*) reaffirmed that recommendations for compensation by the National Human Rights Commission (NHRC) in encounter cases are **binding and legally enforceable**, not merely advisory.
- **Judicial Skepticism of Death Penalty**: While *Prakash Kadam* remains a valid precedent for sentencing, data from **early 2026** shows the Supreme Court has become increasingly cautious, having not confirmed a single death sentence for three consecutive years due to concerns over flawed investigations and "serious procedural lapses" in lower courts.

Article 22 of the Indian Constitution serves as a critical check on state power by providing fundamental safeguards against arbitrary arrest and detention. While it outlines basic procedural rights for ordinary arrests, it also permits "preventive detention"—detention based on the apprehension of a future crime—subject to specific constitutional limits.

1. Protections in Ordinary Arrests (Punitive Detention)

Under Articles 22(1) and 22(2), every person arrested under ordinary criminal law is entitled to:

- **Right to be Informed**: The arrestee must be told the "grounds of arrest" as soon as possible.
- **Right to Legal Counsel**: The individual has a fundamental right to consult and be defended by a legal practitioner of their choice.
- **24-Hour Production Rule**: The arrested person must be produced before the nearest Magistrate within 24 hours (excluding travel time).
- **No Detention Without Judicial Authority**: No person can be kept in custody for more than 24 hours without a specific order from a Magistrate.

2. Preventive Detention Safeguards

Preventive detention is unique to India among many democracies and is often called a "necessary evil". Articles 22(3) to 22(7) provide its framework:

- **Three-Month Limit**: A person cannot be detained for more than **three months** unless an **Advisory Board** (consisting of persons qualified to be High Court judges) finds sufficient cause for extended detention.
- **Communication of Grounds**: The detaining authority must communicate the grounds of detention "as soon as may be" to allow the person to make a representation against the order.

- **Public Interest Exception**: The authority may withhold specific facts if disclosure is deemed contrary to the public interest.
- **Parliamentary Power**: Parliament has the authority to prescribe the maximum period of detention and the procedure for Advisory Board inquiries.

3. Recent Judicial Expansions (2024–2026)

The Supreme Court has recently significantly strengthened these rights, particularly regarding the **form** in which an arrestee must be informed of their grounds:

- **Mandatory Written Grounds**: In the landmark **Mihir Rajesh Shah v. State of Maharashtra (2025)** and **Prabir Purkayastha v. State (2024)** rulings, the Court held that informing an arrestee of the "grounds of arrest" is not a mere formality but a **mandatory constitutional requirement**.
- **The "Two-Hour" Rule**: Written grounds must now be provided to the arrestee in a language they understand, ideally at the time of arrest. In exigent circumstances, they must be provided **at least two hours prior** to being produced before a magistrate for remand.
- **Universal Application**: This requirement for written grounds now applies to **all offenses** under the Bharatiya Nyaya Sanhita (BNS) and to special laws such as the UAPA or PMLA, resolving previous ambiguities.

In addition to the constitutional protections in **Article 22**, the legal landscape for arrest and detention has been updated by the **Bharatiya Nagarik Suraksha Sanhita (BNSS), 2023**, which replaced the CrPC.

Key Enhancements to Arrest Protections

- **Mandatory Written Grounds**: Following the Supreme Court's 2024–2025 rulings (e.g., *Prabir Purkayastha*), the "right to be informed" now strictly requires that the **grounds of arrest be provided in writing** to the arrestee.
- **Right to Inform a Relative**: Under **Section 36 of the BNSS**, the police are now legally mandated to immediately inform a named relative or friend of the arrest and the place where the person is being held.
- **Health and Safety**: The police must ensure the health and safety of the person in custody. For female arrestees, arrests must be made by a **female officer**, and except in exceptional circumstances, no woman can be arrested after sunset or before sunrise.

Preventive Detention Limits

While the Constitution allows for preventive detention, the Courts have added strict layers of "Procedural Safeguards":

- **Strict Construction**: Because it bypasses a trial, courts interpret preventive detention laws very strictly. Even a minor delay in considering a detainee's **representation** can lead to the detention order being quashed.
- **Subjective Satisfaction**: The authority must prove that the detention is necessary to maintain "public order" or "national security," not just "law and order" (which are treated as less severe).

The "Magistrate's Duty"

When an arrestee is produced within 24 hours, the Magistrate is not a "rubber stamp." They must:

1. Verify if the **grounds of arrest** were communicated.
2. Ensure the person was not subjected to **custodial torture**.
3. Check if the **Arrest Memo** was properly prepared and signed.

The Supreme Court in *Prabir Purkayastha v. State (2024)* established that under UAPA and other special laws, the grounds of arrest must be communicated to the detainee in writing before they are produced before a Magistrate. The ruling, relying on *Pankaj Bansal v. Union of India*, held that arrests are invalid unless written grounds are provided, a principle now codified under Section 38 of the Bharatiya Nagarik Suraksha Sanhita (BNSS).

The **Prabir Purkayastha v. State (2024)** judgment is a watershed moment because it elevated the "right to know" from a procedural formality to an absolute constitutional mandate, even under stringent anti-terror laws like the **UAPA**.

The Supreme Court's decision to invalidate the arrest rested on three critical failures of due process:

1. The "Communication" vs. "Information" Distinction

The Court clarified that under **Article 22(1)**, "informed of the grounds" does not mean a mere oral statement.

- **The Rule:** The grounds of arrest must be communicated **in writing** to the arrestee or their counsel.
- **The Failure:** Providing an unsigned, incomplete remand application via WhatsApp *after* the arrest did not constitute "informing" the accused of the specific reasons for his deprivation of liberty.

2. Undermining the Right to Legal Counsel

The surreptitious timing of the remand (6:00 AM–6:30 AM) was seen as a move to bypass the accused's legal defense.

- **The Rule:** An accused has the right to be defended by a lawyer of their choice at the **earliest opportunity**, especially during the first remand hearing, where the Magistrate decides on the legality of detention.

- **The Failure:** By passing the remand order before the lawyers were properly notified or present, the State violated the constitutional guarantee of legal assistance.

3. Judicial Accountability and the "Mechanical" Remand

The fact that the remand order was signed at 6:00 AM—before the accused was even produced or his lawyers notified—indicated a "mechanical" exercise of power.

- **The Rule:** A Magistrate must apply their mind to whether an arrest is justified before authorizing further custody.
- **The Failure:** The Supreme Court noted that the "haste" and "secrecy" of the proceedings suggested the remand was granted without verifying if the mandatory requirements of Article 22 had been met.

The Broader Impact

This ruling corrected a previous ambiguity from the *Pankaj Bansal* (PMLA) case. It established that the requirement to provide **written grounds of arrest** is "sacrosanct" and applies universally across all criminal statutes, including the **UAPA**, **PMLA**, and now the **BNSS**.

The legal landscape surrounding Articles 21 and 22 has significantly evolved in 2024–2026, with the Supreme Court transitioning from recommending procedural safeguards to mandating them as absolute constitutional requirements.

1. Mandatory Written Grounds of Arrest (2024–2026)

The precedent set in **Pankaj Bansal v. Union of India (2023)** has been expanded and clarified across multiple jurisdictions and statutes:

- **Universal Application**: In 2024, the Supreme Court ruled that the requirement to provide written grounds of arrest at the time of detention now applies to **UAPA (terror cases)** and **CGST Act** offenses, ensuring that special laws do not bypass Article 22(1).
- **Strict "Time of Arrest" Requirement**: Recent rulings in **2025 and 2026** (e.g., *Mihir Rajesh Shah v. State of Maharashtra*) emphasize that failing to provide written grounds **at the time of arrest** makes the detention illegal, regardless of subsequent remand orders.
- **Retrospectivity Limit**: The Court clarified that this mandatory "written" rule applies prospectively to arrests made after the *Pankaj Bansal* judgment (October 3, 2023).

2. Evolution of Legal Aid (2025–2026)

The principles from **Hussainara Khatoon (1979)** and **Anwar Ali Sarkar (1952)** have been upgraded to ensure that legal aid is not just provided, but is of high quality:

- **"Effective" Legal Representation**: In **Ashok v. State of Uttar Pradesh (2024)**, the Court held that inadequate or inexperienced legal aid violates Article 21 and may result in the accused's acquittal.
- **Mandatory Duty of Prosecutors**: As of 2025, Public Prosecutors have a positive duty to inform the court if an accused is unrepresented and must recommend the

appointment of a legal aid lawyer before any proceedings continue.

- **Competence Standards**: Supreme Court Justices in early **2026** asserted that "legal aid to the poor must not become poor legal aid," emphasizing that state-provided lawyers must meet the same standards of diligence as private counsel.
- **New Dimensions of Article 21 (2025–2026)**
- The "Right to Life" continues to expand to meet modern technological and biological needs:
- **Right to Digital Access (April 2025)**: The Supreme Court declared digital access a fundamental right under Article 21, particularly for persons with disabilities, ensuring they cannot be excluded from essential services like digital KYC.
- **Menstrual Health and Hygiene (2026)**: In *Dr. Jaya Thakur v. Government of India*, the Court recognized menstrual hygiene as a fundamental right under Article 21, mandating the provision of free sanitary products in all schools.
- **Right to Die with Dignity (2026)**: The Court authorized the first practical application of passive euthanasia in the *Harish Rana* case, confirming that withdrawing futile medical treatment for patients in a permanent vegetative state is part of the right to live (and die) with dignity.

3. Impact of the Bharatiya Nagarik Suraksha Sanhita (BNSS), 2023

Effective **July 1, 2024**, the BNSS has codified many of these judicial guidelines:

- **Section 36 (BNSS)**: Formally codifies the *D.K. Basu* requirement to inform a relative or friend of the arrest.
- **Section 43(3) (Handcuffing)**: Controversially allows the use of handcuffs for "serious offences" (such as organized crime or terrorism), which some legal experts argue contradicts the Supreme Court's previous stances on human dignity.

In the **Bharatiya Nagarik Suraksha Sanhita (BNSS), 2023**, which replaced the CrPC on **July 1, 2024**, the definitions previously found in Section 266 are now located in **Section 301**

Detained:

This includes individuals held under any law that allows for preventive detention, such as the National Security Act.

Prison:

This has a broad meaning and includes:

Any place declared by the State Government, by general or special order, to be a subsidiary jail.

Any reformatory, Borstal institution, or other similar institution.

Understanding Police Use of Force

Various names in different countries, such as police brutality, police violence, police criminality, police misconduct, and police use of deadly force, also refer to the phenomenon of custodial crimes. The term "Police Brutality" is a phrase from everyday speech; thus, its meaning is not defined. In general, it connotes the use of excessive force by the police against members of the public. It is accepted that many uses of force by the police cannot be labeled "police brutality" or "excessive" because the use of force is sometimes necessary for police work.

The police are the officials in modern society who are commonly called upon when the state has to use its ultimate power of coercion against its citizens, either for reasons rooted in enforcing lawful orders or simply to maintain order. Thus, the power to use force is essential to the functioning of police. Fyfe and Skolnick (1993 have made an important distinction between the "unnecessary" use of force, which may be excessive because of poor training, negligence, or the misperception of a situation, and "police brutality," which is defined as a "conscious and venal act". The term "brutality" does not seem to imply a deliberate violent act. Nevertheless, in everyday practice, the distinction is not usually made between force that is unnecessary under the circumstances. Still, it is not deliberately so, and the deliberate use of force by the police is viewed as excessive, which is commonly called "Police Brutality."The United Nations has established standards for the use of force by Law Enforcement officials (which includes police).

According to the UN Code of Conduct for Law Enforcement officials (1991), they may use force only when strictly necessary and to the extent required for the performance of their duty.

Police Brutality may be divided into brutality that occurs as part of the order-keeping and crime prevention functions of the police, on the one hand, or brutality that occurs during the investigative functions, on the other hand. The former usually occurs in the street and takes the form of beating or, in extreme cases, a shooting, and the latter usually occurs inside a police station or police custody as a version of torture.

What is Torture?

Legally, custody is defined as "any point in time when a person's freedom of movement has been denied by enforcement agencies, like during transport before registering a case, or during arrest, prosecution, sentencing, and correctional confinement."

Death in custody is defined as "death occurring in some sort of custodial detention, like police cell or prison."

There have been numerous examples where police have abused their legitimate power, significantly impacting people's lives.

The cops, supposed to be the guardians and custodians of the law, have acted inconsistently, violating Article 21 of the Indian Constitution, and have failed to protect the people's most basic right to life. Custodial violence has recently gained prominence as a source of worry, because citizens' guardians perpetrate it[5].

In the U.N. Convention against Torture and Other Cruel, Inhuman or Degrading Treatment or Punishment, Article 1 defines "Torture" as, "any act by which severe pain or suffering, whether physical or psychological, is intentionally caused on an individual for such purposes as gaining from that person or a 3rd person evidence or a confession, punishing the person for an act he/she or a 3rd person has committed or is suspected of getting committed, or intimidating or coercing him or a 3rd person, or for any reason depending on discrimination of any kind, when such pain or suffering is inflicted by or at the instigation of or with the consent or acquiescence of a public official or other person acting in the legal capacity"[6]

Torture necessarily causes pain that's hard to tolerate. Physical pain resulting from torture can be equal in severity to pain involving serious physical injuries, like failure of body parts or

---

5 Bansal YS, Murali G, Singh D. Custodial deaths-an overview of the prevailing healthcare scenario. J Indian Acad Forensic Med.2010:32:315-315.

6 Prikryl J. Abu Ghraib: A Global Family Portrait, The Believer, 3/2 (March 2005)

organs, damage to biological processes, or even death. Whereas psychological pain or distress that results from psychological torture might end in substantial psychological damage over a serious time duration that could last for months or years.

Keeping in mind the importance of human rights, many conventions or legal declarations in India and around the world have stressed the non-use of violence and banning the use of "torture" in any form. However, despite several commitments made by organizations to eradicate torture, today's reality is that torture has become widespread worldwide, way more than in the past. "Custodial torture" may be an unprotected violation of human self-respect and humiliation that ruins the individual's personality to a large extent. It is a deliberate assault on human dignity. Whenever this self-respect is hurt, civilization takes a step back in humanity's progress on every occasion of human rights violation[7] Overall, custodial crimes will inflict physical suffering as well as mental anguish on an individual who is confined within the four walls of a locked-up station house. The magnitude of trauma a person endures, whether it is a physical attack or rape in police custody, exceeds what is permitted by law[8]

Custodial violence and police power misuse are not only strange to India, but they have spread worldwide.

It has also been a more significant priority issue for international society because this problem is universal, and the challenges generated are almost global. This gross human physical and

---

7. Basu DK, Ashok K. Johri v State of West Bengal, State of UP on 18 December, 1996.
8. Baxi PM, Public Interest Litigation 18, Second Edition, Asoka Law House, New Delhi, 2006, p.22.

psychological violation became very grim and alarming in developing nations such as India.

According to the Universal Declaration of Human Rights (UDHR), despite the prohibition against violence, custodial crimes continue. During the 1960s and early 1970s, the controversial detention and torture of Naxals without trial caused the formation of the Association for the Protection of Democratic Rights (APDR). Custodial torture isn't limited to vicious people like saboteurs, radicals, extremists, bandits, and other hardcore criminals, as certain police officials would like to point out.

Even if they are hardcore criminals, the question that arises is whether the police have the legal authority to impose brutal punishment. Socially and economically deprived people of our society, such as members of scheduled tribes and scheduled castes, tribal women, daily workers in farms, migrated workers, etc., are more prone to be victims of this torture[9]

Some commonly used torture techniques by the police are beating, electric shock, disallowing sleep, solitary confinement in a dark place, and undressing (or stripping) in front of others. The Indian Constitution has bestowed numerous rights on Indian citizens, and their significance requires no further explanation.

Therefore, the courts of law should strive to prevent state enforcement officers from violating the rights of citizens in India.

As against the typical belief, custodial deaths might either be due to natural or unnatural causes.

Natural deaths could also be attributed to disease or alcohol/drug toxicity that existed earlier, within the deceased

---

9. Saini RS. Custodial Torture in Law and Practice with Reference to India 36 JILI (1994) at 166.

person, before the custody and worsened afterward, or it might have progressed after the person was taken into custody [10]

Per NHRC recommendations, all custodial deaths must be reported in less than 24 hours. A panel of specialist physicians must perform post-mortem inspections, which are mandatorily recorded via video. The NHRC reports from 2001–2002 to 2006–2007 showed an upsurge in custodial deaths everywhere in India. Although natural causes caused most custodial death cases, medical treatment negligence or poor healthcare amenities were among the several reasons for these deaths occurring in custody[11][12]

Effective police behavior is claimed to be an outcome of adopting well-developed scientific methods for managing people, processes, policies, and the art of policing. There are several kinds of policing, like democratic, friendly, business-like, and forceful. The style of officers that they adopt during a particular situation or circumstance comes from practical police training.

However, different provisions in the law grant police power to use force only in three circumstances. Firstly, to apprehend a person who resists an endeavor to arrest him or attempts to evade arrest under Section 46 of the Code of Criminal Procedure, 1973; secondly, for the dispersal of an unlawful assembly under Section 129 of the Code of Criminal Procedure, 1973; and thirdly, in the exercise of the right of private defense under Sections 100 and 101 of the Indian Penal Code, 1860. However, police generally believe

---

10. Shakya NK, Siddiqui MN, Shakya P, Singh NB, Gupta OP, Ahmad N. Custodial deaths- aretrospective study. Indian Journal of Applied Research 2018;8(5):67-69

11. National Human Rights Commission Annual report 2002-2003, nhrc-nic.in/annualreports/2002- 2003 (Accessed on June 06,2018)

12. Bansal YS, Murali G, Singh D. Custodial deaths – an overview of the prevailing healthcare scenario. J Indian Acad Forensic Med.2010; 32:315-315.

that the use of force is necessary for detecting and preventing crime; hence, third-degree or torture is considered an effective instrument for seeking confession (Bawa 1999).

Magnitude

A total of 4484 custodial deaths have been reported in the last few years, and another 233 were alleged police encounters. Reliable information on custodial crimes is scarce and difficult to obtain. When it occurs, it is often incomplete because the crime in custody takes place within closed quarters and is very serious. The accountability systems are so inadequate that the police act with virtual impunity, even when the problem is not so serious.

Furthermore, almost all charges of police criminality are contested because it is usually possible for the police to offer a plausible justification for their action.

It is impossible to estimate how many people were tortured in the last century, decade, or year. However, from the beginning of 1997 until the mid-2000s, Amnesty International received reports of torture or ill-treatment committed by state officials in more than 150 countries.

In more than 70 countries, such torture and ill-treatment appeared to be widespread or persistent. In more than 80 countries, people reportedly died as a result of torture.

Moreover, the standard methods of torture and ill-treatment used by state agents or police in almost all countries across the globe include:

1. beating (more than 150 countries),
2. electric shocks (more than 40 countries),
3. rape and sexual abuse in custody (more than 50 countries),
4. suspension of the body (more than 40 countries),

5. beating on the soles of the feet (more than 30 countries),
6. suffocation (more than 30 countries),
7. mock execution or death threat (more than 50 countries).

Other methods included submersion in water, stubbing out cigarettes, sleep deprivation, and sensory deprivation[13] According to the UN Special Rapporteur on torture, various methods of torture are used in police custody.

The Asian Human Rights Commission conducted a study in 2006 across eleven countries: Bangladesh, Burma, Cambodia, India, Indonesia, Maldives, Nepal, Pakistan, Philippines, Sri Lanka, and Thailand. The study found a consistent pattern of police inflicting torture on individuals in custody throughout the Asian region, including extrajudicial killings, torture, violence, and disappearances. Despite these findings, states assert that their actions are necessary to fulfill their duties as a state, even when they may amount to crimes against humanity.

In India, no reliable or authentic statistics are available regarding custodial crimes in police custody since most of these incidents are not recorded.

Incidents of torture and injury in urban areas are brought to public notice by the media. In contrast, many such incidents occurring in rural areas of our vast country remain unnoticed.

In this state of affairs, it is difficult to pinpoint the exact number of incidents of torture and death in custody[14]

In a significant development in 1997, the National Crime Records Bureau (NCRB), Ministry of Home Affairs, Government of India, added a new chapter on "Custodial

---

13. Amnesty International 2001
14. Law Commission of India 1994

Crimes" in its annual publication "Crime in India". Similarly, since its inception in 1993, the NHRC has also been compiling data relating to human rights violations in police custody.

NCRB & NHRC data

The present study focuses on one issue that has been tainting the image of police management, i.e., custodial death. It is necessary to explore the matter of custodial deaths from a different perspective, in a more scientific manner, if such incidents need to be eradicated.

Custodial deaths are classified into three categories as shown in Figure 1.1.

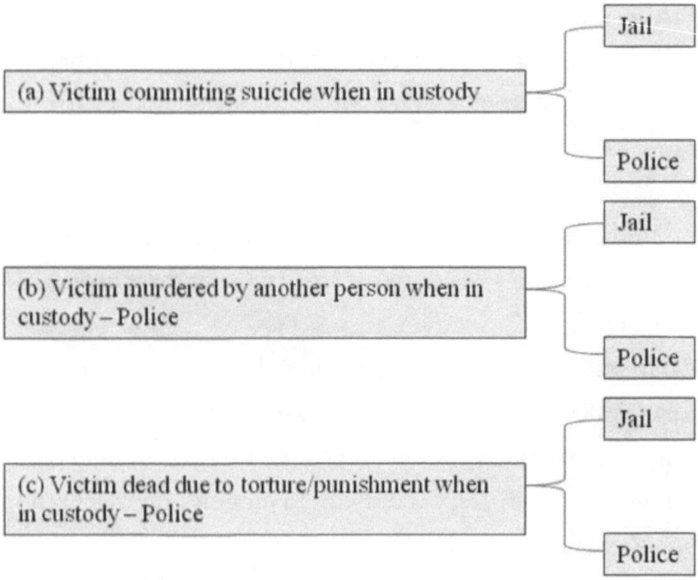

Figure 1.1: Categories of custodial deaths

S. No.	Name of the Unit	2013	2014	2015	2016	2017	2018	2019	2020
1	Srikakulam	0	0	0	0	0	0	1	0
2	Vijayanagaram	0	0	0	0	0	1	0	0
3	Visakhapatnam Rural	0	0	0	0	0	1	0	0
4	Visakhapatnam City	0	0	1	1	0	1	2	8
5	East Godavari	1	0	1	0	0	0	0	0
6	Rajahmundry Urban	0	0	0	0	0	0	10	5
7	West Godavari	0	1	1	0	0	3	2	2
8	Vijayawada City	0	0	0	0	0	0	0	0
9	Krishna	0	0	0	0	0	0	0	0
10	Guntur Urban	1	0	0	0	0	0	0	1
11	Guntur Rural	0	0	0	0	0	1	1	1
12	Prakasam	0	0	0	1	1	1	0	3
13	Nellore	0	0	1	0	0	0	1	0
14	Thirupathi Urban	0	0	0	0	0	1	0	0
15	Chittor	0	0	0	0	0	1	0	0
16	Anantapuramu	0	0	1	0	0	0	0	4
17	Kadapa	0	0	0	1	0	0	2	1
18	Kurnool	1	0	1	0	1	0	0	0
19	RP Vijayawada	0	0	0	0	0	2	0	0
20	RP Guntakal	1	0	0	0	0	0	0	0
	Total	4	1	6	3	2	12	19	25

Table 1.2: Total Custodial Deaths in residual AP from 2013 to 2020, District-Wise,

Source (Primary Data)

Custodial Deaths are categorized into three distinct groups, each being a unique and complex event. Resources for every category of custodial death might be different, and police involvement and legal implications differ. The study focuses on a specific category - death in police custody due to torture - due to its high incidence in the state of Andhra Pradesh, where the study was conducted. This allows for a more precise and more in-depth understanding of custodial deaths in India. Andhra Pradesh is chosen as the focal point of the study because it has a high number of custodial deaths both historically and presently[15]

Sl. No.	Head	2013	2014	2015	2016	2017	2018	2019	2020
1	Committed suicide by hanging	0	0	1	0	0	3	2	2
2	Committed suicide by poisoning	1	1	0	1	0	1	0	0
3	Committed suicide by burning	2	0	0	0	0	0	0	0
4	Due to police firing	0	0	0	0	0	0	0	0
5	Due to torture	0	0	0	0	0	0	0	0
6	Due to ill health	0	0	3	1	2	4	16	21
7	Due to other reasons	1	0	2	1	0	4	1	2
	Total	4	1	6	3	2	12	19	25

Table 1.3: Total Custodial Deaths in residual AP from 2013 to 2020, Reason-Wise

Source (Primary Data)

15. Amnesty International Annual Report, 1992, p.34-35. https://www.amnesty.org/en/documents/po110/0001/1992/en/ (Accessed on September 18, 2020)

This study sheds light on the individuals and officers who have committed and are responsible for torturing victims, and highlights some of the main factors that contribute to custodial deaths.

The primary source of data was collected from individuals who are responsible for custodial deaths. Data for this study were collected through various means, including clinical and psychological tests, as well as demographic, organizational, and legal compliance reports. These variables provide valuable information that helps us better understand the human and organizational factors involved in custodial deaths. By recognizing and addressing these factors, police management can take proactive measures to prevent these tragic events from occurring in the future.

One of the primary objectives of the present study was to evaluate and analyze the risk factors that could be used to forecast and, if possible, to prevent custodial deaths by modifying the work environment. Human factor assessment is brought into this study, as any management study is incomplete without directly studying the human beings and their workplace. To ensure the continuity of this research, a brief introduction to the human factors involved in custodial deaths is provided as follows.

The study aims to assess variables and factors related to four critical areas – organizational, psychological, medical, and legal compliance – as per the guidelines of DK Basu. Identifying risk factors, such as an individual's proneness to aggression and violence beyond the sanctioned limits and losing self-control, may help reduce incidences of custodial deaths.

The following pages highlight the importance of examining the concepts of aggression, violence, and anger, as they are often exhibited by police officers involved in custodial deaths.

This "manifest behavior" is frequently characterized by aggression, which may stem from various "pull and push factors." It is crucial to understand these underlying factors to prevent future incidents of custodial deaths.

Distinctions regarding forms of aggression include antisocial, prosocial, and sanctioned aggression.

Generally, aggression is undesirable and harmful. Some aggressive acts are good. Analysis of aggressive acts reveals that many of them are guided by social rules and are therefore described as prosocial. For instance, acts of law enforcement, suitable parental and teacher discipline, and obeying orders of officers or commandos during wartime are considered necessary. Society generally appreciates the police officer who shoots the terrorist who has killed innocent victims. Malicious criminal acts that harm innocent people, violating social norms, are anti-social acts.

Some aggressive acts observed between the pro-social and anti-social aggression spectrums are classified as "sanctioned aggression." Aggression of this sort includes acts that are not necessary for societal customs but are within their bounds; they do not violate traditional moral standards. A coach, for example, who disciplines a disobedient player by making him run around a kilometer field 20 times is well within his rights [16]

Use of force

Sudden custodial restraint deaths have occurred during a skirmish between the convict and the police in several unpredictable arrest scenarios. They can also happen in prison correctional facilities and mental healthcare facilities.

---

16. Taylor SE, Peplan LA, O Sears AD, Social Psychology; ed 12th, New Delhi: Pearson Education Inc. 2006.

When officers employ force and restraint measures, it is to stop the violent behavior of an individual. If that person dies during the encounter, the police agency is bombarded with several questions by the people and society. Some of these questions involve:

1. What sort of force techniques did the officers use?
2. What sort of restraint equipment did the officers use?
3. Were alternative restraint or force techniques available?
4. Did the restraining officers contribute to the individual's death?
5. What sort of position was the person forced to assume? And for how long?
6. Did the officers perform any medical/psychological assessment of the person?
7. Did the officers provide or delay emergency medical aid for the person?
8. What was the way of monitoring the person?
9. How was the person, and to what location was he transported?

Definition of safety in custody

It is a process that aims to enable the police service to provide a safe and secure environment for persons detained in police custody. This includes meeting expectations and inspiring confidence in the community and the judiciary. The police must acknowledge their duty of care owed to all detainees. This process's ultimate goal is to eliminate death incidents in custody. The method also aims to provide the highest achievable levels of safety for detainees.

Aims of Torture

The main objectives of torture are to;

1. Yield information
2. Extract a confession
3. Obtain evidence or a witness to convict others
4. Seek vengeance
5. Maintain fear and terror in the society
6. Destroy the character

Custodial Deaths In Andhra Pradesh

Custodial deaths in Andhra Pradesh continue to be a matter of grave concern for all of us. Such incidents shake the basic edifice of the world's largest democracy.

Despite so much hue and cry by human rights groups, the press, media, courts, and the human rights commission, custodial deaths in Andhra Pradesh continue to be an eyesore for the entire criminal justice system.

Andhra Pradesh continues to be among the top in India in custodial deaths. The Law Commission has observed that custodial crimes disproportionately affect vulnerable and marginalized people/groups, particularly those who are weak and poor. The patterns of deaths are uniform, and generalization is possible.

The victims are generally petty offenders. In most cases, the causes of death are reported as heart failure, alcoholism, suicide by hanging, or consuming pesticides. The standard methods of suicidal deaths involve using a lungi (a piece of clothing wrapped around the waist and worn by men in India) or a waist belt and hanging inside the lock-up, or jumping from the building to commit suicide.

In a democratic society, the police are empowered to enforce laws against crime and serve as the enforcers of governing laws aimed at maintaining social order and ensuring public safety.

To accomplish these objectives, the police have been assigned several powers and authorities that are not accessible to the ordinary public.

The police are the only civilian profession provided with legitimate and physical means to enforce the law, which includes the use of state-authorized force as needed.

The power of the police in civil society is considerable, making it crucial for democracies to prioritize oversight and regulation of police actions. The police should be held accountable for all acts of commission and omission. Although the Law Commission of India recommended that legislation be passed to check custodial deaths, in its absence, the rich and the influential were getting away while the poor were becoming victims. India has been a party to the International Covenant on Civil and Political Rights and the United Nations Convention against Torture since 1979. However, custodial deaths continue to plague the police force.

With numerous developmental activities underway, including foreign investments, tourism, and World Bank loans, these initiatives are ultimately tied to international human rights standards. Custodial deaths are a poor indicator or index of human rights standards.

Hence, in the coming days, as India rapidly emerges as a global superpower, there is an urgent need to enhance the nation's human rights standards by examining the existing systems within law enforcement agencies and proposing remedial and corrective measures."Human development index," which is directly associated with human rights violations in the form of custodial deaths, is a vital aspect to be considered.

Considering the global perspective, if India is to play a significant role in the United Nations (with permanent membership, for example), it must improve its human rights standards. Amnesty International and other human rights watchdogs continue to paint a negative picture of India at the international level, deriding India's interests in the international arena.

Reports of post-mortem documents being altered or manipulated to aid the police and the omission of relevant injuries in medical examiner's reports have come to light. Following improper arrest procedures, not following or implementing the Supreme Court directives and guidelines of the D. K. Basu case, and inhuman interrogation techniques being followed instead of scientific and skillful interrogation are some of the facets studied in this book. Despite the role played by human rights watch groups, judicial commissions, commissions of inquiry, human rights commissions, magisterial inquiries, courts, and others, much remains to be done. There seem to be some structural deformities in the police organization, including a lack of process standardization concerning arrest, interrogation, supervision, and responsibility, which is studied in detail.

The state of United Andhra Pradesh has an area of 2,75,045 sq. meters with a population of 8,46,65,533. In the United AP, the average number of cases of all kinds (Special, Local Laws, and Indian Penal Code) is about 8,34,030.

The total strength of the police was around 79,296. The percentage of civil police to total police was 84:1. Of these, only 6,779 are empowered to investigate, i.e., they hold a rank above that of Assistant Sub-Inspector (ASI) in the Civil Police.

There are about 28.8 police officers per 100 sq. km. area and 98 police officers for a population of 1,00,000. On average, we have 3.4 IPC cases to handle per civil policeman.

 Rolf Anton Groos, Inspector	 Norway	In Norway, custodial deaths are relatively fewer, and in most instances, suicide is reported as the primary cause of death. With regard to property offences, our detection rate stands at approximately 40%, while the recovery rate is around 30%.
 Felix, Inspector	 Ghana	In Ghana, an average of two to three custodial deaths are reported annually. The reported causes of death in most cases include suicide, torture, and severe physical assault while in custody. In certain serious cases involving offences such as murder and armed robbery, reasonable force may be used during interrogation, as permitted under the law. With respect to property offences, the detection rate is approximately 50%, and the recovery rate is about 45%.
 Ralph Gloven, Sr. Inspector	 Sweden	Custodial deaths have been reported. In the majority of cases, the cause of death has been hanging while in custody, as well as complications resulting from drug abuse and alcohol consumption. The crime detection rate is 60%, whereas the recovery rate is 20%.
 Nick Robertson, Inspector	 UK	In the United Kingdom, custodial deaths are relatively rare. The majority of these cases are attributed to suicide or pre-existing medical conditions. The crime detection rate is 47%, while the property recovery rate stands at 40%.
 Ms. Cornelia, Inspector	 Croatia	There have been no reported custodial deaths in our country. However, in a few isolated instances, suicides have occurred, largely attributed to mental health issues such as depression. With respect to property offences, the detection rate is approximately 50%, while the recovery rate is around 35%.

 Fitz Macariola Sub-Inspector	 Philippines	In the Philippines, a number of custodial deaths have been reported. The principal causes are alleged torture and medical complications while in custody. In respect of property offences, both the detection rate and the recovery rate are approximately 50%.
 Frank Denz Sub-Inspector	 Denmark	In Denmark, custodial deaths are not reported. However, there have been occasional cases of suicide. In relation to property offences, the detection rate is approximately 50%, while the recovery rate is around 30%.
 John Heidke Spl. Agent, FBI	 USA	In the United States, custodial deaths have been reported. The predominant causes include medical conditions, suicides, and firearm-related incidents. In respect of property offences, the detection rate is approximately 40%, while the recovery rate is around 50%.
 Viktor Kostenko, SP	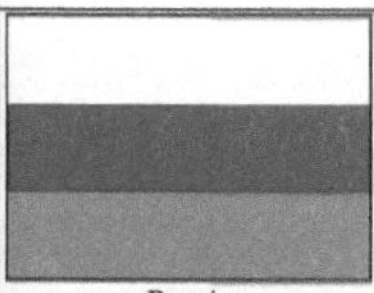 Russia	In Russia, a limited number of custodial deaths have been reported within the department. The principal causes are alleged torture and medical complications while in custody. Regarding property offences, the detection rate is approximately 20%, whereas the recovery rate is around 50%.
 Brajnik Matej, Inspector	 Slovenia	In Slovenia, custodial deaths are not reported. However, there have been occasional cases of deaths on medical grounds. In relation to property offences, the detection rate is approximately 40%, while the recovery rate is around 40%.

International legal custody landscape

Total police expenditure is Rs. 1,116.97 crores per annum, and the cost per policeman per annum is Rs 1,40,735 as per 2014 Andhra Pradesh state pre-bifurcation data The UN mandates 222 police officers for every 100,000 of the population, whereas in

India, we are at 138 per 100,000 of the population. In AP, we have 93 police officers for every lakh of the population.

Arrests

In the erstwhile United AP, 2,27,935 persons were arrested every year (2014), which is 8.6% of the total arrests in the country (2014). Under IPC arrests, there were 2,09,499 males and 18,436 females.

Females formed only 8% of the total arrests. Under Special and Local Laws, 5,94,876 males were arrested (2014), and only 9,166 females were arrested. Females form only 1.5% of the arrests under special and local laws. As the arrests are more in number, the interface of police with citizens is more, and hence the share of custodial deaths/violence in AP.

Bail

The total number of IPC arrests, including those carried forward in jail, was 2,94,397 in 2014. Of them, 13,014 (2014) were released on bail before trial; 2,00,905 were charge sheeted; and 80,478 were under arrest/detention. Total special and local laws arrests, including carry-forward, are 6,12,377; out of which 602 are released before trial, 6,05,621 are charge-sheeted, and another 6154 continue in detention in cases under investigation.

Deaths in police and judicial custody

Andhra Pradesh ranked number one in custodial deaths in 2017 compared to other states and union territories, according to the latest National Crime Records Bureau (NCRB) data. In 2017, 27 people died in police custody, a 350% increase compared to 2016, when only six had died. Twenty accused died before being remanded to judicial custody, and seven died in judicial custody.

According to the NCRB, four had committed suicide while in police custody. The data revealed that eight had died due to ill health, and 15 custodial deaths were put in the 'others' category. Magisterial inquiries were ordered in six out of 27 deaths. Only one charge sheet was filed in these cases in 2017.

In its 2016 report, NCRB stated that six prisoners had died in judicial remand and four were declared dead because of "injuries sustained during the police custody due to physical assault by police, and the other two were categorized as natural deaths due to illness." Despite the state reporting very high custodial deaths in 2017, none of these cases have been declared deaths caused by police torture. The NCRB reports also included rape cases that took place in police custody. Three cases were registered in 2017, two of which were committed by police personnel, while the other was committed by hospital staff. Following AP, Maharashtra and Gujarat take second and third place for the most number of custodial deaths. Overall, 100 custodial deaths have been reported from across the country.[17]

Reasons for custodial deaths

The reasons for custodial deaths, apart from torture, are:

1. In the course of hospitalization or treatment,
2. Caused by accidents
3. Caused by a mob attack or a riot
4. Caused by other convicts
5. Due to suicide
6. Fugitive action
7. Sickness or natural death

---

17. Crime in India, Statistics, NCRB, National Crime Records Bureau, New Delhi, Ministry of Home Affairs, 2016.

Investigative workload on the Andhra Pradesh police

In the United Andhra Pradesh, out of a total of 1,556 police stations, there are 343 police stations where 0-60 IPC cases are reported annually; in 405 police stations 61-100 cases are reported; in 502 police stations 101-200 cases are reported; in 171 police stations 201-300 cases; in 57 police stations 301-400 cases; in 39 police stations 401-500 cases; in 30 police stations 501-1000 cases, in 9 police stations more than 1001 cases are reported.

Eighty percent of the custodial deaths are reported in police stations where more than 500 cases are registered. In the United Andhra Pradesh, 68 police stations have less than 10 men, 829 police stations have 11-20 men, 263 police stations have 21-30 men, 167 police stations have 31-40 men, 81 police stations have 41-50 men and 148 police stations have more than 51 men.

Eighty percent of the deaths are reported in police stations with more than 20% vacancies.

In the State of Andhra Pradesh, there were four zones, 10 ranges, 26 districts, 153 subdivisions, 496 circles, 1,159 rural police stations, 397 urban police stations, and 23 women's police stations.

Custodial deaths were reported in equal numbers in rural and urban police stations. One death was reported in the women's police station as well.

The year-wise details of cases reported – investigation burden and investigated cases – in the present Andhra Pradesh are given in the following Tables 1.4 to 1.6 and Figures 1.2 to 1.4.

Type of Cases	2014	2015	2016	2017	2018	2019	Average share of the state percentage (2017-19)
IPC	114604	110693	106774	132336	126635	119229	3.7%
SLL	25278	15155	22615	15666	18068	26522	1.4%

Table 1.4: Year-wise cases reported-investigation burden in Andhra Pradesh

Source: NCRB, IPC – Indian Penal Code, SLL – Special and Local Loss

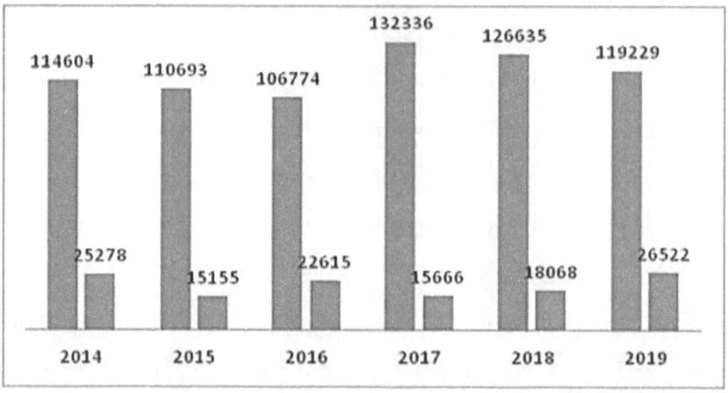

Figure 1.2: Year-wise cases reported-investigation burden in Andhra Pradesh

Source: NCRB, National Crime Records Bureau 2016, Red- SLL & Blue- IPC

Type of Cases	2017	2018	2019	Share of state percentage (2017-19)
IPC and SLL	148002	144703	145751	2%

Table 1.5: Total IPC and SLL Crimes (2017-2019)

Source: NCRB, IPC – Indian Penal Code, SLL – Special and Local Laws

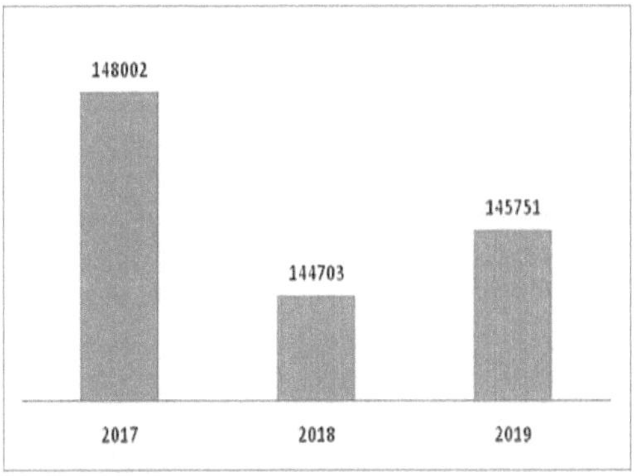

Figure 1.3: Total IPC and SLL Crimes (2017-2019)
Source: NCRB, National Crime Records Bureau 2016

Cases in A.P up to 2016	Total Arrests	Total Crimes	Total Chargesheets
IPC	3737370	2975711	3271262
SLL	2392637	1855804	2264834

Table 1.6: Arrests in Investigated cases in Andhra Pradesh
Source: NCRB, National Crime Records Bureau 2016

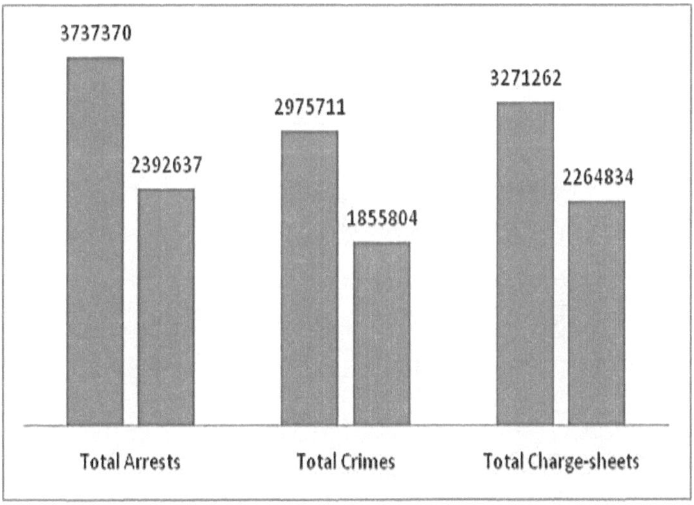

Figure 1.4: Arrests in Crimes Investigated cases in Andhra Pradesh
Source: NCRB, National Crime Records Bureau 2016

The total number of investigated IPC cases, including arrests, crimes, and charge sheets, was 37,370, 29,711, and 32,262, respectively. Similarly, the total number of investigated SLL cases, including arrests, crimes, and charge sheets, was 23, 92, 637, 18, 55, 804, and 22, 64, 834, respectively.

Medico-Legal Investigation And Forensic Pathology

"Forensic pathology" studies the relationship between the conditions that lead to death and the pathological and toxicological results of post-mortem examination.

Restraint Stress

It is pretty challenging to explain the custodial death during police restraint wherein the pathologist doesn't find any significant anatomical or structural injuries on the body[18] Hans Selye, in his book "The Physiology and Pathology of Exposure to Stress," coined the concept of "stress syndrome" as a medical term.

He demonstrated this concept through animal experiments by exposing them to various physically harmful stimuli. Essential findings of his study were,

1. ulceration in the stomach,
2. enlargement of the adrenal cortex,
3. gastrointestinal ulceration,
4. and shrinkage of the thymus and lymphatic nodes [19]

Unpredictable and sudden custodial deaths due to stress could usually happen because of physical restraint. Forensic pathologists are vested with and expected to find the causes of sudden death with no significant bodily changes during autopsy.

---

18. Cannon WB, Voices from the past "voodoo" death. AM J Health. 2002;92:1593-1596.
19. Selye H. The physiology and pathology of exposure to stress. In: A Treatise Based on the Concepts of the General Adaptation Syndrome and the Diseases of Adaptation. Montreal: Acta Inc. 1950.

The risk of physical restraint grasp can result in intense pressure, which may lead to airway injury, including fracture or breakage of the laryngeal cartilage or hyoid bone.

Given the anatomic location of the carotid arteries along the lateral aspect of the subject's neck, the hold may induce loss of consciousness from arterial compression[20]

Deaths in custody investigations

The death of an individual at the time of arrest or in police custody has the potential for a generation of civil litigation, criminal charges against law enforcement personnel, and, on occasion, riots. Though there is no misconduct by the police, some sections of society don't trust the police.

This distrust is generally aggravated by the sensationalism driven by television channels and newspapers. In-depth investigations and meticulous analyses of the incidents are lacking in the news media[21] Aristotle identified that people often confuse the proximity of an action with causality, an error in logic.

Therefore, if the death investigation does not fulfill the initial assumptions, then people claim that it is covering up the case.

Custodial deaths are usually of 3 categories:

1. Those that happen during arrest,
2. Those that take place during the transportation of a convict to prison or hospital.
3. Those that occur when the inmates are in a big house or jail.

---

20. Reay DT, Eisele JW. Death from law enforcement neck holds. Am J Forens Med Path. 1982;3:253- 258
21. Ross DL, Chan TC, Forensic Science and Medicine: Sudden Deaths in Custody, Totowa, NJ : Human Press Inc., 2006.

The causes of custodial deaths could be due to disease, accidental suffering, suicide, homicidal shock, or the sequential events of physiological responses during a stress situation. The medico-legal inquiry of custodial deaths usually comprises three components: the investigation, the autopsy, and subsequent laboratory tests.

Many injuries occur in custody/custodial violence, which precede arrest

Currently, there is no nationwide or jurisdictional system in place to systematically monitor injuries that occur in custody, except for reporting to a magistrate during remand proceedings.

1. During the custody itself
2. Due to improper care during custody
3. An injury or self-harm attempted during detainment
4. Injury while a fugitive escapes from police custody

Therefore, the medico-legal doctor on duty must conduct an independent evaluation of the detainee and submit the report in a sealed cover directly to the magistrate for review.

Incidents – Post Mortem findings are significant

To bring in objectivity, the following should be done during the post-mortem by the forensic pathologist:

1. High-quality videography, including close-ups of wounds and suspected areas, as well as long shots and contextual audio with relevant remarks, should be recorded immediately and uploaded promptly.
2. Previous history of illness should be documented with evidence, reports (epilepsy, hypertension, heart attack, diabetes, etc.)

3. Mandatory microscopic histopathological examination, accompanied by photographs of relevant biological tissues with labels, must be conducted and appended following a tamper-proof chain of custody. Additionally, toxicology reports of the viscera must be obtained.

   Eg: Suicidal hanging (ante mortem or post-mortem).

Medico-legal and ethical aspects of torture

Under the Hippocratic Oath, doctors are prohibited from using their professional knowledge to harm their patients, which was reconfirmed in the Geneva Declaration passed by the World Medical Association. However, despite this, it is a sad truth that doctors sometimes involve themselves directly or indirectly in the perpetration of torture, especially military doctors, police, prison doctors, and forensic experts.

The World Medical Assembly (WMA), in Tokyo (1975), adopted a special resolution regarding this[22]

Hanging/Ligature/Strangulation: Post Mortem Report Analysis

1. The ligature material is termed concerning its nature of material, position, knot-type, loop circumference, length of short and long free ends, foreign materials, etc.

   The material must be returned to the examining officer without disturbing the knot after taking video and photographs.

22. 29th World Medical Assembly, Tokyo, Japan, October 1975.

2. The ligature mark is described in detail about its pattern, nature, direction, extent (complete or incomplete), and correlated with the material, if available. The location of the mark is measured with respect to the chin, angle of the jaw, ears, and occipital protuberance, together with dimensions.
3. Dry salivary marks are identified, and their position, size, and direction are described.
4. The condition of the eyes and pupils is described.
5. The color of lips and nails is mentioned.
6. The position of the tongue is recorded.
7. The distribution of post-mortem marks is described, and the condition of fixation of stain is measured and documented.
8. The presence of injuries on the body is examined and analyzed to determine whether they could have resulted from hanging or struggle.
9. Blood, semen marks, and stool on the body are explained, and their source is identified and detailed.
10. The neck is dissected in detail in a "bloodless field". Soft tissues are examined for injuries and leak of blood. The hyoid bone, thyroid cartilage, cricoid cartilage, and tracheal rings are inspected for fracture and explained.
11. Injury to the cervical bone and spinal cord is examined.
12. Disease, injury, and poisoning of internal organs are examined.
13. Internal organs are preserved to prevent decomposition.

Feasibility and utility of the monitoring system

It is quite possible to observe the nature and extent of injuries that occur in police custody. The monitoring system plays a crucial role in understanding and comprehending the custodial process. It will also be an essential tool for performance monitoring.

It could suggest harm minimization practices in the police, such as audio/video recording of every movement of the accused while in custody or during transportation from prison to court, or from prison to prison, or from a police station lock-up to a hospital, prison, or court.

Based on the injury monitoring trend, data can be a helpful guide to prevent and warn against custodial violence. We can evolve strategies for safe custody.

Harm minimization practices

1. IP-based audio/video communication in lock-ups with cloud storage.
2. Graded scientific interrogation practices.

Legal provisions

- With increasing incidents of terrorism in the country, the police have become even harsher in certain situations. Under Section 31 of the Prevention of Terrorism Act (POTA), 2002 (now repealed), a confession made by a person is only admissible as evidence during a trial if it is made in the presence of a police officer of rank no lower than Superintendent of Police.

  It is usually found that there is a clear violation of Section 25 of the Indian Evidence Act, which gives "License to Torture" to extract confessions. Under the Terrorist and Disruptive Activities (Prevention) Act (a precursor to the

POTA), about <1% of 76,000 persons detained from 1985 to 1995 were convicted. About 80% of these convictions took place based on extracted confessions after torture.

- The police and armed forces enjoy virtual immunity under Section 197 (2) of Criminal Procedure Code (Cr.P.C), which states "No Court shall take cognizance of any offence alleged to have been committed by any member of the Armed Forces of the Union while acting or purporting to act in the discharge of his official duty, except with the previous sanction of the Central Government."
- Most state governments have implemented similar requirements under Section 197(3) of the Criminal Code. P.C.
- Section 6 of the Armed Forces Special Powers Act (AFSPA), 1958, which is applicable in most rebellion sensitive states also offers that "no prosecution, suit or other legal proceedings shall be instituted, except with the previous sanction of the Central Government against any person regarding anything done or supposed to be executed in use of powers offered by this Act".[23]
- According to Section 19 of the Human Rights Protection Act 1993, the NHRC cannot interfere in the allegations of human rights violations committed by the armed forces.

Custody record

1. "Arrest Memo" – Modifications to include the details of GPS/GIS/photograph at the time of arrest must be included and updated in the existing arrest memo.

---

23. Section 164 CRPC

2. Whenever an arrest is being made, live photos and videos of the incident, including the accused and their surroundings, must be taken with a GIS/GPS-enabled camera or smartphone.

Decision to arrest

Arnesh Kumar Judgement (Sec. 41 (a) Cr.P.C Conditions): In this case, the Hon'ble Apex Court of India passed the following instructions/ guidelines to the Government of India, states, and judiciary for arresting an accused and sending him/her for remand:

1. All state governments should educate their police officers not to arrest spontaneously when a case is registered under Section 498-A of the IPC, but to satisfy themselves about the requirements for arrest under the limitations laid down in Section 41, Cr. P.C.
2. All police officers shall be provided with a checklist having specific sub-clauses under Section 41 (1)(b)(ii).
3. The police officer shall submit the checklist duly filled and provide the reasons and resources that compelled the arrest while forwarding or presenting the accused to the magistrate for further detention. Arrests are only made in cases where the punishment is more than seven years; otherwise, the investigation officer must explain the imminent reasons.
4. The Magistrate, while approving the detention of the accused, shall examine the report provided by the police officer in the terms aforementioned. Only after recording to its satisfaction will the magistrate authorize detention.

Pre-custody risk assessment

The time available to perform this risk assessment usually depends on various circumstances. In response to an incident, the procedure for assessing risk to target suspects should begin by collecting available information before approaching the scene.

This risk assessment made during travel or on the streets need not be recorded. The operation should involve a detailed risk assessment and management plan to address the risks associated with target suspects.

The Intelligence, Intention, Methodology, Administration, Risk Assessment, Communication, and Human Rights (IIMARCH) model provides a valuable template for this process.

De-Arrest

If an arrested suspect has not been involved in the offense that has occurred, or reasons for the arrest cease to exist, the police officer must release the person.

Suppose a person has been detained to prevent any breach of social harmony. In that case, the detainee must be de-arrested if the social instability has ended or is unlikely to recur.

However, a custody record must be maintained for the detainee at the police station even after they are de-arrested (released).

The custody record (Arrest Memo-Form 61)

The following information must be recorded in the custody record:

1. Reasons for arrest.
2. Reasons for authorizing detention.
3. Search (level of search and persons present) Form 59.

4. Items or belongings of the detainee were seized following the search.
5. Additional clothing is supplied to the detainee.
6. Risks identified, and control and/or support measures.
7. Medical inquiry form.
8. Time placed in cell, cell number, and cell searched.
9. The whys and what-fors for a juvenile kept in a special cell.
10. Medical care and treatment plan.
11. The use of any force or restraint should be justified and explained.
12. Other pertinent facts, such as details of the detainee's actions and psychological attitudes.

Factors Influencing Aggression Leading To Torture And Custodial Deaths

According to Ghosh (1983), custodial crime in police custody is a symptom and not the disease. The disease lies elsewhere. It is merely a reflection of the social milieu in which the police work. Its causes are multifaceted. This aside, various studies undertaken by government and non-government organizations have identified the following causes of custodial crimes:

Legal Cause

The legal system and social psychology provide a unique opportunity for police management and organization to understand behavior in social contexts, social justice, and personal and public attitudes toward punishment. It is interesting to note that social psychologists share their knowledge with legal and police management, which involves "amicus curiae" or "friend of the court" briefs. Amicus briefs summarize relevant bodies of psychological science to provide judges with a scientific context for deciding a particular case.

Teams write amicus briefs from expert psychologists and attorneys. The American Psychological Association (APA) has filed these briefs in almost 150 cases decided by appellate courts, including the US Supreme Court. These 150 cases have involved some of the most significant and controversial public policy issues of our time, including affirmative action, abortion, employment discrimination, child sexual abuse, same-sex couples, and the death penalty[24].The first and foremost cause or root of the problem lies in a highly eccentric provision contained in the Indian Evidence Act 1872, namely, Section 27.

In the scheme of the act, a confession made by a person in police custody is not admissible in the court of law as evidence under Section 25 of the Indian Evidence Act. However, by way of a provision, Section 27 lays down that if a person in the custody of a police officer makes a statement leading to the discovery of a fact, the same is admissible, whether or not it amounts to a confession.

Many judges, journalists, lawyers, civil libertarians, writers, politicians and police officials themselves are deeply concerned about the widespread torture, custodial rapes and deaths in custody in India.

Chief Justice R.S. Pathak of the Supreme Court of India said in 1988 – "We are gravely concerned at the increasing number of deaths which are reported of persons detained in police lock-up". Chief Minister of West Bengal Jyoti Basu proclaimed in 1987, in response to 43 deaths in the country, that "Deaths in police custody

24. APA Amicus Briefs by Issue
http://apa.org/about/offices/ogc/amicus/index-issues (Accused on October 18, 2020).

are unthinkable in any civilized society. It is illegal and sickening. Nothing could be worse"[25]

It was also noted that few police officers are brought to trial, and virtually none are convicted (under Section 176 of the Code of Criminal Procedure) for committing human rights violations.

"The Statesman", the popular national daily reported in August 1989 that, "the main reason why barbarous third-degree methods are still used, despite being illegal is that the police know fully well that they are (a) protected species and no harm will come to them if the odd prisoner dies in the lock-up." (Amnesty International, 1992)

Official police bodies have also condemned torture. The National Police Commission (NPC) was established in 1979 to enquire "into the system of investigation and prosecution of custodial deaths. The use of improper methods and the extent of their prevalence".

After one year of work, the NPC reported, while condemning torture in the strongest terms, that "...nothing is as dehumanizing as the conduct of police in practicing torture of any kind on a person in their custody. The image of the police in the eyes of the public has suffered significantly from the prevalence of these practices in varying degrees over several years. We make with concern the inclination of even some of the supervisory ranks to countenance this practice in a bid to achieve quick results by shortcut methods."[26]

---

25. Amnesty International Annaul Report 1992, p.34-35.
https://www.amnesty.org/en/documents/poll0/0001/1992/en/ (Accused on September 18, 2020) 26
26. NPC, fourth report (June 1980, at 27 26) cited in Amnesty International, p.34

To keep a check on and reduce torture deaths in custody, the Supreme Court/High Court issued guidelines called the DK Basu case guidelines.

These guidelines are intended to be followed and incorporated into every investigation conducted at a police station. The procedure of investigations with 11 principles was made mandatory. Even if one principle is flouted, it is considered non-compliant and a serious legal violation, which deserves a penalty. Paragraphs 36 to 40 of the DK Basu vs State of West Bengal (AIR 1997 SC 610) case contain the final directions issued with the decision. They read as follows: "we, therefore, consider it appropriate to issue the following requirements to be followed in all cases of arrest or detention, till legal provisions are made in that behalf, as preventive measures[27]. Our concern is with matter that is more substantial. The fact that a statement can be rendered admissible, if it is represented to the trial court as a 'discovery statement' and presented at the trial in the form of a confession marked as a discovery statement, a fact that will be known to every police officer, acts as a lever to the police officer to use unfair means to procure such a statement." The police are aware that this is a convenient way of circumventing the restrictions based on practical wisdom, generations of experience, and deep thought. It is unfortunate, but true, that Section 27 of the Indian Evidence Act has caused significant harm by creating a desire to extract confessions, which can lead to the use of subtle or disguised action, physical or mental torture, cruelty, or any other form of abuse of custody[28].

---

27. Basu DK vs. State of West Bengal, AIR 1997 SC 610, at 615.
28. (Law Commission of India 1994)

Another reason for the continuation of torture and custodial violence is that police officials believe that they are immune to using torture in defense of national interest, public purpose, and good faith while exercising sovereign functions of the state[29]

Indian legislation contains various provisions that provide immunity from prosecution to specific groups of officials for any offense committed in the discharge of their sovereign functions. This way, police officers enjoyed impunity during and after the militancy periods in Punjab, the terrorism situation in Jammu and Kashmir, the North-Eastern states, and the rest of India[30]

It is reiterated here that the present study focuses on assessing offenders, or police officials, who tortured victims who died as a consequence. Note that the offenders are on trial in the state of Andhra Pradesh. The four major areas under which factors were assessed are organizational, psychological, medical, and legal.

In left-wing-infested Telangana districts, many youths brought in for interrogation had become impotent. The stigma associated with visiting a police station has reached such an extent that families are hesitant to offer their daughters as potential brides to the young men who had been taken in as suspects to a police station, resulting in decreased marital prospects.

Organizational Cause

There have been instances of aggression in the workplace among employees, and one of the primary sources has been identified as frustration[31].

29 .(Nair 1999)

30. (Amnesty International 1992, 2001b, 2003; Human Rights Watch 2006)

31. LeBlane M M, Barling J. Understanding the Many Faces of Workplace Violence. IN S. Fox & P.E. Spector (Eds.), Counterproductive work behavior: Investigations of actors and targets. American Psychological Association. 2005;30:41-63.

It was noted that employees seldom kill or assault their colleagues. This may be due to the reason that employees realize that there is a high chance of losing their job if physical aggression is not controlled, which is true for the police organization as well. They are not aggressive towards in-house members but seem to be aggressive towards members of the public who happen to be so-called law offenders and are under their custody in a police station or jail. However, some of the factors that are relevant to cite given the present study, that have emerged out of workplace aggression are:

1. An individual's alcohol consumption is associated with aggressive behavior.
2. Perceiving that one's work situation is unjust or that one's supervisor is over-controlling.
3. Displaced aggression is presumably focused towards persons who are supposed to be less dangerous (in police situations, it could be aggression towards authority/senior/boss to the offender who is being interrogated, who happens to be a soft target) (LeBlanc et al., 2005).
4. Uncongenial workplace environment with undesirable factors, including noise pollution, air pollution, crowding, hostile and aggressive behavior, and other negative influences[32]
5. Bandura (1965) demonstrated, through his experimental research, how observing aggression and violence can lead to similar behavior. Studies have shown that violence can have a substantial impact on real-world situations, including

32. Lobnikar B, Pagon M. The prevalence and the nature of police cynicism in Slovenia. Document No.:207979, December 2004.

police work. Modeling aggressive behavior is not uncommon among superiors within the police station. Additionally, research on modeling suggests that even news reports of violence can have a "contagion effect" or "copycat effect," in which some individuals mimic what they have seen. They may imitate the behavior because they believe it is a good idea. For instance, after watching a movie about bank robbery, someone might imitate the act. The phenomenon of "contagious violence" can also be seen in mob violence.

Work Pressure: One of the causes of custodial crimes is the tremendous pressure on police to detect cases whenever there is a surge in crime, and particularly heinous crime. The First Report of the National Police Commission has observed that, unfortunately, several police officers, under the pressure of work and a desire to achieve quick results, deviate from the path of patient, systematic, and scientific interrogation. They resort to the use of physical force in different forms to pressure the witness/suspect/accused to disclose all the facts known to them.

Lack of Supervision: Administrative reasons, such as inadequate supervision of these officers at the police station level, may contribute to the commission of custodial violence. Officers stationed at police stations often believe that they and their activities are not being closely monitored by supervising officers. They take the liberty of working recklessly, including the perpetration of custodial crimes. UPTO this correction is done 23.2.23.

Outdated Police Structure: The issue of custodial atrocities stems from the Police Act, 1861. It is a fundamental law and has remained unchanged, mainly due to the lack of political will to redefine the role and responsibilities of police officials in light of recent developments.

The British expanded their empire in India with a policing model deemed ideal for colonial rule. The model was based principally on the experience the English had had. At the same time, they tried to enforce order in Ireland (which rejected rule from Westminster) through the Irish Constabulary established under the Constabulary Acts 1822 and 1836.

This model of the Irish Constabulary sought legitimacy at Westminster rather than among the indigenous population. It was an alternative to an army of occupation with no community mandate whatsoever.

At the structural level, it was highly centralized, with a recognized chain of command from an individual constable to the chief constable, who in turn was responsible to the chief secretary and the lord lieutenant.

Another significant characteristic of the model was that it firmly established the principle that the constable was answerable to the chief constable rather than the law, with the chief constable himself being responsible to the central government.

This Irish blueprint was considered the ideal mechanism for solving a specific set of law and order problems. It is clear that from the colonies' point of view, there was considerable attraction to an arrangement that provided the "Para-Military Model" organization and trained them to operate as agents of the central government.

This was in a country where the population was predominantly rural, communication was poor, social conditions were essentially primitive, and the recourse to violence by members of the public who were "against the government" was not infrequent.

It was natural that such a force had been taken as a suitable model for adaptation to colonial conditions.

This force was organized on the "Para-Military Model" and trained to operate as an agent of the central government.

This was in contrast to the purely civilian and localized forces of Great Britain, which were organized on the London Model.

Psychological factors

Several relevant psychological factors are considered in the present study. The factors include cognitive, stress-related, personality, and tolerance, among others.

Cognitive: An individual's cognitive capacities, information-processing strategies, and learning processes play an essential role in aggression. An individual who has been oriented to behave in an impulsive way of life is more likely to react on impulse. This is referred to as an individual adopting an impulsive cognitive style. Impulsive cognitive style individuals may resort to non-thinking or reflective behavior, which can lead to aggressive behavior under stress, fear, and high arousal.

Reaction to ambiguity: In an experiment on individuals talking to another person on the phone, hissing and popping noises were introduced when the phone line went very low.

The reaction to this was often anger and annoyance. Over-attribution to vagueness or ambiguity could lead to either withdrawal or intolerant behavior. If extrapolated to police investigations, when an officer perceives that the offender is vague in their communication and their intentions are unclear regarding crucial facts, they may react with annoyance and anger.

Attribution: Yet another analysis is attribution; over-response to apparent provocations is strongly mediated by over-perceptions concerning the intentionality of these actions.

If actions appear intentional or purposely enacted, we respond with anger, which affects the likelihood of such treatment being repeated. If, instead, they seem to be unintentional, the result of an accident or factors beyond others' control, we are less likely to lose our temper and behave aggressively.

In short, our ascriptions regarding the reasons behind provocative actions by others play a pivotal role in determining how we respond to such treatment[33]

Frustration: There is widespread acceptance that humans are aggressive when their goals are thwarted. Out of this has emerged the model frustration–aggression hypothesis[34]

The assertions are that frustration always leads to some form of aggression, and aggression always stems from frustration.

It is only one of the many factors that can potentially lead to aggression.

Further research has shown that "frustration leading to aggression could depend on two conditions, its intensity and its perceived legitimacy."

When frustration is intense and perceived as unfair or random, it tends to increase the likelihood of potential aggression.

In contrast, when frustration is weak or observed as justified and legal, it may have less of an impact on the succeeding aggression[35].

---

33. Baron RA and Byrne D. Social Psychology, understanding Human Interaction, 5th Ed. London: Prentice – Hall Internatinal Inc, 1998, p.307.
34. Dollard J. Miller NE, Doob L.W, Mowrer OH, Sears RR. (1939). Frustration and Aggression. New Haven, US : Yale University Press, 1939.
35. Kulik J.A, Brown R. (1979). Frustration, attribution of blame, and aggression. Journal of Experimental Social Psychology, 1979; 15 (2): 183-194.

[36]In the context of police lock-up interrogation, the entire field force is challenged by different people playing different roles, riding on different emotions, and having different agendas and goals. Police, tasked with eliciting information, may become annoyed and suspicious.

They need to use discretion to separate lies and false information from the truth while complying with their supervisor's instructions. They need to comply with these, especially while experiencing pressure and discomfort.

The perception of victims as non-communicative and stubborn would likely lead to a punitive situation. This could potentially lead to an escalation of anger or aggression to levels higher than optimal and a physiological state of arousal. The victim being punished could be equally frustrated because, along with physical pain being inflicted, often derogatory and humiliating verbal abuse is experienced. In this case, frustration, which is also a form of physiological arousal, can lead to aggression directed toward the self. The atmosphere of lock-up gets compounded with human negativity and may result in a disaster such as custodial death.[37]

In the present study, frustration is assessed as part of stress along with anxiety, overload, and self-concept.

Personality Assessment

The Type A personality behavior pattern has been focused on since studies have shown a significant relationship between Type A, coronary disease-prone disorders, blood pressure, etc.

---

36. Worchel S. The effect of three types of arbitrary thwarting on the instigation to aggression. J Pers. 1974;42 (2):300-318.
37. Parameswaran EG, Beena C. An Invitation to Psychology, Tata McGraw-Hill, New Delhi, 1988.

Type A possesses characteristics such as excessive competitiveness, exaggerated time urgency, hyperactivity, and high levels of hostility and aggression. Type A individuals are shown to be involved in aggressive encounters more frequently than others who do not share these traits.[38] Due to the greater likelihood of Type A personalities' involvement in hostility and aggression, the investigator of the present study assessed Type A patterns through a questionnaire on the sample.

Gender Differences in Aggression

Information on gender differences in aggression is necessary, as the research reveals an interesting analysis.

Crime statistics show that males are expected to be more aggressive than females detained for violent acts.

Eagly and Steffen (1986) concluded that males do appear to be more aggressive than females.

However, the size of the difference is found to be small[39]. Gender differences in the context of risk factors are studied, as 10% of the sample consists of women police personnel. Other psychological factors measured in this study as part of stress factors are work overload, anxiety, self-perception/concept, and feelings of loneliness and boredom.

Medical Cause

In the present study, the sample was assessed clinically under the medical category. The parameters included blood pressure, the

---

38. Carver CS, Glass DC, Coronary-prone behavior pattern and interpersonal aggression. Journal of Personality and Social Psychology, 1978;36:361-366.
39. Eagly AH, Steffen VJ, Gender and aggressive behavior: A meta-analytic review of the social psychological literature. Psychological Bulletin, 1986;100 (3):309-330.

presence of ulcers, and the presence of heart ailments. Since blood pressure and heart ailments are directly or indirectly related to stress and aggression, these conditions were considered.

Here, it is worth noting that a well-established principle in psychology is that heightened arousal intensifies ongoing behavior and bodily and psychological reactions, including changes in blood pressure, respiration, and endocrine function. Under such conditions, the vigor of the current response, whatever it may be, tends to increase.

For instance, a police officer involved in interrogation tackling a complex case and going through heightened arousal may increase the intensity of aggressive practices on the offender (third-degree).

However, Zillmann's (1983) research contends that heightened arousal does not necessarily or automatically facilitate assaults against others; instead, such effects occur only under specifically limited conditions.[40] Though there is a paucity of empirical evidence, the observations and experience of the investigator of this research wish to point out that basic medical and physiological parameters, if not within the normal range, would contribute to the tendencies or predisposing psychological factors such as Type A personality, intolerance to ambiguity, impulsive style of functioning, etc.

In addition, when the work environment is not congenial, the officer is highly vulnerable."

---

40. Zillmann D. Transfer of excitation in emotional behavior. In J.T. Cacioppo & R.E. Petty (Eds.), Social psychophysiology: A sourcebook. New York: Guilford Press, 1983, p.215-240.

Social Cause

Custodial atrocities and brutality are rampant because of society's impractical demands and expectations to take stern action. A large section of society also feels that, despite their excesses, the police carry out the necessary and unpleasant task of preserving and protecting the state.

The nature of crime problems is complex, and the judicial process is painfully slow, taking years to decide on cases and often releasing the accused on technical grounds. As a result, the public is often desperate for peace.

They approve of police excesses if they can restore tranquility and punish those responsible for terrorizing and victimizing innocent citizens, such as terrorists, gangsters, dacoits, and professional criminals. The police officers who confront and kill these criminals in real or fake encounters earn people's appreciation.

The condoning public attitude toward police highhandedness is used as an alibi for justifying police torture.

The Padmanabhaiah Committee on Police Reforms (2000) has observed, "a large section of people strongly believe that police cannot deliver and cannot be effective if it does not use strong-arms methods against the criminals and anti-social elements of society.

And these people include India's political class, the bureaucracy, and large sections of the upper and middle class. In their own perception, the policemen feel that they are doing a job.

They resort to torture for 'professional objectives' to extract information or confession in order to solve a case, in order to recover stolen property or weapons of offence; in order to unearth other crimes that an arrested hardened criminal may have committed; in order to ascertain the whereabouts of other criminals; and in order to locate hide-outs another professional objective that the police often follows, which is to terminate the criminality of a professional criminal, who could be a burglar, a robber or a gangster, or even a terrorist by maiming him, by making him lame, rendering him incapable of committing further crime."

Economic Cause

Indian Police Commission (1902-03) found strong evidence of widespread corruption and police harassment throughout the country. The Report of the Commission narrated, "the forms of the corruption are very numerous. It manifests itself in every stage of the work of the police station. The police officer may levy a fee or receive a present for every duty he performs. The complainant has often to pay a fee for having his complaint recorded. He has to give the investigating officer a present to secure his prompt and earnest attention to the case. More money is extorted as the investigation proceeds.

When the officer goes down to the spot to make his investigation, he is a burden not only to the complainant, but to his witnesses, and often to the whole village.

People are harassed sometimes by being compelled to hang about the police officer for days, sometimes by attendance at the police station, sometimes by having him and his satellites quartered on them for days, sometimes by threats of evil consequences to themselves or their friends (specially to the women of the family) if they do not fall in line with his view of the case, sometimes by invasion of their houses by low caste people on the plea of searching the property, sometimes by unnecessarily severe and degrading measures of restraint. From all this deliverance is often to be brought only by payment of fees or presents in cash."

The Third Report of the National Police Commission (1979-1981) highlights two main points. The police powers involve the exercise of considerable discretion in the day-to-day work of the police. This discretion gives scope for corruption and malpractices, which are often accompanied by extortion and harassment of the public.

The power of arrest is the most significant in this category and deserves a close examination from the perspective of reducing the scope of several malpractices.

The Commission further stated that around 60 percent of the total arrests made by the police are unnecessary and unjustified. It is evident that a substantial portion of the arrests were associated with minor prosecutions, and it is estimated that 43.2 percent of the expenditure in the connected jails was for such prisoners, who, in the ultimate analysis, may not have needed to be arrested at all.

Political Cause

Even six decades post-independence, the police in this country are perceived as authoritarian agents of the state rather than agents of the law.

Political interference occurs at all levels, from the local to the highest echelons and in everyday functioning. The incentive for bad officers is to benefit from powerful patronage. Honest officers who discern their duty as serving without bias, fear, or favor find themselves labeled as uncooperative, complicated, and unhelpful and are sidelined into non-operational roles. Allegiance to power centers outside the police means that the chain of command is weakened; lines of control become blurred within the force, and the ability of superior officers to marshal their forces or hold them accountable for wrongdoing is severely compromised.

Political interference can have a chain reaction that becomes institutionalized in a negative manner, resulting in the subversion of existing structures of supervision and control within the establishment.

The police are unable to resist outside influence, whether from powerful societal or political elements or political superiors, due to the power of transfer and the ability to damn or advance individual officers' career paths.

Transfers have become negotiable instruments. It's a constant threat that hangs over their heads like the Sword of Damocles.

Eager to please, at times, police themselves tend to resort to politicking and hobnobbing with functionaries outside the system to secure personnel favors and benefits. All these make the possibility of professional policing a distant dream.

The report of the Shah Commission (1978), while investigating police atrocities during the emergency, observed that the police committed wide-scale atrocities during that period. The way the police were used and permitted to be utilized for various objectives, including how certain police personnel acted as if they were not answerable to any public authority.

The decision to arrest and release certain persons was entirely based on political considerations that were favorable to the ruling party and subverted the rule of law. Similarly, the NHRC has observed time and again that today, the country is witnessing the disturbing spectacle of the politicization of crime and the criminalization of politics.

The report of Vohra Committee (which the Commission submitted in counter affidavit in the matter of Prakash Singh & Others vs. Union of India, writ petition no.310 of 1996 of the Supreme Court) recognized that the ominous trend of criminal, political, and bureaucratic nexus assuming alarming proportions, combined with the politicization of the police, pose real threats to the very survival of democracy.

The Commission further observed that the insulation of the investigative function of the police from political and other extraneous pressures is essential to restoring confidence in the police and reducing complaints of human rights violations by members of the force.

Consequences

Custodial crimes have multiple consequences for individual personalities, family life, and the social functioning of communities and society. Torture is always aimed at the victim's physical and mental vulnerabilities. This is because these vulnerable points are generally consistent across people from all societies.

The physical injuries, sometimes present for entire lifetimes, have the effect of continuing the torture long after the detention. Pain, scars, and deformities will be continuous reminders of the torture. When government officials use rape, the suffering inflicted might go beyond the suffering caused by classic torture, partly because of the intention and often resulting in isolation of the survivor. In some cultures, rape victims may be rejected or formally banished from their community or family.

This rejection greatly hinders the psychological recovery of the victims and often condemns them to destitution and extreme poverty. Moreover, because of the stigma attached to sexual violence, officials deliberately use rape not only to humiliate and punish victims but also to destroy entire families and communities.

The arrest and detention in police custody itself psychologically impact the detainees. The anxiety, fear, and stress of being arrested and detained cause mental pressure, trauma, and stress on the detainee. The suspect or accused person arrives at the police station in a state of shock, and this varies enormously from person to person in terms of their capacity to cope with the situation.

The detainee spends much of their time in police custody, where the interrogation occurs. The police interrogate arrested persons in secret without recording the arrest. The detainee is under tremendous psychological strain during interrogation due to poor mental and physical condition. The interrogation process and the surrounding circumstances in custody can affect the mind of the arrested person, causing them to crumble. It builds pressure on the mental state of the person being interrogated.

The torturer aims to destroy the victim's mind by torturing the body. Torture in police custody is considered an instrument to impose the will of the strong over the weak. Torture is despair, fear, rage, and hate. In all custodial crimes, what is of genuine concern is not the infliction of pain but the mental agony a person undergoes within the four walls of the police station or lockup. Whether it is the murder of a man or the rape of a woman in police custody, the extent of trauma a person experiences is beyond the purview of the law (D.K. Basu vs. State of West Bengal, AIR 1997 SCC 610).

Torture creates enormous fear and insecurity in victims and their environment, and the spillover effect is on individuals, families, and the community. The social impact of torture includes feelings of insecurity, a sense of alienation, stigma, apathy toward democracy and governance, a feeling of being alienated by the country, a lack of social support, such as shelter, food, livelihood, education of children, and marriage. Custodial violence or police brutality not only affects the immediate victims and their families but also has a broader impact on society.

When people perceive police officers' actions as unfair, unreasonable, unnecessary, or harassing, particularly against minority communities, it can trigger riots, unrest, and societal disturbance. This perception can lead to the destruction of public property, violence, and casualties, causing significant harm to the affected communities and society at large.

The International Rehabilitation Council for Victims of Torture (IRCT) has developed various rehabilitation models that are implemented in centers and programs worldwide. One such model is the holistic approach, which considers several aspects such as psychological, somatic, social, legal, spiritual, and cultural factors for the rehabilitation of torture victims.

It is also of conceptual importance to note that torture survivors should not be considered sick, but rather as having normal reactions to a very abnormal event.

1. The primary treatment and principles are:
2. To treat physical and psychological symptoms at the same time.
3. to secure the patient's trust and confidence;
4. to respect the individual;
5. to avoid a situation that reminds the patients of torture and to inform the victims of torture.

Human Rights Violation, Code Of Conduct, And Compensation To Victims

Code of conduct for the police to prevent allegations of human rights violations

1. The Police must bear a faithful commitment to the Indian Constitution and uphold and endorse the rights of citizens as guaranteed by it.

2. They should enforce the law firmly and impartially, without fear or favor, malice or cruelty, or questioning the requirements of the law.
3. They should be aware of and value their limitations in terms of their responsibilities and powers. They should not usurp or even seem to usurp the functions of the judiciary and sit in judgment on cases to avenge individuals or punish the guilty.
4. As and when practicable, the police should use methods of persuasion, guidance, and warning while safeguarding the law and order. When the use of force is inevitable, they should use the minimum force to face or prevent the circumstances.
5. The primary role of the police is to prevent crime and maintain public order. They should realize that their efficacy is vested in the absence of crime and disorder, rather than in the cases where there is a visible indication of severe police action while dealing with such problems.
6. They should realize that they are also the citizens of this country. The only variation is that, on behalf of the society, they are employees vested with the power to pay more attention where a normal citizen cannot perform. Hence, they should act accordingly.
7. The efficiency of police performance depends on the magnitude of cooperation received from the people, which is dependent on the ability to gain public support for their actions and conduct, and retain confidence, value, respect, and admiration from the public.
8. The welfare of the public is the primary objective of the police, and therefore, they should be caring and

sympathetic towards all citizens. Regardless of people's social status and wealth, they should maintain friendships and offer the best individual services, providing necessary help.

9. The police should prioritize their duties over personal gain and maintain composure in dangerous and challenging situations. They should be prepared to make the ultimate sacrifice in the process of protecting the citizens.
10. The police should be mature enough, gentle, courteous, dependable, and unbiased. They should work with dignity and valor, developing their character and earning the trust of the people.
11. Maintaining integrity is the most important fundamental requirement and expectation of the police force. To gain respect, the police must maintain their private lives with meticulous care, be honest in their actions and thoughts, and exercise self-discipline, both personally and professionally.
    By doing so, they can gain the public's confidence and be regarded as model citizens.
12. The police should maintain the highest standards of discipline and faithfulness in performing their duties according to the law. They should respect lawful directions and the commanding ranks. They should practice absolute loyalty to the police force and continually improve their performance through consistent training and preparedness to serve society.

As members of a secular and democratic country, police officers should prioritize the greater good over personal interests and foster a sense of unity and brotherhood among all citizens of India, regardless of their diverse backgrounds. They must refrain from engaging in derogatory activities towards women and marginalized communities.

Human Rights of the Police/ Accused

Human Rights, including the rights of the accused, are usually found in the Indian Constitution and Law. The following is a demonstrative list:

1. Protection against arbitrary or unlawful arrest (Article 22 of the Constitution and Sections 41, 55, and 151 Criminal Procedure Code (Cr.P.C).
2. Protection against arbitrary or unlawful searches (Sections 93, 94, 97, 100 (4) to 81 and 165 Cr.P.C).
3. Protection against "Double Jeopardy" (Article 20 (2) of the Constitution and Section 300 Cr.P.C).
4. Protection against conviction or enhanced punishment under ex-post facto (Article 20 (1) of the Constitution);
5. Protection against arbitrary or illegal detention in custody (Article 22 of the Constitution and Sections 56, 57, 58, and 76 Cr.P.C)
6. Right to be informed of the grounds, immediately after the arrest (Article 21 (1) of the Constitution and Section 50 Cr.P.C as also Sections 55 and 75 Cr.P.C).
7. Right of the arrested person not to be subjected to unnecessary restraint (Section 49 Cr.P.C).
8. Right to consult a lawyer of his own choice (Article 22 (1) of the Constitution and Section 303 Cr.P.C).
9. Right to be produced before a Magistrate within 24 hours of his arrest (Article 22 (1) of the Constitution and Sections 57 and 76 Cr.P.C).

10. Right to be released on bail, if arrested (Sections 436, 437 and 439 Cr.P.C and Sections 50 (2) and 167 Cr.P.C).
11. Right not to be a witness against himself (Article 20 (3) of the Constitution).
12. Right to get copies of the documents and statement of witness on which the prosecution relies (Sections 173 (7), 207, 208, and 238 Cr.P.C).
13. Right to have the benefit of the presumption of innocence till guilt is proved beyond a reasonable doubt (Sections 101-104 Evidence Act);
14. Right to insist that evidence be recorded in his presence except in some exceptional circumstances (Section 273 Cr.P.C also Section 317 Cr.P.C).
15. Right to have due notice of the charges (Section 218, 228 (2), etc. of Cr.P.C).
16. Right to test the evidence by cross-examination (Section 138 Evidence Act);
17. Right to have an opportunity for explaining the circumstances appearing in evidence against him at the trial (Section 313 Cr.P.C).
18. Right to have himself medically examined for evidence to disprove the commission of offence by him or for establishing commission of offence against his body by any other person (Section 54 Cr.P.C).
19. Right to produce defense witnesses (Section 243 Cr.P.C).
20. Right to be tried by an independent and impartial Judge (The Scheme separation of Judiciary as envisaged in Cr. P.C., also Sections 479, 327, 191, etc. of Cr.P.C).
21. Right to submit written arguments at conclusion of the trial in addition to oral submissions (Section 314 Cr.P.C).

22. Right to be heard about the sentence upon conviction (Section 235 (2) and 248 (2) Cr.P.C).
23. Right to fair and speedy investigation and trial (Section 309 Cr.P.C).
24. Right to appeal in case of conviction (Sections 351, 374, 379, 380, Cr. P.C. and Articles 132 (1), 134 (1), and 136 (1) of the Constitution).
25. Right not to be imprisoned upon conviction in certain circumstances (Section 360 Cr P.C.C and Section 6 of the Probation of Offenders Act).
26. Right to refrain from police intrusion on his privacy (Article 31 of the Constitution).
27. Right of release of a convicted person on bail pending appeal (Section 380 Cr.P.C).
28. Right to get a copy of the judgement when sentenced to imprisonment (Section 363 Cr.P.C).

Compensation to victims

Section 357 (1) of Cr.P.C provides that when a court imposes a sentence which includes a fine, the court may direct that the fine amount should be utilized.

1. In meeting the expenditures of prosecution.
2. In making disbursements for the damage incurred by the victim.

Section 357 (3) of Cr. P.C. provides that the court can order the accused to pay to the victim, by way of compensation, when a fine is not part of the sentence.

Police Management Issues, Police Lock-Up, Treatment of People in Custody and Under Trial Detainees

Improving the organization and management of the law enforcement system in India. An evaluation report by BPRD 2000[41].

1. To make public-police interaction more meaningful, there is a need to reinforce good relationships between the police and the community.
2. Community Liaison Groups (CCLGs), which can strengthen the relationships between the police and the community, need to be reorganized and revitalized. A careful selection of CLG members should be made. This cannot be confined to SPs and SHOs; necessary measures should be identified to keep this mechanism active.
3. The selection of CLG members must be conducted in a more planned and careful manner so that it does not remain an exercise confined to SPs and SHOs only. Steps should be taken to maintain the good condition of this CLG mechanism.
4. As per the Supreme Court's directives based on the DK Basu vs. State of West Bengal case, the rights of the detainees should be appropriately displayed on the notice board of police stations.
5. There is a need for access to police through community representatives.
6. The police should maintain contact with relevant interest groups regarding the case.

---

41. BPRD Report, Research Studies on Police and Prison Issues (1970-2016) Compendium. Bureau of Police Research & Development, Bureau of Police Research & Development, New Delhi: Ministry of Home Affairs, 2017

7. Ensuring that the police make contact with various interest groups in a non-conflict situation (perhaps just going to talk to them about the new approach).

Stress, Health, And Performance

Police personnel face various challenges.

1. Irregular working hours.
2. Leave Problems
3. No social life.
4. No promotion.
5. Family Neglect and Separation.
6. Risk to life
7. No government Support.
8. Inadequate infrastructure.
9. Pressure of officers.
10. Political influence.
11. Frequent transfers.
12. Attitude of officers.
13. Children education.
14. Mess inadequate.
15. Poor salaries.

Recommendations

1. There is a need for open dialogue involving all ranks of police personnel, including effective communication with them and establishing a proper grievance redressal system that is accessible to them, as is present in the Indian Armed Forces. They generally practice monthly badakhanas and sainik durbars or sammelans.

2. Malignant problems that the police come across should be solved by making structural changes in the organization, within the police system, to deal with work and family stress conditions.

Psychological Problems In Police Personnel – An Epidemiological Study

BPRDR Reasons reported for stress and psychological problems are[42 43]:

1. Heavy workload and long working hours without breaks.
2. Conflicting orders from senior officers confuse police officers. This hampers their performance and leads to performing a stressful job.
3. Harassment by senior officers can lead to significant stress and anxiety.
4. A greater proportion of police personnel in Delhi (52%), Bangalore (95%), and Hubli (85%) are unable to stay with their families. Hence, they are more stressed out in their jobs.
5. Unable to avail of leave facilities as their services are needed in emergencies or festivals, this also leads to a significant cause of stress.
6. Meager job incentives and lower security lead to low morale among police officers.

---

42. Hiss J. Kahana T. Medicolegal investigation of death in custody: a postmortem procedure for detection of blunt force injuries. Am J Forensic Med Pathol 1996: 17:312-14.
43. Tedeschi LG. Methodology in the forensic sciences. Documents of human right abuses. Am J Forensic Med Pathol. 1984;5:301-303.

Recommendations:

1. There exists a greater extent of psychological issues with police officers, and they shall be trained in strategies for stress management in both their job and personal lives.
2. Police hospitals should recruit psychologists and counseling officers to identify and mitigate psychological stress among police forces by providing regular annual check-ups.
3. Detainees in police custody are usually deprived of any objects to avoid possible suicidal attempts. Items such as belts, suspenders, and cords are usually denied to detainees. The police lock-up is designed to avoid any such suspension points like hooks, door handles, hangers, rods, and bars to avoid any possibility of prisoners killing themselves. It was found that bedding cloths, handkerchiefs, and other clothing have also been used for self-hanging. Hanging need not occur from high suspension points such as ceiling fans, and the prisoners have committed suicide by attaching ligatures to beds, chairs, lock-up doors, or any unexpected objects in the cell.
4. Some of the alleged cases of suicides by hanging in police custody were homicides committed by police personnel. These homicides can be identified through autopsy, as there are usually no physical marks of struggle, scratches, or other signs of violence. It is not possible to hang a conscious person against their will without leaving any evidence of restraint. However, the suggestion that the hanging was caused by ligature strangulation can be disproved by the rising angle of the ligature mark, which is typically found under the angles of the jaw and has a defect in the skin mark where the suspension point pulls the ligature away from the surface. On the other hand, homicidal strangulation usually encircles the neck, and a

crossover point is often seen, with the level being lower and near the horizontal.

5. In cases where the true hanging mark is caused by a rope with a slip knot, there is a possibility of skin compression and a full circle scuff. When the suspension point of hanging is low, it can be achieved using a doorknob or bed frame, where the direction of pull can be oblique, and if the body rests against the direction of pull, the restraint marks can be almost horizontal. It is essential to have an expert assess the crime scene in these situations to avoid confusion, as was the case with Rudolph Hess in 1988, who was an inmate prisoner in Berlin's Spandau prison.

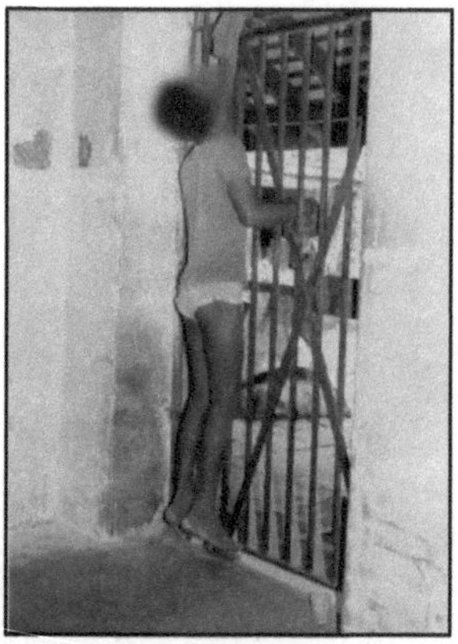

6. Death in prison can also occur due to natural causes, such as cardiovascular issues, emotional distress, or physical distress as an after-effect of arrest. These factors can affect blood pressure, adrenaline response, and heart function, and may lead to cardiac arrest, particularly in individuals with pre-existing health conditions.
7. The past health history of an inmate, including conditions such as diabetes, asthma, epilepsy, and others, can potentially lead to sudden death. It is crucial to gather medical history, autopsy evidence, and arrest memos, as directed by the National Summit on Wrongful Convictions in 2013, to investigate the cause of death in such cases[44].

44. National Summit on Wrongful Convictions: Building a Systemic Approach to Prevent Wrongful Convictions Report from the International Association of

The International Association of Chiefs of Police (IACP), the Department of Justice's Office of Justice Programs (OJP), and the Innocence Project joined forces to announce the release of the report of the National Summit on Wrongful Convictions: Building a Systemic Approach to Prevent Wrongful Convictions. The summit report was a result of a National Summit on Wrongful Convictions that the IACP held in concurrence with OJP in 2012. The summit brought together 75 subject matter experts from all key disciplines to address and examine the causes of, and solutions to, wrongful convictions across the entire justice system (National Summit on Wrongful Convictions, 2013).

The report comprises 30 recommendations for practicing fair arrests, rectifying unlawful arrests, supporting technology and forensic medicine, and re-investigating wind-up cases. The summit report emphasizes the required modifications in investigative protocols, policies, strategies, training, administration, and assessment.

"*This groundbreaking report lays out a strategy for law enforcement to take a leadership role in preventing and responding to wrongful convictions,*" said Chief Walter McNeil, Quincy, Florida, Police Department, and former IACP President.

In a first step towards addressing such concerns, the writer examines the Indian police officer's approaches to interviewing and compares these results to the attitudes of citizens and lawbreakers.

Unambiguously, the beliefs of participants about the human rights of suspects and the use of threatening and non-intimidating interrogation strategies are to be considered.

Chiefs of Police/ U.S. Department of Justice, Office of Justice Programs Wrongful Convictions Summit August 2013.

This information will offer insight into the beliefs related to using threatening and non-intimidating interrogation methods by Indian police officers. This will be useful in developing better training methods that lead to higher professional standards, recognition of fundamental human rights philosophies, and increased empathy for how frightening tactics can lead to failures of justice[45] Previous research by Alison and Furnham (1994) in the UK, involving 43 police officers, 49 offenders, and 58 citizens, examined their outlook towards delinquency, pre-trial jury partiality, and punishment. The results showed that lawbreakers tend to view criminals as victims of unfavorable situations[46] The offenders believed that the criminals were not morally accountable for their actions because prevailing social circumstances were the root cause of their deviation[47] Criminals believed they preferred compassionate legal methodologies that involved lenient punishments. In a nutshell, police officers considered criminal activity an inherent attribute of an individual, whereas criminals believed that the choice to commit a crime was a deliberate act.

Lock-up

As per the Cambridge dictionary, a "Lock-up" means a small room, used as a prison, usually in a small town, in which criminals can be kept. As per Part I Vol. II A of A.P. Police Manual

45. Sarangi, IPS Director General (Investigation) at NHRC https://nhrc.nic.in/press-release/new-dg- investigation-nhrc (Accessed on October 18, 2020).

46. Furnham A, Alison L. Theories of Crime, Attitudes to Punishment and Juror Bias Amongst Police, Offenders and the General Public. Personality and Individual Differences, 1994;17 (1):35-48.

47. Hollin C. Psychology and crime: An introduction to criminological psychology. London: Routledge, 1989.

(Investigation) Police Standing Order 456-1, a person who is arrested and not released on bail shall be detained in a secure zone of the police station reserved for such purposes, under consistent watch (Police Standing Order 456-1, Andhra Pradesh).

A detainee that the station house official (SHO) considers dangerous and fears will abscond should be kept in the lock-up under constant and practical observation. This should be done immediately after an exhaustive search, and necessary entries should be made in the detainee's search register and the guard or watch sentry relief book.

The person called to a police station for questioning to verify his complicity in any offense shall not be kept in lock-up without effecting an arrest. Detainees known to be goons, rowdies, risky criminals, organized gang members, militant groups, and those liable to escape and charged in notorious offenses of homicide, assault, rapes, kidnapping for ransom, etc. should be kept in the lock-up rooms.

Detainees in police custody should not be allowed to leave the lock-up after sunset, except in emergencies, with sufficient escorts, which should be recorded in the general diary (GD) and the Sentry Relief Book. Anyone in police custody before remand is entitled to see their relatives and an advocate. They should not, however, be allowed to talk to members of the public.

If the arrested person desires that one of his relatives be permitted to remain with them, then the request should be considered unless there are compelling security reasons.

As per Running Current No. 449/ J3/62, dated 10.10.62 of the Director General of Police, Andhra Pradesh, and Police Standing Order 460- 1-A, once a person is in the custody of the police, the responsibility for their life and security lies with the law enforcement authorities.

The primary concern is the physical safety of the person in custody. This includes protection from injury and death, whether caused by oneself or due to any other reason.

As it is difficult to measure an individual's psychological state, it is essential to understand that the prevailing psychological state of a detainee would be full of fear, shock, trauma, a sense of guilt and shame, etc. Therefore, suicidal tendencies may develop. Hence, the lock-up should be devoid of any objects or belongings that will provide an opportunity to attempt suicide. They should be under continuous observation at all times by at least one police officer.

The detainee's residence should be under vigil and in full view of the police personnel on duty, including the station writer, head constable, or duty officer. The workplace should be set up to provide a clear view of the lock-ups. The detention room should be immediately searched if any suspicious attempts or actions are noticed. The person in custody may cause self-injuries or commit suicide, which can be assumed to have been caused by the police.

Hence, it is crucial to have timely involvement, a contemporary record of events, and a proper reporting system for such attempts by prisoners.

No investigating officer (IO) should employ any force or cause any physical injury during an interrogation of the detainee. If such injuries are generated, the responsible police officers are prosecuted for killing, and the burden of evidence of their innocence lies on them.

Article 5 of the Universal Declaration of Human Rights says: "No one shall be subjected to persecution or cruel, inhuman or degrading treatment or punishment in custody."

The police lock-up, if it has a detainee, shall not be closed at dawn. The bedding of the arrestees should be brought out of the cell, shaken well, and left out for some time in the sun.

In lock-ups where there are no toilet facilities, the used vessels shall be removed and the toilets shall be thoroughly cleaned. Wherever toilets are provided, they should also be thoroughly cleaned and maintained. The detainees shall be taken to the common restrooms and washrooms. The food should be provided daily at 10 am or as early as necessary before attending court, and again at 5 pm or as soon as possible if they are brought to the police station after 5 pm.

The detainees should be fed at government cost if their relatives do not provide them with food, which should be checked for poisonous substances. Strict compliance with these orders is vested in the station in charge.

Depending on the need, a separate escort should be provided to the convicted and under-trial prisoners. A conveyance must be provided in the case of women prisoners if the travel distance exceeds 2 km, or for any valid health reasons.

Scale Of Accommodation For Arrestees

As recommended by the Government Order (G.O.s 1672, Judl., Dt. 11.7.1969 and 325, Home (Judl.) Dt. 9.2.1918), a 16 cubic meter of breathing space and four square meters of ground space should be kept as the minimum standard for each prisoner in lock-up. According to the Public Works Department, Government of India, PWD Circular, Memo No. 3266 G, dated July 19, 1917, the lock-up room design should ensure sufficient ventilation, light, and safety measures. There should be concealed electric wiring and roof-embedded lights with switches provided outside the lock-up.

The lock-ups should be devoid of rods or hooks on the ceiling and walls. The walls and ceilings should be smoothly finished and painted white color.

The right guaranteed by Article 21 of the Constitution of India cannot be denied to detainees, under-trial prisoners, and convicts, except according to the procedure established by law, by placing reasonable restrictions as permitted by the law (D.K.Basu Vs. State of W.B. 1997 Crl. L.J. 743). Police, anywhere in the world, work under various challenging conditions, including high work pressure, irregular working hours, and the existing security scenario of VIPs, while performing multifaceted duties. With more and more liberalization and enforcement of fundamental rights, it is becoming difficult to detect crimes committed by hardcore criminals, terrorists, extremists, drug peddlers, and smugglers within the ambit of the Law.

The Latin word, maxim salus populist suprema lex (the safety of the people is the supreme law) and salus republicae est suprema lex (safety of the state is the supreme law) co-exist and are essential and relevant, and lie at the heart of the principle that the welfare of an individual must yield to that of the society[48 49].

The State must act "right, just, and fair." Using any form of torture to extract information will result in an offense under Article 21 of the Constitution of India. A crime suspect must be interrogated using sustained and systematic interrogation techniques by the law.

---

48. Cicero. On the Republic on the Laws, London: Loeb Classic Library, 1989, p.467.
49. Jonathan Law, A Dictionary of Law (8 ed.), London: Oxford University Press 2015.

One can't be tortured using third-degree methods to confess to the crime. Their constitutional rights can't be violated except as permitted by the law.

Emerging technologies towards smart lock-ups[50]

The advent of digital transformation has brought about a significant revolution in how we organize and manage our daily lives.

However, when we imagine a prison in India or any developing nation, the common perception is of a rundown facility with outdated infrastructure designed to isolate detainees from the outside world. On the other hand, inefficient monitoring and security systems can lead to a host of illegal activities, physical abuse, and suicidal tendencies among inmates.

The emergence of novel technologies has brought a significant revolution to the way law enforcement agencies operate.

However, many detention centers in developing nations like India still operate with inefficient monitoring and security systems, which can result in illegal activities, physical abuse, and even suicides. Such activities can lead to legal problems for the responsible officers. The implementation of the Internet of Things (IoT), artificial intelligence, facial recognition, and innovative prison layouts can help transform prisons and lock-ups into fully automated IoT solutions - "Smart Lock-up Facilities." By connecting different devices and services throughout the detention facility, IoT-based monitoring and control systems can facilitate real-time monitoring of prisons and lock-ups, intercept prison activities, and prevent criminal and suicidal behaviors.

---

50. Bundinski M. Berat N. Business and Technology. IoT in Prisons: From a Dusty Old Lockup to a "Smart Penitentiary Facility", June 24, 2019.

Upgrading the existing prisons and lock-ups in India with such technology can create a safer environment for detainees, visitors, and vehicles.

Detention before trial (police custody) has been one of the most neglected areas in the whole administration of the criminal justice system. In the past, attention has been focused almost exclusively on detention after trial (judicial custody), which has a more significant impact on people's lives than detention before trial (Friedland, 1965; Adam, 1998).

The institution of police custody plays a crucial role in the administration of criminal justice. The police agency is authorized to arrest an accused or suspected person and to carry out searches and seizures of property in the course of implementing the justice process.

Complaints of abuse of power and torture of suspects in police custody, who have the power to detain a person during interrogation and investigation, have led to the rise of custodial crimes. This has profound implications for the administration of justice and the public's trust in law enforcement agencies.

"Custodial violence" and "abuse of police power" are not only peculiar in India, but they are widespread phenomena. It has been a concern of the international community because the problem is universal, and the challenge is almost global.

Although various efforts have been initiated at international, regional, and domestic levels, which set out international standards, best practices, benchmarks, basic principles, and guidelines, they have not proved to be effective enough to curb the menace of torture in custody.

The prohibition on torture is a fundamental principle of international human rights law, firmly established and absolute.

All states and territories under their jurisdiction or effective control are bound by this prohibition, which applies in all circumstances, whether in times of war or peace. States must rigorously uphold this prohibition in all its forms, combat the impunity of perpetrators of torture, and provide redress for abused detainees and all victims and survivors of torture. Any deviation from this prohibition not only violates fundamental human rights but also undermines the credibility and integrity of the justice system (UN 2005).

It is noteworthy to mention that India has signed the UN Convention against Torture and Other Cruel, Inhuman or Degrading Treatment or Punishment (1984) on 14th October, 1997.

However, custodial torture is endemic even in India. In the past, several committees and commissions have been established by the government to initiate the process of reforming the institution of police custody and investigate the causes of custodial crimes.

However, little progress has been made in this direction. In most cases, either these reports have not been released or their recommendations have not been implemented. Some of these reports include the Sarkaria Commission, Bhargava Commission, Tarkunde Commission, Deb Commission, Shah Commission, National Police Commission, Law Commission, and National Human Rights Commission.

The issue of custodial crime has been examined by both internal and external sources, as documented in the literature. However, internal studies conducted by public authorities, such as commissions and committees appointed by governments, have been subject to numerous limitations.

These studies often do not provide a comprehensive picture of custodial crime, and their findings are not readily available to the public due to the sensitivity of the issue. Furthermore, many of these studies are based on secondary data or surveys, which may not accurately reflect the on-ground reality of the situation.

External sources, on the other hand, have historically paid little attention to the problem of custodial crime.

Until the end of the 1960s, the issue was largely ignored by scholars and was not a significant focus of academic studies.

Academics in both universities and research centers, as well as other professional bodies, were primarily focused on studies that were relevant to government policies. These studies did not shed much light on the crucial problem of governmental lawlessness.

The problem of custodial violence was not a primary research agenda, and only a few stray studies, seminars, or symposia have analyzed this issue (Desai, 1986).

Official statistics compiled by the National Crime Records Bureau (NCRB), Ministry of Home Affairs, Government of India, attribute the causes for custodial deaths as illness/natural deaths, escaping from custody, suicides, attacks by other criminals, riots, accidents, and demise during treatment or hospitalization. No single case of torture causing death in police custody is reported by the NCRB from 1999 to 2007.

In contrast, the NHRC, since its establishment in 1993 up to 2018-2019, has been reporting several cases about violations of human rights due to torture in police custody. An important observation made by the NHRC over the years is that large numbers of such complaints are reported from the state of Andhra Pradesh.

The Commission's latest report highlights that despite the establishment of its own human rights commission, Andhra Pradesh continues to witness the trend of custodial crimes. These crimes have a devastating impact on the victims' families and communities. Therefore, it is crucial to fully comprehend the process that leads to custodial crimes in police custody, with a specific focus on the state of Andhra Pradesh.

There is a paucity of reliable data, scholarly literature, and studies to comprehend the problem of custodial crimes, their causes, consequences, and preventive measures in the country. Studies in this domain have primarily focused on custodial deaths.

Other forms of custodial crimes such as rapes, arbitrary arrests and unlawful detentions, and disappearances in custody, etc., are almost unexplored. Most of these studies are based on secondary data. Very few studies in different states provide insight into the causative factors and preventive measures. However, an in-depth analysis of field reality is missing in the literature.

Despite the prevalence of custodial crimes in the state of Andhra Pradesh, no comprehensive study has been conducted on their causes, consequences, and preventive measures.

There has been a lack of critical research on the managerial perspectives of police administration and strategies to counter the threat of custodial deaths. To fill this gap, the present study, conducted by an IPS officer, aims to gain insights into the phenomenon of custodial crimes in police custody in Andhra Pradesh. The author had access to records and was able to interview guilty police officers using a questionnaire. This study is a modest attempt to understand and address the issue of custodial deaths in police custody in Andhra Pradesh.

Scope of the Study

This research aims to conduct a sample survey of the data on custodial deaths in United Andhra Pradesh, India, and analyze the current situation of the custodial environment. It proposes managerial and technological remedies to address issues with existing facilities in prisons and lock-ups, with a focus on crucial aspects and recommendations to turn the existing lock-up into a "Smart Lock-up Facility." The research explores the use of managerial strategies to improve police administration principles in light of current custodial deaths in Andhra Pradesh. It also brings out organizational approaches to handling the problem of custodial deaths.

It formulates effective police management practices in Andhra Pradesh to prevent custodial deaths through better police management policies.

References

1. Human Development Report, 1990
2. National Human Development Report 2001
3. International Commission of Jurists 2003
4. Crime in India 1997 published by National Crime Records Bureau
5. Bansal YS, Murali G, Singh D. Custodial deaths-an overview of the prevailing healthcare scenario. J Indian Acad Forensic Med.2010:32:315-315.
6. Prikryl J. Abu Ghraib: A Global Family Portrait, The Believer, 3/2 (March 2005)
7. Basu DK, Ashok K. Johri v State of West Bengal, State of UP on 18 December, 1996.

8. Baxi PM, Public Interest Litigation 18, Second Edition, Asoka Law House, New Delhi, 2006, p.22.
9. Saini RS. Custodial Torture in Law and Practice with Reference to India 36 JILI (1994) at 166.
10. Shakya NK, Siddiqui MN, Shakya P, Singh NB, Gupta OP, Ahmad N. Custodial deaths- aretrospective study. Indian Journal of Applied Research 2018;8(5):67-69
11. National Human Rights Commission Annual report 2002-2003, nhrc-nic.in/annualreports/2002- 2003 (Accessed on June 06,2018)
12. Bansal YS, Murali G, Singh D. Custodial deaths – an overview of the prevailing healthcare scenario. J Indian Acad Forensic Med.2010; 32:315-315.
13. Amnesty International 2001
14. Law Commission of India 1994
15. Amnesty International Annual Report, 1992, p.34-35. https://www.amnesty.org/en/documents/po110/0001/1992/en/ (Accessed on September 18, 2020)
16. Taylor SE, Peplan LA, O Sears AD, Social Psychology; ed 12th, New Delhi: Pearson Education Inc. 2006.
17. Crime in India, Statistics, NCRB, National Crime Records Bureau, New Delhi, Ministry of Home Affairs, 2016.
18. Cannon WB, Voices from the past "voodoo" death. AM J Health. 2002;92:1593-1596.
19. Selye H. The physiology and pathology of exposure to stress. In: A Treatise Based on the Concepts of the General Adaptation Syndrome and the Diseases of Adaptation. Montreal: Acta Inc. 1950.

20. Reay DT, Eisele JW. Death from law enforcement neck holds. Am J Forens Med Path. 1982;3:253- 258.
21. Ross DL, Chan TC, Forensic Science and Medicine: Sudden Deaths in Custody, Totowa, NJ : Human Press Inc., 2006.
22. 29th World Medical Assembly, Tokyo, Japan, October 1975.
23. Section 164 CRPC cases data. www.ecops.appolice.govin (Accused on October 18, 2020).
24. APA Amicus Briefs by Issue http://apa.org/about/offices/ogc/amicus/index-issues (Accused on October 18, 2020).
25. Amnesty International Annaul Report 1992, p.34-35. https://www.amnesty.org/en/documents/poll0/0001/1992/en/ (Accused on September 18, 2020)
26. NPC, fourth report (June 1980, at 27 26) cited in Amnesty International, p.34
27. Basu DK vs. State of West Bengal, AIR 1997 SC 610, at 615.
28. Law Commission of India 1994
29. Nair 1999
30. Amnesty International 1992, 2001b, 2003; Human Rights Watch 2006
31. LeBlane M M, Barling J. Understanding the Many Faces of Workplace Violence. IN S. Fox & P.E. Spector (Eds.), Counterproductive work behavior: Investigations of actors and targets. American Psychological Association. 2005;30:41-63.

32. Lobnikar B, Pagon M. The prevalence and the nature of police cynicism in Slovenia. Document No.:207979, December 2004.
33. Baron RA and Byrne D. Social Psychology, understanding Human Interaction, 5th Ed. London: Prentice – Hall Internatinal Inc, 1998, p.307.
34. Dollard J. Miller NE, Doob L.W, Mowrer OH, Sears RR. (1939). Frustration and Aggression. New Haven, US : Yale University Press, 1939.
35. Kulik J.A, Brown R. (1979). Frustration, attribution of blame, and aggression. Journal of Experimental Social Psychology, 1979; 15 (2): 183-194.
36. Worchel S. The effect of three types of arbitrary thwarting on the instigation to aggression. J Pers. 1974;42 (2):300-318.
37. Parameswaran EG, Beena C. An Invitation to Psychology, Tata McGraw-Hill, New Delhi, 1988.
38. Carver CS, Glass DC, Coronary-prone behavior pattern and interpersonal aggression. Journal of Personality and Social Psychology, 1978;36:361-366.
39. Eagly AH, Steffen VJ, Gender and aggressive behavior: A meta-analytic review of the social psychological literature. Psychological Bulletin, 1986;100 (3):309-330
40. Zillmann D. Transfer of excitation in emotional behavior. In J.T. Cacioppo & R.E. Petty (Eds.), Social psychophysiology: A sourcebook. New York: Guilford Press, 1983, p.215-240..
41. BPRD Report, Research Studies on Police and Prison Issues (1970-2016) Compendium. Bureau of Police Research & Development, Bureau of Police Research &

Development, New Delhi: Ministry of Home Affairs, 2017

42. Hiss J. Kahana T. Medicolegal investigation of death in custody: a postmortem procedure for detection of blunt force injuries. Am J Forensic Med Pathol 1996: 17:312-14.
43. Tedeschi LG. Methodology in the forensic sciences. Documents of human right abuses. Am J Forensic Med Pathol. 1984;5:301-303.
44. National Summit on Wrongful Convictions: Building a Systemic Approach to Prevent Wrongful Convictions Report from the International Association of Chiefs of Police/ U.S. Department of Justice, Office of Justice Programs Wrongful Convictions Summit August 2013.
45. Sarangi, IPS Director General (Investigation) at NHRC https://nhrc.nic.in/press-release/new-dg- investigation-nhrc (Accessed on October 18, 2020).
46. Furnham A, Alison L. Theories of Crime, Attitudes to Punishment and Juror Bias Amongst Police, Offenders and the General Public. Personality and Individual Differences, 1994;17 (1):35-48.
47. Hollin C. Psychology and crime: An introduction to criminological psychology. London: Routledge, 1989.
48. Cicero. On the Republic on the Laws, London: Loeb Classic Library, 1989, p.467.
49. Jonathan Law, A Dictionary of Law (8 ed.), London: Oxford University Press 2015.
50. Bundinski M. Berat N. Business and Technology. IoT in Prisons: From a Dusty Old Lockup to a "Smart Penitentiary Facility", June 24, 2019.

1

LITERATURE REVIEW

Custodial deaths are one of the most egregious intersections of state power, institutional apathy, and individual vulnerability. Custodial deaths do not occur in isolation. They are increasingly recognized as manifestations of an inadequate and dysfunctional structure of policing and the criminal justice system. In India, custodial deaths have been receiving more attention, awareness, and scrutiny from civil society, legal institutions, and human rights organizations in recent years. The intensification of scrutiny of custodial deaths, particularly, has come about as patterns have emerged around the victims' socio-economic and demographic profiles, the nature of the environments within the custodial settings and or situations, and the fuzzy or opaque accountability arrangements when custodians do kill in custody.

Literature in this domain spans multiple disciplines—ranging from criminology and public administration to psychology and information systems. While some scholars emphasize the systemic nature of police violence and institutional impunity, others examine the organizational behaviors, decision-making biases, and cultural factors that shape police conduct.

Simultaneously, emerging research in technology and data governance opens new avenues for transparency and reform in custodial settings.

In this chapter, I have collated relevant studies and theoretical frameworks that help explain why custodial deaths exist and continue to occur. By locating the problem of custodial death within broader forums of state power, procedural justice, and public accountability, we can identify not only the immediate sources of custodial death but also the institutional logics that sustain custodial death. The literature we have reviewed provides a conceptual understanding and a critical lens for proceeding with empirical and policy discussions.

Although natural causes cause most custody-related deaths, we cannot ignore deaths caused by negligence in provision of medical aid or the inaccessibility of healthcare settings. Data on custody-related deaths is critical when looking to improve upon prison medical services or develop strategies to avoid future deaths. These studies may also help prison services determine where to allocate their healthcare funding and services best. However, there remains a lack of updated morbidity and mortality data in India to make this determination.

1. Police Management and Organizational Behavior

Globalization has led to a new approach to public management, known as New Public Management (NPM). Several European countries seriously examined police management within the context of NPM. Discussions and analyses focused on the implications of police management reforms for law enforcement and future police management scenarios (Cope et al., 1977).

Various police management styles and models have been proposed to boost police performance, including in investigations. Gotheschalk (2006) highlights that police officers encounter enormous and impressive amounts of information during their work. Knowledge management in law enforcement progresses through several stages: the "Offices-go-Technology System," "Officer-to-Officer System," "Officer-to-Information System," "Officer-to-Application System," and "Officer-to-Public." Providing relevant training and education—from constables to higher-ranking officers—can help foster a positive departmental environment and enhance the police department's public image.

COMPSTAT, a competency mapping technology used within the Command Accountability System, and the OODA (Observe, Orient, Decide, Act) loop— a decision-making and organizational learning model developed and widely adopted by the military—offer valuable insights into COMPSTAT's effectiveness. This police management system significantly accelerates the dissemination of accurate crime analysis data, supporting decentralized decision-making and problem-solving efforts to reduce crime and meet organizational objectives. Walsh and Henry (2008) note that effective police management relies on both COMPSTAT and the OODA loop in police performance management. Implementing these tools to handle critical incidents—such as violence and suicide attempts—within jails and police stations may help prevent undesirable events.

2. Psychology of Aggression and Risk

It is necessary to point out how decision-making processes surrounding custodial deaths, especially involving torture, can be framed around decisions either to decrease the level of torture or escalate it during an interrogation to find the truth.

Social psychologists have studied the "risky shift," and the phenomenon has been observed in practice across a range of real-life experiences and fields including politics, governance, and other increasingly complex systems. Stoner (1968) points out that research findings have shown that group decisions are generally riskier than individual decisions, and additional studies suggest that when group members initially favor risk, group decision-making becomes even riskier.

In contrast, when the initial opinions of the group favor conservation, the group decision results in a shift toward more extreme conservationism. Such a finding showing discussion leading to more extreme decisions is called "Group polarization", according to Levine and Moreland (1998).

This phenomenon can be exemplified by instances of custodial deaths, such as a case cited by Amnesty International (1992, Pg 34-35). It reports that at the state level, police officials admitted to using torture. For instance, after a rise in deaths at police stations in Andhra Pradesh during 1985 and 1986, the Andhra Pradesh Police Association publicly urged officers to stop using torture and to adopt modern scientific investigation methods. In response, Delhi's Police Commissioner, Mr. Vijay Karan, announced on 1 May 1988 that he aimed to ban torture and third-degree methods. During his tenure, the use of torture during interrogations was prohibited in Delhi police stations, which appeared to reduce custody deaths significantly—by half in 1989-1990 compared to previous years. However, the number of deaths in police custody in Delhi increased substantially again in 1991 after Vijay Karan's term ended. This highlights the critical role of decision-making in influencing organizational performance.

Many officials fear that the lack of new investigative techniques promotes police misconduct and abuse of power. The Director General of the British Police explained that officers are not supported in taking alternative paths and also lack modern, scientific interrogation techniques to adopt. Based on this, we can generalize that several factors exist to promote custodial deaths, including lack of training, non-compliance with interrogation procedures, shift work circumstances, and political influences. Additionally, building on the topics of police management and Custodial Deaths from earlier discussions, the researcher has written about relevant 'human factors research' pertinent to the issue at hand.

The study of aggression is a vital aspect of social-psychological research. Almost everyone has experienced being either a victim or an initiator of intense aggression or violence at some point. As society grew more complex, the methods of using weapons of aggression also advanced. The frequency of conflicts involving weapons to express aggression has increased significantly. Despite extensive knowledge about aggression and violence, ongoing research is necessary to understand these behaviors in specific contexts and situations. Much human behavior, especially aggression, is often attributed to our animal instincts. According to Lorenz et al. (2002), aggression frequently originates from innate causes. He suggests that an instinctual drive compels us toward aggression, sometimes even destructive toward others. Morris (1994), in his book "The Naked Ape," argues that many of our aggressive behaviors are genetically programmed responses to particular environmental cues and signals from others.

Recent experiments, as noted by Berkowitz (1965), suggest that reducing physiological tension—caused by injuring the anger trigger—happens when the aggressor learns that aggression is often rewarded (within the social learning framework). This tension relief or gratification resembles a reinforcement mechanism and does not imply a long-term decrease in the likelihood of aggression; individuals who find aggression rewarding are more prone to attack again. This reinforcement may also explain why Lorenz (1963) and Storr (1968) viewed appetitive behavior as strong evidence of spontaneous aggressive drive. Moreover, recent studies on the nervous and endocrine systems in animals have contributed to a more comprehensive understanding of their aggressive behavior. Moyer (1968) believes that the endocrine system releases hormones into the bloodstream or lymphatic system. Hormonal differences between males and females correspond to differences in aggressive tendencies. Thus, virkkunen et al. (1995) discovered that while the rate of testosterone secretion corresponded to overt hostility in young men, it did not do so for older men.

In light of the above research, an effort is made to relate the variables of the sample, such as age, Physiological parameters (including blood pressure, diabetes, and ulcers). Etc. In addition, other psychological factors under study included cognitive and stress factors.

Todd (2001) discussed cognitive factors, focusing on cognitive style, and highlighted an essential element: "available heuristics." Heuristics are cognitive shortcuts that help people make quick inferences about their environment. This idea explains why, in problem-solving, people sometimes make rapid, unconscious decisions, which can cause issues later. Custodial torture is widely regarded as one of the most severe forms of human rights violations. It is prohibited by the Constitution of India, the Supreme Court, the National Human Rights Commission (NHRC), and the

United Nations. However, police officers across the country continue to violate these prohibitions. Consequently, there is a need to balance individual human rights with societal interests in crime prevention through a pragmatic approach (Joginder Kumar v. State of Uttar Pradesh, (1994) 4 SCC 260).

3. Torture and Human Rights Violations

Saggi (2020) noted that when officers are regularly exposed to descriptions of violence victims' aggression in civil society, as well as visuals of successful and unsuccessful police interrogations, they tend to internalize these vivid details into mental shortcuts. These become quickly accessible for future reference or during current problem-solving situations, such as interrogations that could lead to Custodial Deaths. Ruiz et al. (2014) outlined several other factors that might contribute to Custodial Deaths, although these have not yet been studied in this specific context.

- Prior dislike for the person, group (like black, religion, caste, etc).
- Escalation (victim interrogation responding aggressively or refusing information.
- Displaced Aggression.

Additionally, other contextual elements may influence the behavior of custodial staff:

- **Perceived Safeness** – When the detainee is perceived as weak and unlikely to retaliate, officers may feel more emboldened to use excessive force.
- **Visible Pain Responses** – Physical signs such as prayers, groans, or pleading can sometimes provoke further abuse, rather than empathy, due to a misinterpretation of vulnerability.

- **Perceived Strangeness** – Cultural or behavioral differences (such as unfamiliar rituals, calmness, or silence) may be misinterpreted as defiance or manipulation, further aggravating the situation.

Finally, the researcher wishes to highlight that enhancing the management of individuals in custody and the investigation procedures can be achieved through disciplines that have aided in understanding and predicting human behavior across various situations. These include Psychology, Social Psychology, Criminology, Law, Medical Sciences, and Information Technology (IT). These fields provide services and processes that enable faster, simpler, and more efficient analysis and knowledge creation. Consequently, "knowledge management" is highly pertinent to police management.

4. Role of Knowledge and Technology in Prevention

Since knowledge management supports overall police management and investigations, including those related to custodial deaths, the researcher has explored this topic in detail. Gottschalk (2006) notes that the importance of knowledge management in policing "Europol" is centered at the Knowledge Management Centre (KMC) in The Hague, Netherlands, where Europol regularly updates its database. The Centre aims to stay at the forefront of scientific and technological advancements, as well as other specialized fields that support law enforcement. It is argued that knowledge is the most vital resource in police investigations, with many investigators asserting that effective investigations rely heavily on the availability of knowledge.

5. Empirical Evidence from India and Abroad

Professor Graham Towl, formerly Chief Psychologist at the UK Ministry of Justice, analyzed death cases in state custody from 2000 to 2014.

The study included sections on the prevalence of deaths in custody, deaths by setting in 2014, and self-inflicted deaths over the period.

Data revealed 8,129 deaths across 15 years, with 73% (5,918) men and 27% (2211) women. There was a 21% decline in total deaths in 2014 (479) compared to 2000 (607). Most deaths (59%) occurred among patients detained under the Mental Health Act (N=4,801), followed by Prisons (34%, N=2,728). Overall, deaths among detained individuals seem to decline annually, though prison deaths have increased since 2006. Over the period, the White ethnic group had the highest number of deaths; deaths caused by natural causes were most common among MHA detainees, while other causes, including homicide, were more frequent in prisons. In 2014, 479 deaths were recorded in custody, a 15% decrease from 2013. Natural causes accounted for 67% (N=323), and self-inflicted deaths for 23% (N=111). White males constituted most deaths. Age was only documented for 194 individuals, with those aged 61 and older — primarily detained under the MHA — being the largest group (N = 121), primarily due to natural causes. Between 2000 and 2014, there were 1921 self-inflicted deaths across all settings; 82% (1,572) were men, and 18% (349) were women, representing a 27% decrease from 2000 to 2000. Prisons had the highest proportion of self-inflicted deaths during this period; however, these deaths' share of all deaths decreased from 55% (N=81) in 2000 to 35% (N=84) in 2014.

Jhamad et al., 2014 conducted a retrospective analysis of custodial-related deaths based on autopsy reports at AIIMS, New Delhi, covering 13 years (1999-2011). The study identified 15 cases, all male, with most aged 25-35 years (8 cases). Of these, nine involved Hindus and 6 Muslims.

Ten deaths were due to natural causes, while three were from unnatural causes—one from hanging, one from a fall, and one from blunt injuries. In two cases, the cause was undetermined.

In India, prison overcrowding persists, and despite medical screening, infectious diseases like TB remain prevalent. The National Human Rights Commission is working to improve jail conditions.

Vipra's 2016 study revealed that 1,275 people died in police custody in India from 2001 to 2013. Less than half of these custodial deaths resulted in official cases, according to the National Crime Records Bureau (NCRB). The number of deaths in judicial custody—such as in prisons-reported by the National Human Rights Commission (NHRC) is significantly higher, with about 12,727 deaths recorded between 2001 and 2010. Since 2000, the fewest deaths occurred in 2010 (70), while the highest was in 2005 (128). On average, around 98 people die annually in police custody across India. Maharashtra, Andhra Pradesh, and Gujarat experienced the most custodial deaths from 2001 to 2013, whereas Bihar reported only six such cases.

Human Rights Watch's report highlighted that nearly 600 individuals died in Indian police custody from 2009 to 2015, many after being tortured. The report states that police often ignore arrest procedures and torture suspects to death, frequently attributing these deaths to suicide or illness. Such killings usually go unpunished. Although torture is illegal in India and many countries now recognize that it rarely yields accurate information, many Indian police openly admit to using the 'third degree'—which can range from slaps to severe beatings—to obtain confessions. Citing government data, the report noted that 97 people died in police custody in 2015, with 67 cases involving failures to present suspects before a magistrate within 24 hours or deaths occurring within that period. HRW emphasized the need for strict enforcement of arrest guidelines, including informing families, conducting medical exams, and ensuring suspects are promptly brought before magistrates.

The Asian Centre for Human Rights (ACHR) report, "Torture in India 2011, indicates that the National Human Rights Commission (NHRC) in India has recorded 14,231 deaths in custody from 2001 to 2010, comprising around 1,504 deaths in police custody and 12,727 deaths in judicial custody. It notes that these figures relate only to reported cases and do not represent the total number of custodial deaths. The ACHR report notes that custodial deaths are linked by reports to deaths from torture, deaths from lack of medical attention, and deaths relating to deplorable conditions. Once a person is in custody, they become the responsibility of the authorities, police, or personnel of the jail, who are responsible for the person's life, health, and safety (Rebecca & Vijay, 2013).

Shakya et al. (2018) conducted a retrospective study on death patterns in custody, analyzing medico-legal autopsy reports at IMS, BHU, Varanasi, from July 2006 to June 2016. They identified a total of 235 custodial deaths in Varanasi, considering factors such as age, sex, religion, and death pattern. Of these, 225 were males and 10 females. Hindus were the most involved (202), followed by Muslims (31) and others (2).

The majority of deceased individuals were from Uttar Pradesh, with five from Uttarakhand, and one each from Bihar, Jharkhand, West Bengal, Haryana, and Punjab. Deaths among convicted prisoners (187) exceeded those among under-trial prisoners (48). Out of the total, 210 deaths occurred in jail and 25 in hospital.

Causes of death included 197 natural, 28 unnatural (mostly suicides), and in 10 cases, the cause was undetermined.

Mandar et al. (2016) conducted a retrospective autopsy-based study on custodial deaths in Aurangabad over 10 years (1999-2008). Out of 90 custodial deaths, 89 were males, with the highest number (33.3%) in the 31-40 year age group. Natural causes accounted for 62 (68.9%) deaths. Among the unnatural deaths (30%), suicides made up 59.3%, homicides 25.9%, and accidents 14.8%. Pulmonary tuberculosis was the leading cause of natural death, followed by ischaemic heart disease. Poisoning was the primary method of suicide. The study highlights the importance of better medical services and tuberculosis control in prisons. Increasing suicidal awareness among detention staff could help identify prisoners at risk early.

Naik et al. (2016) presented a case report involving a 32-year-old male prisoner brought in for autopsy. According to the investigating officer, the individual was detained for a cognizable offence. The following day, he was found partially hanging from a prison bar with a loincloth (lungi). The body was brought in dead for the autopsy. The use of modern technologies, such as CCTV cameras, can help address these issues. To prevent deaths, it is essential to develop and enforce existing guidelines. This case highlights the importance for police to motivate and monitor prisoners to prevent suicidal behavior actively.

Bardale and Dixit (2015) studied files on deaths in custody over a decade. Compared to the general population, individuals in custody have a higher suicide rate, raising concern given their marginalized status. Data from the National Crime Record Bureau of India (2009–2011) indicates that approximately 27.48% of custodial deaths are due to suicides in police lock-ups, meaning about a quarter of arrested individuals face suicide risk—an alarming figure. The study found that 78.57% of these deaths occurred in the 21–40 age group. Older inmates have a lower suicide rate than younger ones and the general population. Hanging is the most common method, constituting 42.85% of suicides, followed by poisoning at 35.71%. The prison or lock-up environment itself may elevate suicide risk, as many inmates perceive their suffering as worse than death.

Amrit (1999) outlined the standard procedure for autopsies in cases of custodial deaths. Such autopsies should be conducted by a Revenue Divisional Officer, Sub-Collector, or Deputy Collector, also known as Additional District Magistrates. As per the Government Orders (G.O.s 1672, Judl., Dt 11.7.196 and 325, Home (Judl.) Dt 9.2.1918), each prisoner in a police lock-up must have at least 16 cubic meters of breathing space and four square meters of ground space. The Public Works Department, through Circular Memo 3266 G, dated July 19, 1917, states that lock-up cell designs must ensure proper ventilation, lighting, and safety. Electrical wiring should be concealed, with lights embedded in the ceiling, and switches placed outside the lock-up. Ceilings and walls should be smooth, polished, and regularly whitewashed, with no rods or hooks present. The rights guaranteed under Article 21 of the Indian Constitution cannot be denied to detainees, under-trial prisoners, or convicts, except through lawful procedures, with reasonable restrictions as permitted by law (Basu, 1997).

Digital transformation has radically changed how we organize and oversee our daily lives. When imagining a prison in India or other developing countries, it is often seen as a dusty, outdated facility with archaic infrastructure. Its purpose is to isolate detainees from the outside world.

However, inefficient monitoring and security measures can lead to illegal activities, physical abuse, and suicidal acts, which can cause legal issues for the officers involved. New technologies, methods, and ideas have brought significant changes to law enforcement agencies. Innovations in emerging technologies are expected to shape future policing, supporting and enhancing police operations and connections that help maintain social order more effectively (Mirkov & Gelles, 2020).

Bulman (2009) recorded several new technological developments. The National Institute of Justice (NIJ) utilized countersigned recommendations to fund various projects aimed at enhancing prison security. Scanning and detection devices can determine the location of cell phones, and possibly the location of areas or items, such as a knife. There are also radio wave devices to track movements of staff and incarcerated persons inside the prison facility. New computer programs can also analyze and forecast occurring problems. Furthermore, new technology has provided cost savings and improvements in facility operations (Sarah, 2003).

Encouraging the utilization of IoT and monitoring and control systems to enable real-time oversight of prison facilities and vehicles, to identify wrongful actions, and even to prevent actions such as suicides, would enhance the safety of inmates, visitors, and staff.

A Death on the Edge of Custody: Chittoor District (2023)

Most of the data and research on custodial deaths are confined to events known to have occurred in custody (e.g., at police stations or jails), but there is a series of real-life examples which occur in a legal and procedural grey area; those events which occur after things like physical police contact, or psychologically and procedurally influenced in some manner by custody, without being in the physical four walls of a lock-up.

The following case from the Chittoor district in Andhra Pradesh (2023) conveys this blurriness. The case is collated as a series of events by the district authorities. It lays bare how institutional practices and physical proximity to custody can obscure the line of what constitutes a "custodial death." The case establishes that the deceased was technically "out of custody," but the variety of factors leading up to his death drew close connections to law enforcement contact.

On the night of September 27, 2023, during a routine drunk-driving check at Reddygunta on the outskirts of Chittoor, Andhra Pradesh, traffic police intercepted a lorry (bearing registration number TN 50 1618) en route from Tiptur to Guwahati, carrying a load of coconut powder. Rajendran, a 55-year-old man from Katpadi and the second driver of the vehicle, was found to be intoxicated.

The Reserve Sub-Inspector (RSI) on duty instructed the lorry to be taken to the local police station, where the vehicle's documents were collected. Both the driver and co-driver were released shortly thereafter, with instructions to return the following morning and produce the required records before a magistrate of the second class.

Rajendran had joined the journey at Katpadi, already under the influence of alcohol. The primary driver and owner of the vehicle, Swamigan, had driven the lorry from Tiptur to Katpadi, after which Rajendran joined the journey.

Following their release, the drivers parked the lorry approximately 100 meters away from the Two Town Police Station and decided to sleep inside the vehicle overnight. They intended to appear before the magistrate the next morning, pay the requisite fine, and continue toward Guwahati.

The following morning, however, Rajendran was discovered dead, having hanged himself from the vehicle using a rope.

Initial observations by traffic police suggested no signs of foul play. Notably, the primary driver, Swamigan, had reportedly spent the night within the police station premises. A formal complaint was filed against him, in which he confirmed that no police misconduct was involved. The deceased's family was informed and was en route to Chittoor at the time of reporting.

As the body was found outside the police station and not within formal custody, the authorities proposed registering the case under Section 174 of the Criminal Procedure Code (suspicious or unnatural death). However, depending on further legal consultation with the Public Prosecutor, a reclassification under Section 176 (death in custody) was also being considered.

The district police reported no anticipated law-and-order issues but confirmed they would closely monitor the situation.

— Filed by Rajasekhar, Superintendent of Police, Chittoor.

Custodial deaths are always a result of a complex layering of systemic failure, biases, institutional culture, and boundaries.

Medical neglect, which is always preventable, is rarely recognized as a cause.

Organizational elements, such as training, political dynamics, and peer pressure, are contributing to the evolution of the conversation toward increased violence. Even with promising avenues to explore, such as COMPSTAT and knowledge management systems, the organizational landscape of police operations in India lacks the use of these systems.

The frameworks of aggression and group polarization help to interrogate further the persistent abuse happening in contemporary police systems, but are rarely incorporated into training or policy discussions.

The path to reducing custodial deaths lies in acknowledging their complexity. Reforms must integrate multidisciplinary knowledge—from law, psychology, and medicine to technology and data science.

Only through a combination of legal accountability, institutional reform, and a shift in professional culture can custodial settings become safer and more just. This review lays the groundwork for empirical analysis in subsequent chapters by framing the key drivers and consequences of custodial deaths.

2

FEW INCIDENTS OF CUSTODIAL DEATHS

Added the following for structure:

Custodial deaths can be defined as deaths of individuals in the custody of law enforcement or correctional authorities, which often point to a larger problem of police brutality, institutional negligence, and a lack of accountability.

While there are cases where custodial deaths are the result of negligence or systemic shortcomings, there are also cases where custodial deaths arise as a result of excessive force, torture, and depriving individuals of medical assistance promptly. Here are a few examples that illustrate the different types and contexts of custodial deaths:

1. Case - Telangana's Ranga Reddy district

On November 27, 2019, a woman veterinary doctor was sexually assaulted and abused, and murdered in Telangana's Ranga Reddy district. On November 29, 2019, four suspects were arrested by the Hyderabad police, and during their seven-day police custody, they were taken to the scene for reconstruction.

However, during the reconstruction, the suspects snatched weapons from the police, fired at them, and tried to escape.

The police fired back, and all four suspects died in the encounter. This incident elicited varied reactions, with some celebrating the police's actions while others expressed concern and criticized them.

Samajwadi Party MP Jaya Bachchan and BSP President Mayawati praised the police.

At the same time, activists such as Vrinda Grover and Kavita Krishnan (Secretary, All India Progressive Women's Association) criticized the encounter, stating that it was not justice but a means to silence demands for accountability and justice for women.

2. Case - Mohammed Zakir

Mohammed Zakir, a 34-year-old auto driver, was the youngest of his eight siblings and had a wife and two children. In July 2010, he was arrested by Andhra Police along with four others for allegedly aiding Mohammed Viqaruddin, who was accused of killing three police officers in Hyderabad and one in Ahmedabad. Zakir was also accused of being a member of the alleged fundamentalist outfit, Darsgah Jihad-O-Shahadat (DJS). He had helped Viqaruddin rent a house. Police officers apprehended Zakir in July 2010 while he was on his way to work early in the morning in Warisguda. His family was not informed about his arrest for several months. Eventually, his family discovered that he had been held in Cherlapally prison in Hyderabad. On April 7, 2015, Zakir and four others, who were under trial, were being transported from Warangal prison to the Hyderabad court by the Warangal prison escort team when they were shot dead near Aler in Telangana's Nalgonda district.

3. Cr. No.5/90 u/s 176 CrPC of Nagaram PS Guntur T (C) Guntur Dist.

Nagaram PS arrested Nalluri Baburao under Cr. No. 4/90 u/s 457, 380 IPC on February 18, 1990, at 10 p.m. and was kept in the lockup. On February 19, 1990, at around 3 p.m., PC 1580 B. Nirmal Babu, who was on station watch duty, discovered that Baburao had hanged himself with his lungi on a window in the PS and died. It is important to note that the custody of the deceased began from the time of his arrest on February 18, 1990, and the police are responsible for the safety of the person they arrested (in this case, Sri Nalluri Baburao).

4. Cr.No. 24/90 u/s 174 CrPC of Husnabad PS of Karimnagar Dist.

On March 8, 1990, at around 5 p.m., Uppulati Chandraiah was brought and locked up in the police station.

Around 7.30 a.m. the following day, CI Mogalaiah arrived at the police station and brought Chandraiah to the SI's room. The SI was on leave at the time, so the beating and torture were conducted by one probationary SI and two police constables. During the torture, the sarpanch of Rekonda came to the police station in connection with the release of another person from police custody. Chandraiah was beaten severely and had bleeding injuries all over his body. At around 9 p.m., the wounded Chandraiah was moved to the front room of the police station and locked up in the police cell of Husnabad. PC 313 Galaiah was the night sentry at the police station. At around 3 a.m., the following morning, Chandraiah died in the police lockup. A judicial inquiry was ordered, and the CB CID subsequently investigated the case. Departmental action was taken against the police personnel involved. This is a clear case of torture and cruelty in custody.

5. Cr. No. 39/90 u/s 174 CrPC of Raikal PS

Gurrappu Lingam committed theft at his employer's house. As a result, the village elders held a panchayat and decided that he should pay Rs. 5,000/- towards stolen articles and Rs. 500/- as a penalty. However, Gurrappu Lingam sold his land and did not pay his employer. On May 13, 1990, the SI of Raikal PS was informed about the incident and called Gurrappu Lingam to the police station for interrogation. During the interrogation, Lingam confessed to the offense, and the SI recovered the stolen "silver kadas" from his house. Later, CI Korutla instructed the SI to take Lingam to Korutla PS for further questioning. While on their way back to Raikal PS, Lingam expressed that he was feeling restless, so the SI took him to Bethany Nursing Home. Unfortunately, Lingam did not respond to treatment and died.

The medical officer stated that the cause of death was "neurogenic shock," indicating primary and secondary injuries resulting in a neurological shock, which is a form of custodial death. The CID investigated the case and concluded that there was no evidence to prove that Gurrappu Lingam died due to torture by police personnel.

6. Cr. No.93/93 u/s 174 CrPC of Mahaboob Nagar (R) PS, Mahaboob Nagar Dist.

On July 18, 1990, at about 4 p.m., the deceased Lambadi Mothi was arrested by the SI while he was travelling on a rickshaw with a load of iron pieces tied in a gunny bag under suspicious circumstances. The ASI interrogated him and concluded that the iron pieces were stolen. A case was registered under Cr. No. 84/90 u/s 379 IPC at Mahaboobnagar (R) PS, and Mothi was released with instructions to come whenever called by the police.

On August 7, 1990, Mothi was called to the PS and allowed to sleep in front of the lockup room after having meals. At about 4 a.m., he woke up and shouted that some insect had bitten him. The ASI sent him to the Government. The hospital in Mahaboobnagar, where the Casual Duty Medical Officer attended to him. However, he passed away on August 11, 1990, in the hospital. As the insect/snake bite occurred in police custody, this case qualifies as a custodial death.

7. Cr. No. 106/90 U/S 309 IPC of Medchal PS, Ranga Reddy Dist.

On August 15, 1990, Abubakar and Abdul Akil, r/o. At the Medchal check post, they were caught while trying to dispose of some vehicles, suspected to be stolen. The SI of Medchal registered a case under the Criminal Code. No. 104/90 u/s 41(A) and 102 Cr.PC. On interrogation, it was discovered that both accused had stolen vehicles worth Rs. 1 lakh. Both accused were brought to the PS. While in custody, one of the accused, Abubakar, consumed pesticide poison (monocrotophos) from a plastic tin that had been seized in a prior case and was being preserved in the PS.

Abubakar had forcibly administered some of it to his associate, accused Akil, under threat. The police noticed this too late, and both victims were immediately shifted to the Government civil hospital, Medchal, for treatment. Due to the non-availability of medical officers at the Government hospital, the victims were then taken to a private hospital in Medchal.

First aid was administered before they were immediately shifted to Gandhi Hospital, Secunderabad. Abubakar expired in the hospital. A magisterial inquiry was conducted, and it was found that the availability of pesticide poison to the accused, who were in the custody of the police, resulted in their consumption of it, leading to the death of one of the accused. The inquiry also suggested that action was taken against the police officers who kept the poison carelessly in the police station. Therefore, it is a custodial death.

8. Cr.No. 211/90 u/s 176 CrPC of Ibrahimpatnam PS, Vijayawada City

On September 14, 1990, at around 9:30 p.m., Smt. B. Samrajyam was returning home when the deceased, P. Joji, attempted to assault her sexually. Samrajyam managed to escape and hollered for help, and the deceased fled the scene. The beat PCs brought the deceased to the PS at 02:00 a.m. on October 15, 1990, where the SI noticed injuries on his legs and hands inflicted by members of the public (at that time, he was injured only) because of the above incident. Due to a traffic jam, the deceased was taken to a private hospital.

The doctor advised transferring him to the University General Hospital as he complained of a burning sensation in his stomach and vomiting. However, he was declared dead upon arrival at the hospital, and a case in Cr. No. 211/90 u/s 174 Cr. P.C. was registered at Ibrahimpatnam PS.

A magisterial inquiry revealed that the deceased had been beaten while in police custody and died not only due to the beating but also due to the police's inaction in taking him to the hospital immediately. As a result, the government took departmental action against all police officers and personnel at Ibrahimpatnam PS. This is a custodial death.

9. Cr. No.7/91 u/s 147,148,324,342,302 r/w 149 IPC of Mahanandi PS Kurnool Dist.

The deceased, Boya Krishna, and two others were arrested by SI H.N. Karunakar, his staff, and 20 other private individuals. The three had been accused of threatening people with bows and arrows and robbing them. After the villagers complained, the SI, his team, and 20 others surrounded the accused and beat them.

As a result of the beating, Krishna sustained severe injuries and died. The SI then directed two police officers and four others to burn Krishna's body in the forest and shifted the remaining two accused to Nonepalli. The SI, two Home Guards, and six others were arrested on February 13, 1991. It is suspected that Krishna died as a result of police brutality, and as such, it is a custodial death.

10. Cr. No.15/91 u/s 176 CrPC of Karvetinagar PS, Chittoor Dist.

On March 1, 1991, SI N. Venkatanadha Reddy, one HC, and two PCs were on night rounds between Karvetinagar and Puttur to prevent wire offenses. At approximately 1:30 a.m., they arrested one A. Sanjeevi and recovered a cutting plier, two hacksaw blades, and other items. The accused confessed that he committed wire offenses and sold wire in the Puttur market. Later, around 04:00 a.m., the SI and his team boarded a lorry to Puttur to recover the stolen property. On the way, the accused requested a stop on the pretext of urination and attempted to escape. He jumped into a culvert numbered 59/2, not knowing its depth, and died. As the accused was in police custody at the time, his death is considered a custodial death.

11. Cr. No.19/91 u/s 176 CrPC of Amruthluru, Tenali ®, Guntur Dist.

On the night of March 8, 1991, a theft occurred at the residence of Y. Srimannarayana in Pyaperru village at around 7:30 p.m. During a power outage, an unidentified person entered his house from the back and stole Rs. 150 from his shirt pocket, which was hanging on a hook in his room.

When the intruder tried to enter another room, there was some noise, and the commotion raised the alarm of the householders. Two individuals, Paleti Veeraiah Chowdary and Swarna Nagabhushan, assisted by other villagers, caught the thief as he attempted to escape through the northern door of the house.

The villagers handed him over to the police through the village sarpanch, Movva Sambasiva Rao, who informed the Amruthaluru police station.

HC 2062 of Amruthaluru police station and other constables arrived at Pyaperru village and took the culprit to the police station in a car. A report was filed, which was subsequently registered as Cr. No. 18/91 under Section 380 IPC of Amruthaluru police station at around 1:15 a.m. on March 9, 1991. The stolen Rs. 150 was recovered from the thief, and he was kept in the lockup room of Amruthaluru police station from around 1:00 or 1:10 a.m. on March 9, 1991.

On March 9, 1991, at approximately 1:15 p.m., P.C. 716 Sri K. Brahmam Raju opened the lockup room for interrogation on the instructions of the Circle Inspector of Police, Sri T.V. Saibabu. At this time, the accused, Sri Kavuri Vinaya Babu, was found hanging by a nail with his lungi and a wire in the lockup room. Upon examination, it was discovered that Vinaya Babu had died. The villagers claim that Sri Kavuri Vinaya Babu was beaten to death by the police, who were trying to extract a confession for the offenses he allegedly committed, and that it is not a case of suicide by Vinaya Babu, by hanging himself with his lungi. The police officers, on the other hand, claim that Sri Kavuri Vinaya Babu was beaten by the villagers immediately after being caught red-handed in the act of stealing Rs. 150, that he was subjected to humiliation by the villagers and unable to bear the insult, and that he committed suicide in the lockup room.

The deceased was arrested in a theft case on March 8-9, 1991, and brought to Amruthaluru PS of Guntur District by HC 2062 J. Sangeet Rao, along with three other police personnel at 12:15 a.m. He was confined to the lockup after a due search. The judicial inquiry commission recommended departmental action against the personnel responsible, as the deceased died in police custody.

12. Cr. No.24/91 u/s 398,332 IPC of Domakonda PS, Nizamabad Dist.

Upon receiving information about a dacoity from unknown criminals on the BTS Domakonda Road, S.I. Domakonda and his staff proceeded to the location in a jeep. While en route, two unknown women standing on the street flagged down the jeep.

The S.I. stopped, and suddenly, six offenders wearing lungis and pants attacked the jeep, pelting stones and beating the occupants with sticks. The police party managed to apprehend both women and all the criminals involved in the attack. During questioning, they revealed their names and admitted to committing highway dacoities under the leadership of Akula Balaraju. While questioning was ongoing, A. Balaraju complained of severe chest pain, and the S.I. requested the presence of Surender Reddy, Medical Officer, Primary Health Centre, Domakonda, at 06.30 a.m. Unfortunately, Akula Balaraju passed away in the presence of the medical officer. The deceased's body was referred for a post-mortem examination.

13. Cr. No.26/91 U/S 174 CrPC of Ramakistapur PS, Adilabad District

Bonasa Odellu, s/o Rayamallu, r/o Ramakristapur, was arrested on March 31, 1991, on charges under Section 307 of the Indian Penal Code at PS Ramakristapur (Cr. No. 25/91).

At around 3:00 a.m. that night, the deceased requested PC 967 to take him out to attend to nature's call while PC 433 of APSP was on sentry duty. As the accused was being escorted to the bathroom, he picked up a glass bottle intended for use in the toilet. Instead of entering the toilet, he went into the adjacent bathroom, broke the bottle against the wall, and inflicted a deep cut on the right side of the neck of PC 967. The accused then collapsed in the bathroom while holding the broken bottle in his right hand, and PC 967 could not react in time.

The case has been classified as a "suicidal death." Since the incident occurred within the PS's confines and the deceased was under custody, it is a case of custodial death.

14. Cr. No.62/91 u/s 174 CrPC, Yelamanchali (R), Vizag Dist.

On the intervening night of June 16-17, 1991, at around 1:30 a.m., the accused, Yerakayya, took the "mangal sutra" necklace from Smt. Boja Manikyam's neck while she was asleep. She woke up and raised an alarm, causing the accused to flee. The accused's associate attacked Appa Rao, the victim's husband, with a stick, causing him to lose consciousness.

Villagers caught the accused and beat him, then brought him to Elamanchili Rural Police Station, where he was registered under Cr. No. 60/91 u/s 392 IPC. However, an investigation was not undertaken due to the police force being engaged in related election duties. On June 22, 1991, at 9:00 a.m., the home guards took Yerakayya to answer nature's calls with the assistance of PC 408. Yerakayya then requested a cup of tea and sat on the veranda steps. After drinking the tea, he collapsed and died. The inquiry officer concluded that Yerakayya's death was likely caused by the negligence of police officials, who failed to provide him with timely medical treatment and proper food. The decision to hand over Yerakayya's body to his relatives is also criticized, as it should have been preserved by burying it for further examination if necessary.

15. Cr. N o.102/91 u/s 174 CrPC of Medak Town PS

On the intervening night of July 20–21, 1991, around 30 individuals committed theft in the houses of Shivnoor village in Chegunta Mandal. While investigating the case, CI Medak and the police party went to Gouraras village in Bichkonda Police Station, Nizamabad District, to apprehend the culprits. They caught hold of Yellamma w/o Mallaiah and recovered a golden ornament related to the Karnapalli theft case. Yellamma complained of chest pain during the journey back to Medak and was taken directly to the Civil Hospital, where she died before receiving medical attention. The post-mortem examination conducted by the Deputy Civil Surgeon at the Community Hospital in Medak revealed that Yellamma died due to heart failure. A further medical investigation was ordered, and the report concluded that Yellamma's death was due to heart failure and that no one was responsible for it.16.

16. Cr. No.56/91 u/s 174 CrPC, Vijaypuri P.S., Nalgonda District.

On August 14, 1991, at 6:00 p.m., V. Narayana Reddy and four others from Chelakurthi village forcibly stripped a 40-year-old woman from the same village, tied her hands, and paraded her naked through their village streets.

The victim was also tortured, as they suspected her involvement in the elopement of V. Narayana Reddy's sister, Jaya, with Govindu, who too was from the same village. Additionally, the perpetrators forced the victim to consume arrack before parading her naked in the streets. They also threatened anyone who tried to come to the victim's rescue with dire consequences. Upon receipt of a complaint from the victim, a case is opened in the Criminal Division. No.77/91 U/s 354 and 501 IPC was registered by the S.I. of Police, Alwal, on August 15, 1991. During the investigation, T. Parwatha Reddy surrendered himself on August 19, 1991, to sentry PC 379 at Halia PS in a drunken condition with contusions on his back and lacerated wounds on both elbows. He was in a shirt and underwear. The special party took Parwatha Reddy in the jeep to Chalakurthy and produced him before the investigating officer. S.I. Alwal was coming there in connection with the proposed visit of the Lady Governor to inquire into the incident and console the victims. The S.I. arrested the accused, Parwatha Reddy, and handed him over to the Vijayapuri police for safe custody. Meanwhile, Parwatha Reddy complained of a stomachache. He was immediately shifted to K.N. Hospital, Vijayapuri, but on the way, he breathed his last at about 11:15 a.m. and was pronounced dead in the hospital.

17. Cr. No.80/91 u/s 174 CrPC of Madanapalle 2 Town, Chittoor Dist.

The deceased, Basheer, was caught red-handed stealing a saree from a society colony compound in Madanapalle on August 23, 1991, at about 12:30 p.m. He was beaten by the public and handed over to the police. Before this case, he was involved in another criminal case with the same PS. The SI registered a case, but as his injuries were not severe, he was put in lockup to send him to a government hospital through the court. The next day, Basheer developed fits and died in the hospital. The CID investigated the case and found lapses on the part of the SI, recommending departmental action.

18. Cr. No.90/91 u/s 174 CrPC of Pattabhipuram PS, Guntur Dist.

On August 27, 1991, T. Punnaiah, aged 40 and a former Mutha coolie of Jagan Mohan Rice Mill, along with another coolie, stole a paddy bag from a heap of bags outside the mill. When Punnaiah attempted to carry the bag on his head, he couldn't manage due to being intoxicated and fell. P. Vijaykumar refused to help them and alerted Mutha Mistry and B. Chinna Kotaiah about the theft. This caused the culprits to flee in different directions. P. Vijayakumar and Shaik Hussain pursued Punnaiah, apprehended him, and handed him over to PC 2340 P. Venkatarao, who was on picket duty at the Prakasam center. The deceased was brought to Pattabhipuram Police Station around 2:00 a.m. At approximately 4:15 a.m., sentry PC 2509 A. Azeez discovered the deceased hanging inside the lockup, having tied his full-sleeved shirt around his neck, bent in his knees, and the lockup door. He was promptly transported to G.G.H., Guntur, where the casualty medical officer examined him and pronounced him dead.

19. Cr. No.107/91 u/s 176 CrPC of Gudivada II Town

The deceased, Rajaboyina Kasulu, aged 22, s/o Chinna Raghavulu, a Yadava from Paaulapadu (V), was the alleged accused in Cr—no—56/91 u/s 324, 307, and 506 of the IPC at Gudivada Tq Police Station. The case was reported on September 4, 1991. The ASI promptly arrested Kasulu at his residence, brought him to the police station, and handed him over to PC, the sentry, for secure custody. On September 5, 1991, at 06:45 a.m., PC 1017 M. Kumar Singh, who was on sentry duty from 03:00 to 06:00 a.m., discovered Kasulu hanging lifeless from the door frame of the lockup using his lungi.

20. Cr . No.78/91 u/s 174 CrPC of Nagi Reddy Pet PS, Nizamabad (Cr.No.290/91 u/s 174 CrPC of Market PS, Secunderabad).

The deceased, Laxmaiah's wife, and Chakali Durgaiah argued at their residences in Nagireddypet. Laxmaiah went to the Nagireddypet Police Station and reported the incident verbally.

The station inspector (S.I.) advised him to return later for further inquiry into the matter. On October 4, 1991, around 10:30 a.m., while the S.I. was at the police station, Laxmaiah arrived drunkenly, seeking an update on his earlier report. The S.I., noticing his intoxicated state, requested that he return later. This request angered Laxmaiah, leading him to use abusive language against the S.I. and attempt to approach him. PC 90 Mohan Rao intervened to restrain Laxmaiah, but as the S.I. stood up from his chair, Laxmaiah lost his balance while retreating and fell, sustaining head injuries. Laxmaiah was immediately taken to the government hospital in Yellareddy and later referred to Hyderabad for treatment. He passed away on October 9, 1991, while receiving treatment at Gandhi Hospital in Secunderabad. Consequently, a case was registered under the Criminal Code. No.290/91 at Market Police Station, Secunderabad.

21. Cr. No.47/91 u/s 174 CrPC of K.D.Peta PS, Narsipatnam (C)

Masa Nookaraju, a rickshaw puller and a Harijan (Dalit) community member with a criminal record was detained by the police in K.D. Peta from November 8, 1991, to November 10, 1991. It is claimed that he was subjected to torture during his detention, which ultimately led to his death on November 23, 1991.

During the inquest, the relatives of the deceased were examined, along with the president of the Dr. Ambedkar Dalit Yuvajana Sanghan organization. Based on the statements provided by these individuals, the panchayatadars (a group of local community representatives) formed an opinion. According to their assessment, the deceased had been subjected to torture by the police between November 8, 1991, and November 10, 1991.

As the deceased's health deteriorated, he was eventually handed over to his relatives. According to the police, on November 8, 1991, they located the deceased and brought him to the police station for questioning. He was kept under surveillance until November 10, 1991. After gathering information about his activities during the period he was out of their sight, the police asked him to leave. From November 8 to November 10, 1991, the police claimed that the deceased was neither held in the police lockup nor subjected to any form of torture. Later, on November 23, 1991, the deceased was brought to the police station by his relatives in critical condition and left outside the station. Unfortunately, he passed away in the evening of the same day. The medical examination findings indicate that the cause of death was tuberculosis and was not a result of any excessive force or mistreatment by the police.

22. Cr. No.137/92 u/s 304, 337 IPC of II Town Traffic P, S Vijayawada

The deceased, who was an accused in Cr. No. 171/92 u/s 302 IPC of Chilkalapudi PS of Krishna district, was arrested by Inspector of Police, Machlipatnam Town at Vijayawada. While they were being transported back from Vijayawada in a police jeep, an accident occurred at Poranki village involving a collision with a truck traveling in the opposite direction.

Unfortunately, the deceased passed away at the scene of the accident, while the other individuals in the vehicle sustained injuries.

23. Cr. No.9/92 u/s 302 IPC of NARSAPUR P.S. ADILABAD

On February 24, 1992, police personnel visited the residence of Malayala Chandraiah, a suspect in Cr—no—8/92 U/s 302 IPC, at P.S. Narsapur.

While searching for Chandraiah, they encountered him walking toward his home in an intoxicated state. They apprehended him, but Chandraiah resisted their efforts and fell during the struggle. After overpowering him, they brought Chandraiah to Narsapur Police Station in an auto-rickshaw. Even while boarding the auto, Chandraiah attempted to escape but was unsuccessful. During the journey to Narsapur Police Station, Chandraiah revealed the names of other individuals involved in the murder. The police took Chandraiah to the CCC Narsapur Police Station and assigned a sentry police constable to watch him. They then left the police station to search for the other three suspects. When the head constables returned to the police station around 3 PM, they learned that Chandraiah had already been transferred to Mancherial Hospital, where he subsequently passed away.

The medical officer determined that the cause of death was "shock due to injuries."

24. Cr. No.5/9 u/s 176 CrPC of Kollapur PS, Mahaboob Nagar Dist.

On February 29, 1992, at 04:30 p.m., the CI of Police in Wanaparthy arrested the deceased at Kollapur RTC Bus Stand due to suspicious behavior. In the presence of five witnesses, the CI recorded the deceased's confessional statement and recovered a country-made revolver from his possession. Subsequently, the CI handed him over to the Armed Reserve (A.R.) Sentry PC 1354 for safekeeping, making the necessary entries in the records. The deceased was kept in a private house behind PS Kollapur, where the A.R. party was stationed. At approximately 5:30 p.m. on the same day, the deceased entered the private place under the pretense of attending to nature's call.

He closed the doors and proceeded to commit suicide by hanging himself with his towel, using a wooden peg.

As the deceased did not return, AR PCs 1708 and 1344 went to investigate and discovered the closed doors. Through the window, they observed the deceased hanging lifeless. The medical officer who conducted the autopsy concluded that the cause of death was hanging.

25. Cr. No.19/92 u/s 174 CrPC of Veldurthi PS, Medak Dist.

Mallesham was brought to Veldurthi PS following a complaint accusing him of being involved in the murder of Jagga Chinnamutna Goud in February 1992. On the night of March 11, 1992, the SI interrogated Mallesham at the police station. Subsequently, the SI took him to his residence and contacted Shankar Goud, the Sarpanch of Veldurthy, who was related to Mallesham. The SI requested that Shankar Goud persuade Mallesham to confess the truth about Mutna Goud's murder. While the SI had dinner in the adjoining room, Shankar Goud conversed with Mallesham. Tragically, Mallesham was later found deceased in a nearby well, close to the house where he was being held. Dr. Sudarshan, the Deputy Civil Surgeon at Civil Hospital, Medak, conducted the postmortem examination.

His professional opinion stated that the cause of death was internal head injuries, likely sustained from the fall into the well.

26. Cr. No. 59/92 u/s 176 CrPC of Khammam I Town

On April 3, 1992, around 01:30 p.m., Alamalkunta Yakaiah entrusted his cash bag containing ₹7,000/- (INR 7,000/-) to Changala Mallaiah, who worked as a scavenger at the RTC Depot, Khammam. Yakaiah went to use the lavatory, and upon his return, he requested the cash bag from Mallaiah. However, Mallaiah denied receiving it. Yakaiah promptly reported the incident to the police, resulting in the registration of a case (Cr. No. 58/92 u/s 379 IPC). The Sub-Inspector (SI) interrogated Mallaiah, who eventually confessed to taking the cash bag and handing it over to a Lambada individual. He offered to lead the police to the Lambada. Consequently, the SI, accompanied by PCs 1641 and 757, took Mallaiah in a jeep to various locations in search of the Lambada. Unfortunately, they were unable to locate the individual. During their search, Mallaiah attempted to escape by jumping from the moving jeep, resulting in minor injuries. However, the escorting police officers managed to apprehend and bring him back to the police station by approximately 08:50 p.m. At around 09:00 p.m., Mallaiah complained of chest pain, prompting the SI to rush him to the government hospital. Tragically, the doctors at the hospital declared him deceased.

27. Cr.No. 18/92 u/s 304 (ii) IPC of Bainsa PS

On April 14, 1992, at 10:30 p.m., T. Rajeshwar, along with two other individuals, visited the residence of Pandari, an RTC driver.

They forcefully dragged Pandari out of his house and subjected him to physical assault in the presence of Rajeshwar and two others. Pandari promptly filed a complaint at Bhainsa Town Police Station between April 14 and 15, 1992. Subsequently, SI Ch. V.

Ramanajalu registered a case (Cr No. 17/92 u/s 448, 324, 506 r/w 34 IPC) against five individuals, including Rajeshwar. The SI then directed Pandari to receive medical treatment at the government hospital.

Later, during the night, the SI went to Rajeshwar's residence, brought him to the police station, and, along with PC 791 Padmanabham, subjected him to severe beatings using a stick. On April 15, 1992, a morning reporter from Udayam Daily newspaper and one of Rajeshwar's relatives met with the SI, eventually securing Rajeshwar's release in the evening. Rajeshwar then went to a hotel, but suddenly collapsed. The hotel owner and Rajeshwar's relatives promptly took him to a doctor, who examined him and pronounced Rajeshwar dead.

28. Cr. No.58/92 u/s 176 CrPC of Macherla TN Macherla (C) Guntur Dist.

The deceased was arrested in connection with Cr. Nos. 122 to 127/92 under Section 9(1) of the A.P.G.

Act by Macherla Town PS. Following the necessary procedures, he was placed in the police lockup.

Unexpectedly, the deceased experienced seizures and convulsions, causing him to collapse. The CI of Macherla immediately provided first aid and subsequently summoned a local medical practitioner to the police station for further treatment. The doctor examined the deceased and pronounced him dead. A post-mortem examination was conducted, during which the medical officer determined that the cause of death was "cardiac respiratory arrest."

29. Cr. No.43/92 u/s 176 CrPC of Naidupet PS Nellore Dist.

His father-in-law brought Chavuturu Subbaiah Arundhatiya from Athivaram (v) to Naidupet PS on May 15, 1992. He suspected Arundhatiya's involvement in the alleged murder of his daughter, Subbamma, as per the Cr. No. 34/92 u/s 174 CrPC registered at Naidupet PS. However, on the same day, at around 07:15 p.m., Chavuturu Subbaiah was discovered hanging from the roof inside the lockup of Naidupet PS.

30. Cr. No.56/92 u/s 176 CrPC of Guruzala PS, Guntur

On June 16, 1992, at 11:30 p.m., CI Guruzala and his staff arrested the deceased and brought him to the PS. On interrogation, the deceased confessed to committing the offenses in Cr. No. 20/92 u/s 41 and 102 CrPC of Dachepalli PS and 53/92 u/s 457, 380 IPC of Gurazala P.S. He was brought to PS Gurazala at 12:45 a.m., on June 14, 1992, and handed over to PCs 275 K. Satyanarayana and 2524 R. S. Prasad for keeping the accused under surveillance for further investigation to apprehend the remaining three accused involved in the above case. At about 2:30 p.m., the accused deceased complained of a stomachache, and the PCs allowed the accused to answer calls of nature in the premises of the Sub-Jail, which is adjacent to the lockup and surrounded by a well-built compound wall.

Hoping that there was no scope for Dedukala Siddaiah to escape from the sub-jail, the PCs waited for about 15 minutes.

They then went in search of the deceased and found him hanging from the southern side window of the kitchen with the available coir rope, which prisoners were using for cooking rice.

31. Cr. No.50/92 u/s 174 CrPC of Nagayalanka PS, Krishna Dist.

On the night of July 19-20, 1992, PC 833 B. Yohan from Nagayalanka PS brought the suspect, Dagoni Babu Rao from Kosuru (v), to the Nagayalanka PS and placed him in the lockup. At approximately 09:00 a.m., the station writer opened the lockup door and discovered the suspect hanging by a rope tied to the ventilator bar inside the lockup, struggling to breathe. Acting swiftly, the station writer cut the rope, causing the suspect to fall unconscious. However, the station writer neglected to send the suspect to the hospital for immediate medical attention and failed to report the incident to higher authorities.

Upon examination by the medical officer, it was determined that the deceased had suffered 11 antemortem injuries.

32. Cr. No.55/92 u/s 174 CrPC of Husnabad PS

The accused, Selva Narasaiah from Nizamabad district, and seven others were involved in dacoity cases registered as Cr. No. 47/92 u/s 395 IPC at Husnabad PS and Cr. No. 48/92 u/s 395 IPC at Bejjanki PS. On July 29, 1992, the accused was apprehended, and a pair of gold earrings and other items were seized from him in the presence of two panch witnesses.

Subsequently, the accused was placed in the lockup at Husnabad PS at 04:50 p.m. Later, around 07:00 p.m., the accused informed PC 1575 that he needed to wash up after passing stool in the lockup cell. The PC accompanied the accused to the well situated in the PS's backyard. However, while fetching a bucket of water from the well, the accused suddenly experienced fits, fell to the ground, lost consciousness, and subsequently passed away.

33. Cr.No. 33/92 u/s 174 CrPC of Makavaram PS

During the night of July 29-30, 1992, an unidentified group of individuals killed Lalam Amalavathi and stole items, including gold ear studs.

On August 7, 1992, at approximately 7:00 a.m., HC 592 Suryanarayana from Makavaram PS instructed PC 1076 to accompany Lalam Thatayya (L. Amalavathi's brother) and go to Boyyavara village to bring M. Venkataramana to the PS. PC 1076 located M. Venkataramana at his grandmother's house and requested that he accompany them to the police station. While en route to the PS, Venkataramana informed PC 1076 that he had ingested poison at his residence to commit suicide. He was promptly taken to the PS without delay, and PC 1076 informed HC 592 about the situation. M. Venkataramana provided a written statement in two sentences stating that he had consumed poison in an attempt to end his own life. He was then transferred to the government hospital in Narsipatnam for medical treatment, but unfortunately, he passed away while receiving treatment.

34. Cr. No.177/92 u/s 174 CrPC of Chittoor II Town PS

On August 27, 1992, between 08:30 a.m. and 09:00 a.m., an incident occurred at the clinic of the complainant, Dr. B. Althaf Hussain. The deceased, Peddabba Naidu, attacked the complainant with a knife, causing bleeding injuries to his chest. The intention behind this assault was to commit murder, as the complainant had not operated on the deceased. At around 01:30 p.m., the deceased was brought to the police station, where he complained of dizziness. Subsequently, he was transferred to a government hospital, where he, unfortunately, passed away.

35. Cr. No. 168/92 u/s174 CrPC of Matwada PS

On August 21, 1992, at 05:00 p.m., SI K. Nageswara Rao, along with the staff of CCS Warangal, apprehended the accused, I. Komaraiah, at B. Market, Warangal, proceeded to interrogate him. During the interrogation, the accused confessed to his involvement in various offenses, leading to the seizure of specific properties from his possession.

The accused was then taken to CCS Warangal at 7:00 p.m. on the same day. However, after some time, he complained of experiencing chills and abdominal pain. The CI of CCS immediately arranged for his transfer to MGM Hospital, Warangal, accompanied by police constables.

The accused was admitted to the hospital and received treatment for "PYREXIA" (fever). Unfortunately, he passed away while undergoing treatment on August 22, 1992. The medical officer who conducted the postmortem examination concluded that the cause of death was natural, as no external or internal injuries were detected.

36. Cr. No.264/92 u/s 176 CrPC of Narasaraopet Tn Guntur

The deceased was an accused in Cr. No. 51/92 U/s 13 of the Indian Lunacy Act of Nadendla PS. He was brought to the court of AMM Narasaraopet by escort PCs 2768 and 2475. Per the court's instructions, the prisoner was being taken to appear before the Executive Magistrate in Chilakaluripet.

While they were passing through the market at around 03:45 p.m., the deceased suddenly grabbed the leading chain and positioned himself underneath the bus No. AEZ 1207, which was heading towards Macherla.

As a result, he sustained injuries from the incident. Unfortunately, he did not survive the injuries and passed away at the government hospital in Narasaraopet. A case was immediately registered under the Criminal Code. No. 264/92, and the deceased's body was subsequently moved. The doctor who conducted the postmortem examination concluded that the cause of death was shock and hemorrhage resulting from multiple injuries.

37. Cr. No.83/92 u/s 176 CrPC of Gurajala PS, Guntur Dist.

Badiya Naik was identified as accused #1 in Cr—no—59/92 under Sections 304 and 201 of the IPC at Karampudi PS. On September 22, 1992, at 05:30 p.m., he was apprehended and brought to Gurajala PS at 05:45 p.m., where he was subsequently placed in the lockup at 05:55 p.m. At approximately 06:00 p.m., the deceased attempted suicide by hanging himself from the bars of the lockup door using his lungi. The guard PCs on duty noticed this and promptly intervened, rescuing him from the situation by removing him from the lockup. First aid was administered immediately, and he was then transported to the government general hospital in Guntur, where a case was registered against him under the Criminal Code—83/92 u/s 309 IPC at Gurajala PS. Unfortunately, despite receiving medical treatment, he passed away at the government general hospital in Guntur between September 25 and 26, 1992.

38. Cr. No.331/92 u/s 174 CrPC of R.C. Puram P.S. Ranga Reddy Dist.

On November 3, 1992, a 21-year-old individual named M. Hari Babu was brought to R.C. Puram P.S., under suspicious circumstances, along with a stolen moped, by the BHEL security personnel.

The Inspector of Police, R.C. Puram, arrested Hari and interrogated him at the police station. Additionally, two more individuals were arrested in connection with Cr. No. 329/92 u/s 457, 380 IPC of R.C. Puram PS. At 4:00 a.m., under the watch of PC 2002, all the accused were confined in the PS Lockup. Two other prisoners, O. Narasimha and Dhan Raj, were already in the police lockup. On November 4, 1992, around 7:00 a.m., the accused, Hari Babu, experienced seizures, with white froth appearing from his mouth. His fellow inmates promptly informed the sentry, PC 605 Dasarath, that Hari Babu had consumed some poison. PC 605 immediately called for other staff members and informed the inspector. Hari Babu was swiftly transferred to Gandhi Hospital. However, after a medical examination, the attending physician pronounced him deceased.

39. Cr. No.47/92 u/s 176 CrPC of Udayagiri PS, Nellore Dist.

The victim, Bathala Narayana from Malakondaiah of Bathuvaripalem, was arrested on December 25, 1992, in Cr. No. 33/92 u/s 394 IPC of Duthular PS and gold jewels and HMT watch were seized from his possession by Inspector of Police, Udayagiri. He was handed over to the staff of Duthalur Police Station and placed in the police lockup. On the morning of December 26, 1992, he was found in an unconscious state.

He was shifted to the government hospital, Udayagiri. The Medical Officer examined him and declared him dead. The Medical Officer who conducted the P.M. examination opined that the cause of death was due to shock due to fright pre-disposed by acute starvation.

40. Cr. No.11/93 u/s 174 CrPC of Matwada PS Warangal Dist.

Manupati Isthari was involved in a chit fund business and owed Rs. 2,500 to Dammupati Veeresam. On January 10, 1993, while Manupati Isthari, accompanied by his brother and brother-in-law Sri Kuthati Buchaiah, was returning home from Desaipet, Warangal, they were intercepted by the accused Chindam Babu Rao and three others. The accused demanded immediate payment of the money owed by Isthari. Isthari requested an extension until January 12, 1993, but the accused refused and proceeded to assault Isthari. Buchaiah SB, SI Warangal Tn, and M. Sammaiah intervened but were also attacked. Buchaiah suffered injuries to his back and a fractured jawbone. Subsequently, the accused fled the scene.

A case, Cr. No. 6/93 u/s 325 r/w 34 IPC of Metwada PS was registered in connection with the incident. On January 17, 1993, at approximately 01:00 p.m., Sri V. Bhaskar Rao, SI L&O of Metwada PS, and his team spotted one of the accused, Chindam Babu Rao, near the railway gate of Warangal. The SI attempted to apprehend him with the assistance of constables, but Babu Rao resisted arrest and tried to flee. The SI used force to subdue and apprehend Babu Rao.

Upon complaining about his health, the SI assured him that he would be taken to the hospital from the police station and subsequently brought him to Metwada PS.

Upon arrival, the SI documented the incident in the General Diary (G.D.) and arranged for Chindam Babu Rao to be transported to MGM Hospital, Warangal, for medical treatment, accompanied by HC 1004 M. Kumara Swamy.

Chindam Babu Rao was admitted to MGM Hospital at 2:05 p.m. on January 17, 1993, but he passed away while undergoing treatment.

41. Cr. No.36/93 u/s 304 IPC of Amberpet PS, Hyderabad

On February 27, 1993, around 10:30 p.m., residents of Tirumala Nagar colony apprehended an unknown male individual behaving suspiciously and causing a disturbance in Tirumala Nagar. The SI on duty recorded the incident in the General Diary (G.D.) and proceeded to question the person to ascertain his identity and address. However, the individual, who seemed to be mentally unstable, refused to provide any information. In light of this, the sub-inspector instructed the unidentified person to sleep in a shed near the police station, to send him to a mental hospital in the morning.

Around 7:15 a.m. the following day, some individuals from the police station noticed the unidentified person sleeping near an Eucalyptus tree close to the shed. When the SI intended to transport the person to the hospital, it was discovered that he had passed away. Upon examination, a team of doctors determined that the cause of death appeared to be 'Cerebral Hemorrhage.

42. Cr. No.16/93 u/s 174 CrPC of Tiruvuru PS

On March 9, 1993, K.V. Krishna Rao was brought to Tiruvur Police Station (PS) based on a court warrant. He remained in the custody of the police station until March 18, 1993, without being produced in court, as required. On March 18, 1993, the warrantee experienced epileptic convulsions, resulting in a fall and loss of consciousness. Immediate action was taken to provide medical attention, and he was promptly transferred to the government hospital in Tiruvuru for treatment. As the condition of the warrantee worsened, the medical officer in Tiruvur referred him to

C.G. Hospital in Vijayawada for advanced treatment. Unfortunately, the warrantee passed away during his treatment at C.G. Hospital.

43. Cr. No.69/93 u/s 176 CrPC of Tadepalligudem-T W.G. Dist.

This custodial death occurred on April 8, 1993, within the premises of Tadepalligudem Sub-jail. The deceased, V. Ramalinga Swamy, was an accused in Cr. No. 40/90 u/s 302 IPC of T.P. Gudem (R) PS. While in custody, the accused entered the latrine and subsequently emerged, proceeding towards the well with the company of PC 540 to wash his feet. Upon reaching the well, he intentionally jumped into it, resulting in his demise. PC 540, who was present at the scene, attempted to prevent this action but was unable to do so.

44. Cr. No. 50/93 u/s 176 CrPC Balanagar PS, Ranga Reddy Dist.

On April 10, 1993, at 12:45 p.m., the crime team of Balanagar PS apprehended an individual identified as Nagesh, son of Narasappa, aged 22, hailing from Sholapur and temporarily residing at Madura Nagar, Jagadgirigutta. A case was registered in Cr. No. 48/93 under Section 380 IPC of Balanagar PS, involving stolen property valued at Rs. 5,000, which included a VCP. The accused was produced before Detective Sub-Inspector Balanagar, and the necessary records were documented. Subsequently, the accused underwent a search and was placed in the lockup at 03:00 p.m. on April 11, 1993.

At 08:45 a.m., PC 2069, B. Venkataiah, with the permission of ASI, Crime, accompanied the accused to the adjacent lavatory to attend to nature's call. Upon entering the lavatory, the accused locked the door from inside. As the accused failed to exit the restroom, PC Venkataiah grew suspicious, checked through the ventilator, forcibly opened the lavatory door, and discovered the accused unconscious. Immediately, the accused was shifted to Gandhi Hospital, Secunderabad, where he was pronounced dead.

45. Cr. No.11/93 u/s 323, 324, 304, 201 r/w 34 IPC of Mahadevpur PS.

On June 3, 1993, a case was registered in Cr—no—10/93 under Sections 148, 341, and 506 IPC against the accused and others.

PC 2047, 1594, and 1317 were dispatched to apprehend the accused, Kanne Sammaiah and Sripathi Babu, who were named in the case above. The police officers arrived at the residence of the deceased and Sripathi Babu to make the arrests.

Upon spotting the police officers, the deceased and Sripathi Babu attempted to escape by running toward the Godavari River. The pursuing police officers managed to catch up to them at the riverbank and subjected them to severe physical assault.

Due to the combination of not having consumed food since morning and the exertion of running in the hot sun, the deceased was unable to withstand the assault and tragically lost his life. In an attempt to dispose of the evidence, the police officers disposed of the deceased's body by throwing it into the river.

Lockup deaths in 1993

1. Cr. No. 70/93 u/s 174 CrPC of Jubilee Hills Ps, Hyderabad

The incident occurred when Hanumanth was brought to the police station by PC 7156 and HC 6052 from the Rahmath Nagar outpost of Jubilee Hills PS: his wife, Smt. Laxm accompanied them, complaining of harassment by her husband.

Upon their arrival at the police station at 02:30 p.m., SI Bhoopal Swamy examined Laxmi and subsequently registered a case under Cr no. 69/93 u/s 498(A) IPC at 05:55 p.m.

Following the case registration, Laxmi left the police station to seek refuge at her parents' home. At approximately 06:45 p.m., Hanumanth went into the lavatory of the police station and used his dhoti to hang himself from a wooden beam.

Abdul Sattar, who had been brought to the police station earlier in connection with a pending Non-Bailable Warrant (N.B.W.) under Cr. No. 85/91 u/s 302 IPC of Jubilee Hills PS, noticed the incident and promptly informed the police staff.

2. Cr. No. 70/93 u/s 302, 201 IPC of Railway Police Station Bellampally

On the intervening night of July 11-12, 1993, Sangam Padma, r/o. Yapal committed suicide by coming under the train.

A relative of the deceased suspected foul play and informed Bellampally SI, Sri Babu Jani, of this. The relatives suspected the deceased's maternal uncle, Sangom Nandaiah, and the husband's cousin brother, Lingaiah. / The relative suspected the husband, Lingaiah, and the deceased's maternal uncle, who is also her husband's cousin, Sangom Nandaiah. This information led the Sub-Inspector of the Railway Police Station, Bellampally, along with his staff, to Mandamarri on July 14, 1993, to bring Nandaiah in. He was interrogated by the Sub Inspector and beaten with a lathi. He was detained at the Railway Police Station on July 14, 1993, along with Sangam Lingaiah, the husband of Padma. On July 15, 1993, Sangam Nandaiah was interrogated by the police again and beaten with a lathi and a small vacuum pipe. Due to the injuries he received, Nandaiah was unable to consume the food offered to him by night duty RPC 238 Devadass.

On the night of July 15, 1993, watch RPC found Nandaiah dead in the lockup room. Thereafter, SI RP put the dead body in a gunny bag and shifted the dead body to the Dakshin Express with the help of PCs. After leaving the dead body by the side of the track near Raichni Rly Stn. at a distance of about 8 kms from Bellampally, they returned.

3. Cr. No.56/93 u/s 174 CrPC of Pochampalli PS, Nalgonda Dist.

The police made determined efforts starting from August 5, 1993, to apprehend Gopanna Dalam, a member of the People's War Group militant organization. Raids were conducted, and sympathizers in Pochampalli and other strongholds of the Dalam were interrogated.

During this process, it came to light that a 15-year-old girl named S. Pochamma was also associated with the militant group and had close connections with the Dalam.

On August 12, 1993, Pochamma's parents and the village sarpanch brought her to PS Pochampalli.

The Sub-Inspector (SI) began questioning Pochamma in the presence of her parents and the sarpanch when she suddenly complained of abdominal pain.

Concerned about her well-being, she was promptly taken to a private doctor in Pochampalli along with her parents and the sarpanch. She received treatment for a day and a half.

Pochamma returned home on August 14, 1993, stating that she needed to attend her uncle's funeral. However, on August 16, 1993, she reported feeling unwell again, prompting her parents to transfer her to Osmania General Hospital in Hyderabad for further treatment. Upon admission, Pochamma and her parents mentioned the presence of a fever.

Tragically, despite undergoing treatment, she passed away on August 17, 1993, at 5 a.m. The final postmortem examination concluded that the cause of death was "Septicemia," a condition resulting from infection in the damaged abdominal viscera.

4. Cr.No. 17/93 u/s 174 CrPC of K.Kotapadu PS

On August 28, 1993, around 02:30 p.m., K. Ramakrishna, residing in Rajula Alamanda Village Jami (Mandal), was apprehended under suspicious circumstances. He was found in possession of a stolen 'Hero Honda' motorcycle and confessed to stealing it from a bar in Visakhapatnam City. The bike was seized, and a case was registered in Cr. No. 16/93 under sections 41 and 102 of the Criminal Procedure Code (CrPC) at K. Kotapadu PS. During interrogation, K. Ramakrishna also admitted his involvement in other property offenses. As the police station was housed in a private building without a designated lockup room, K. Ramakrishna was placed in the adjoining room of the PS after a search at 02:45 p.m. Later, at around 05:00 a.m., the sentry PC discovered the accused hanging by his lungi, which was tied to the top of the window bar. The Sub-Inspector (S.I.) registered a case in Cr—no—17/93 under section 174 of the CrPC to investigate the circumstances surrounding the death.

In the subsequent postmortem examination, doctors determined no internal or external injuries on the deceased's body, except for the ligature mark on the throat. Based on their findings, the doctors concluded that it was a clear case of suicidal death caused by hanging.

5. Cr. No.136/93 u/s 174 CrPC of Khammam II Town PS

On September 17, 1993, around 6:15 p.m., SI Khammam I Town PS noticed Shaik Khader Baba, a known criminal and resident of Manikyanagar. He was acting suspiciously near a gold shop in the vicinity of Ravichettu Bazaar Center, Khammam. The SI was accompanied by PCs 68, 278, and 1691. The officers apprehended him and discovered a gold chain in his possession. After further investigation, he confessed to participating in a dacoity within the limits of Khammam I Town PS. Consequently, he was taken into custody, and the recovered gold chain was seized as evidence. The accused was brought to the police station and officially arrested at approximately 06:15 p.m. Subsequent interrogations revealed that the accused was involved in other criminal activities alongside his associates. Later that same day, at 11:15 p.m., the accused, who had asthma, experienced difficulty breathing. Concerned for his health, the SI and PCs 68 and 278 promptly took him to the government headquarters hospital. The attending medical officer examined the accused and inquired about the injuries on his body, which he claimed occurred during his attempt to evade capture. Despite receiving medical treatment, the accused passed away the following day.

6. Cr. No.126/93 u/s 174 CrPC of Yellandu PS

One Padma Ashalu, a practicing RMP doctor, performed an abortion for Vooke Veeramma and Laxmaiah (spouses) on September 11, 1993. Veeramma was 3 months pregnant and wanted an abortion as the couple already had six children. Unfortunately, she died due to complications, including uterine and intestinal rupture. Subsequently, Veeramma's husband lodged a written complaint at Gundala Police Station, leading to the registration of a case no. 19/93. Upon learning about the incident, villagers from Sayanapalli planned to attack the doctor and went to his house the same day.

Fearing for his safety, the doctor went to the Gundala Police Station and sought protection from the Station Inspector.

He remained at the police station voluntarily. Despite the wife and relatives of the doctor requesting the CI and SI to send him for remand due to his chronic health conditions, their request was disregarded. On September 20, 1993, at 01:00 p.m., the SI arrested the doctor and brought him to Yellandu along with his wife and children. Two PCs, 2065 and 1460, escorted them and were stationed at Yellandu PS. Tragically, in the middle of the night, Padma Ashalu developed Dyspnoea and passed away.

7. **Cr. No.88/93 u/s 174 CrPC of Velgode PS Kurnool Dist.**

On December 7, 1993, Golusanna was arrested in Cr. No. 87/93 and brought to the police station by HC 1671 around 02:30 a.m. Approximately an hour later, at 03:30 a.m., Golusanna complained of a stomachache. He was escorted outside to attend to his needs. Around 04:30 a.m., the sentry on duty heard unusual sounds and woke up. To his alarm, he discovered Golusanna attempting to hang himself by tying his dhoti around his neck and the window. The vigilant PC acted swiftly, rescuing him by cutting the dhoti and promptly rushing him to the government hospital. Golusanna was pronounced dead upon arrival.

8. **Cr. No.211/96 u/s 147, 148, 302 r/w 149 IPC of Dhone PS, Kurnool District**

Ediga Venkateswarlu was arrested in Devara Banda village on September 10, 1996, for an offense under the Prohibition Act. He was brought to the prohibition and excise station in Dhone at 03:00 p.m. on the same day and confined to the lockup room. On the morning of September 11, 1996, Venkateswarlu was found deceased in the lockup, bearing antemortem injuries.

At the time, Constable V. Rangaiah was assigned as the sentry constable and was responsible for the lockup.

It is improbable that Venkateswarlu could have been beaten in the lockup without the sentry constable's knowledge or permission. Regrettably, the sentry constable failed to report the alleged beating to higher authorities.

Upon learning about Venkateswarlu's death, a mob vandalized the excise station in an act of protest.

9. Cr. No.166/2003 u/s 176 CrPC altered to 302 IPC of Bapatla Town PS, Guntur Dist.

Velavala Akkaiah, also known as Ankaiah, was a resident of Vellaluru (v). He was one of the accused in Cr. No.57/03 under sections 147, 148, 307, 302 r/w 149 IPC of Bapatla Taluk PS, along with 17 others. On October 26, 2003, the deceased and 16 others were arrested, and on October 27, 2003, they were sent for judicial custody and lodged in Sub-Jail, Bapatla.

During the same period, Sk. Jilani had a pending warrant executed against him in Cr. No.10/96 u/s 8 (b) AP Excise Act of Bapatla Town PS. He was remanded to judicial custody on October 20, 2003, and lodged in the same Sub-Jail at Bapatla. Additionally, Katta Nageswararao, arrested by the Excise Department under the NDPS Act, was also lodged in the same cell in Sub-Jail, Bapatla, alongside the deceased and Sk. Jilani. It was observed that all the prisoners in Sub-Jail, Bapatla, had free movement within the facility.

Later, Shaik Jilani was released on bail on November 28, 2003. On December 14, 2003, around 06:10 a.m., all 25 prisoners, including the deceased, were taken out of the Sub-Jail for whitewashing work. Two warders of the Sub-Jail instructed the deceased and some others, including Katta Nageswararao, to attend to the whitewashing work. At the same time, the remaining 21 prisoners were sent to their respective cells.

Around 08:30 a.m., three inmates were taken out to cook food. Shaik Jilani, who had been released on bail, approached the Sub-Jail from the R&B office side and handed half a bottle of Old Monk XXX Rum to Kotamma, the sister of Katta Nageswararao, who was collecting firewood. Shaik Jilani instructed Kotamma to deliver the bottle to the deceased of Vallaluru and her brother Nageswararao. Upon receiving this information, the deceased, who was engaged in whitewashing work outside the Sub-Jail premises, went inside the kitchen building, consumed some quantity of liquor, and then emerged, falling under a soap nut tree within the Sub-Jail premises.

The deceased displayed symptoms such as passing urine and fecal matter, and white froth came from his mouth. He was immediately shifted to the government hospital in Bapatla, where the medical officer examined and pronounced him dead.

10. Cr. No.124/2003 u/s 309 IPC and Section 176 CrPC of Piduguralla PS, Guntur Dist.

Krishna, a resident of Tangeda village in Dachepalli Mandal, Guntur District, was apprehended by the Police of Piduguralla PS on June 20, 2003, around 01:30 PM on suspicion of being a member of the banned organization People's War militant. He was taken into custody and brought to Piduguralla police station, where he was presented before the Sub-Inspector of Police for questioning.

During the interrogation, Krishna initially identified himself as Perum Venkateswarlu, son of Manikya Rao. However, the Sub-Inspector of the Police suspected that he had provided false information.

Around 2:30 PM, the Sub-Inspector, after confirming the whereabouts of Krishna's wife and children, sent a constable to gather his correct name and address from his wife. According to press reports, fearing that his true identity would be revealed, Krishna climbed up the terrace of the CI office building, which was approximately 40 feet high, and jumped, sustaining injuries to his head and face.

Several individuals witnessed this incident, including fruit and flower vendors, as well as shopkeepers in the vicinity. The Sub-Inspector of Police and his staff immediately took Krishna to the Police Station, where first aid was administered by a person named K. Venkateswarlu, also known as Dr. Busi, an RMP Doctor.

Subsequently, Krishna was transferred to a nearby private nursing home run by Dr. Anjaneya Reddy near the Police Station. Based on the doctor's recommendation, the injured individual was then transferred to Guntur General Hospital, where he was pronounced "brought dead."

In response to the incident, the Sub-Inspector of Police registered a case in Crime No.124/2003 u/s 309 IPC and Section 176 CrPC.

11. Cr. No.294/2003 u/s 224, 379, 307 IPC, Exchange of Fire and 176 CrPC of Guntur Rural PS, Guntur Dist.

In the case of Cr. No.50/03 u/s 302, 307, and 34 of the IPC, the investigation focused on Derangula Laxmi Prasad as one of the accused. On October 31, 2003, at 06:00 a.m., Derangula Laxmi Prasad was arrested at Santhamaguluru crossroad in connection with Cr—no—50/03 of Savalyapuram PS under sections 302, 307, and 34 of the IPC. The arrest occurred in the presence of two mediators, and during this time, the accused confessed to the crime.

He admitted to killing the deceased in Cr. No.50/03 and hiding the knife and blood-stained clothes used during the offense in his room in Hyderabad. He agreed to lead the investigation team to where these items were concealed.

The investigation officer subsequently sent the accused for remand and requested the Munsif Magistrate, Vinukonda, to transfer the accused from judicial custody to police custody to facilitate the pursuit of a confession. Following the Magistrate's order, the accused was taken from Sub Jail, Vinukonda, on November 3, 2003, to be held in police custody. Savalyapuram Police brought the accused to the police lockup at Vinukonda Police Station after conducting a thorough search.

On November 4, 2003, the accused was escorted by PCs 672, 1405, and 3090, along with ARPC 3009 as the driver, in a Tata Sumo Police Vehicle (AP9P 3797) from Vinukonda.

At 10:00 p.m. on November 5, 2003, they seized the knife used in the crime and the blood-stained clothes of the accused from his house in Hyderabad. The seizure took place in the presence of mediators. The journey from Hyderabad commenced at 2 a.m. on November 5, 2003. During the trip, the vehicle made multiple stops at Narketpalli, the outskirts of Suryapet, Kodada, Chillakallu, and near the Muggu Road center in Tadepalli, as requested by PC 672. The final stop occurred between Budampadu and Etukuru by-pass road junction on NH-5. ARPC 3009 was driving the vehicle, with PC 3090 seated in the front beside the driver. The accused sat between PC 672 and the rear side of the middle seat, while PC 1405 occupied the right rear seat.When PC 672 left the vehicle to answer nature's call, he left his loaded 410 musket with a pouch containing rounds on the left side of PC 1405, who was sitting in the right rear seat.

Seizing the opportunity, the accused snatched PC 672's 410 musket, along with the pouch and live rounds. He then opened the rear door, jumped out, and ran into the nearby bushes. PC 3090 and PC 1405 also exited the vehicle, attempting to confront the accused. Despite repeated warnings to surrender, the accused refused and fired the 410 musket at them, attempting to murder them.

Given the life-threatening situation and the fact that the accused possessed a firearm with live rounds, he and his staff had no choice but to exercise their right to self-defense. Consequently, he fired seven rounds from his 9 MM Pistol, PC 3090 fired eleven rounds from his carbine, and PC 1405 fired six rounds from his 410 musket at the accused. The accused cried out and fell to the ground, remaining motionless for approximately 5 to 6 minutes. The team approached.

3

DATA ANALYSIS AND INTERPRETATION OF RESULTS

The objective of this chapter is to analyze, quantify, and interpret the data obtained from various sources. Various appropriate statistical techniques have been used to analyze, quantify, and test the data. The results are presented using tables, diagrams, and pie charts, among other visual aids. Statistical tools such as percentages, chi-square, t-test, and ANOVA are employed to arrive at meaningful and logical conclusions.

In this chapter, data analysis and interpretation are presented with the accused respondents' profiles, risk factors for custodial fatalities, the relationship between organizational culture and custodial deaths, victim compensation issues, and medical considerations. A comparison of the injuries listed in inquest reports and postmortem reports, as well as the physiological and psychological characteristics of the accused responders that may have an impact on incarcerated deaths It also presents data analysis related to organizational vulnerability and compliance with legal procedures.

Socioeconomic profile of the deceased, nature of custodial deaths, NHRC's budget and expenditure, magnitude of risk, descriptive statistics of various risk factors, vulnerability scores, and index of custodial deaths.

The objective is to analyze, quantify, and interpret data obtained from various sources. Data has been studied, quantified, and tested using appropriate statistical techniques. The results are presented in tables, diagrams, and pie charts, among other visual aids. Statistical tools, such as percentages, chi-square tests, t-tests, and ANOVA, are employed to draw meaningful and logical conclusions. Thus, this chapter aims to discuss the study's results.

The data, obtained from various sources using the defined tools, regarding the profiles of the accused and the deceased, as well as organizational and legal aspects, have been analyzed and tested using both quantitative and qualitative techniques to assess impacts or dependencies on custodial deaths.

The results are presented in tables and diagrams and analyzed using statistical methods, including percentages, chi-square tests, t-tests, and ANOVA. The findings are discussed in the following sections.

Data analysis and interpretation of results

Personality, behavior, and risk factors contributing to custodial deaths.

Profiles of the Accused Age

To comprehensively understand custodial deaths, the investigator felt it necessary to present data on demographic variables, i.e., persons accused and suspended for committing custodial deaths.

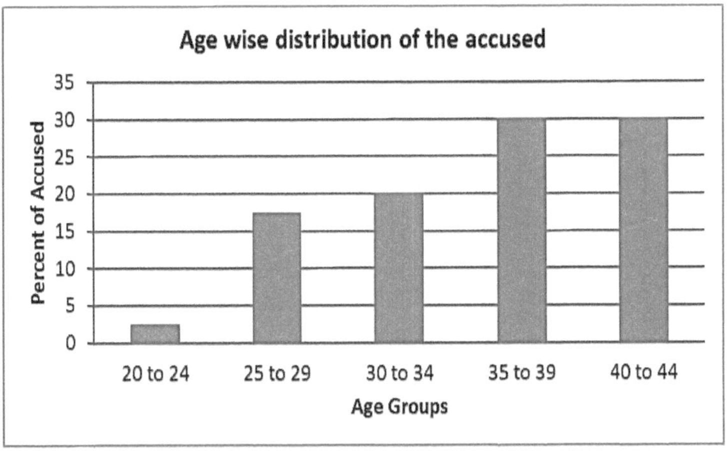

Figure 3.1: Age-wise distribution of the accused
Source: Primary Data

Age (in years)	Frequency	Percentage
20 to 24	1	2.5
25 to 29	7	17.5
30 to 34	8	20.0
35 to 39	12	30.0
40 to 44	12	30.0
Total	40	100.0

Table 3.1: Age-wise distribution of the accused
Source: Primary Data

As shown in Table 3.1, 60% of the sample falls within the age range of 35 to 44 years, while 40% belongs to the 20-34 years age group. It should be noted that young adults and middle-aged police personnel with considerable experience in handling police interrogations have been involved in custodial deaths.

Overconfidence among seniors aged 35–44 and a lack of knowledge about the location of vital organs in the human body are contributing factors to custodial deaths.

Generally, these crime detection units consist of older, experienced police officers, which is reflected in their age distribution. Only 2.5% of the samples belonged to the 20-24 age group, likely recent entrants to the service and possibly still adjusting to police procedures and interrogations (see Figure 3.1). The factors contributing to their limited experience and youth are examined and detailed in the tables and figures provided in this chapter.

Rank	Frequency	Percentage
Circle Inspector	2	5
Sub-Inspector	6	15
Assistant Sub-Inspector	1	2.5
Head Constable	5	12.5
Police Constable	26	65
Total	40	100

Table 3.2: Rank-wise distribution of the accused
Source: Primary data

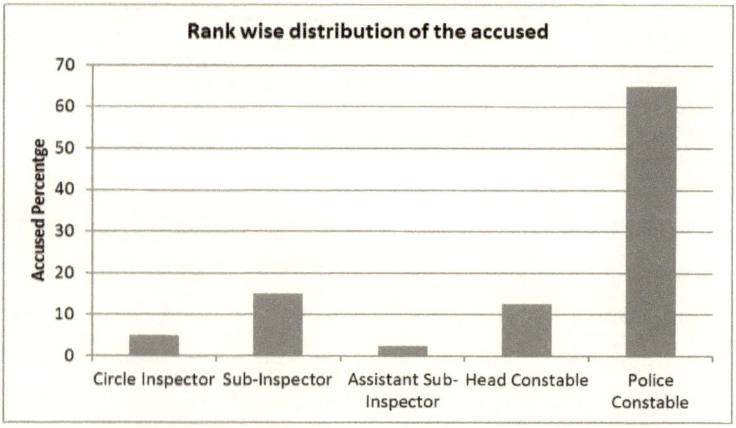

Figure 3.2: Rank-wise distribution of the accused.
Source: Primary Data

Table 3.2 and Figure 3.2 reveal that most custodial death cases involve Police Constables, accounting for 65%, with Sub-Inspectors responsible for 15%. The police management operates within a highly structured, linear, and hierarchical communication system. As the lowest rank responsible for interrogation, constables are more likely to be held accountable for custodial deaths. This structure mandates strict obedience to orders from senior officers.

Multiple interrogation methods are used on suspects, and if an officer issues an order—regardless of legality—the constable is expected to follow it.

Therefore, senior officers must intervene to implement necessary changes. It is worth noting that during an annual crime conference of the Andhra Pradesh Police in 1986, police officers stated that most custodial deaths were caused by pressure from senior officials and local political parties to solve property crimes. The current study shows that in Andhra Pradesh, nine Police Stations and 26 constables are involved.

This workload may be impacting most officers at these stations. It's also essential to explore other factors that may cause some individuals to struggle with accurately assessing the effectiveness of their crime detection efforts using this method. Additionally, they often fail to recognize the victim's vulnerability and misinterpret the signals from a victim who is being tortured.

Gender

Gender	Frequency	Percentage
Male	36	90
Female	4	10
Total	40	100

Table 3.3: Gender wise distribution of the sample

Source: Primary data

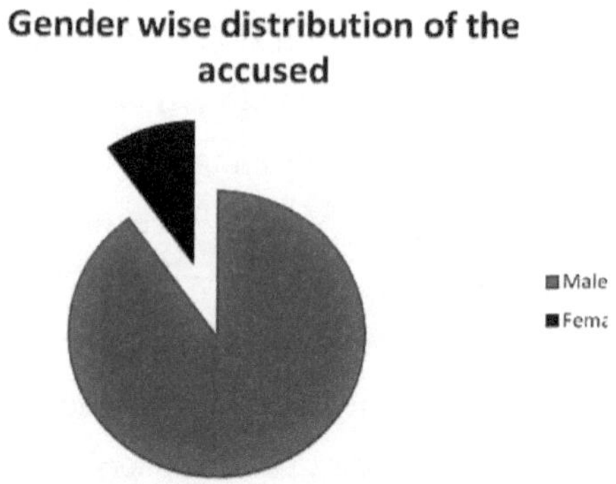

Figure 3.3: Gender wise distribution of the sample

Source: Primary data

Table 3.3 indicates that women make up 10% of the custodial death sample, with most being Police Constables. They may experience similar reasons as those depicted in Figure 3.3.

However, as more women are recruited into police forces, it is essential to study whether gender influences the conduct of operations related to different levels of torture.

Given the limited number of cases, a larger sample size would improve the analysis of gender differences.

Police station

S. No	Police Station	District	Number of People	Male	Female
1	Balanagar	Ranga Reddy	1	1	0
2	I-town PS	Vijayawada	7	7	0
3	Kadiri Town	Ananthapur	8	8	0
4	Nagarampalem	Guntur	5	5	0
5	Ongole Railway Police Station	Ongole Railway PS	3	3	0
6	Prattipadu PS Guntur	Guntur	4	4	0
7	Suryaraopet PS Vijayawada	Vijayawada	4	0	4

8	Tadipatri Tq. PS Anantapur	Anantapur	3	3	0
9	Yadiki PS Ananthapur	Anantapur	5	5	0
	Total		40	36	4

Table 3.4: Sample data collected from different police stations involved in custodial deaths of Andhra Pradesh during the years 1995–2005

Source: Primary data

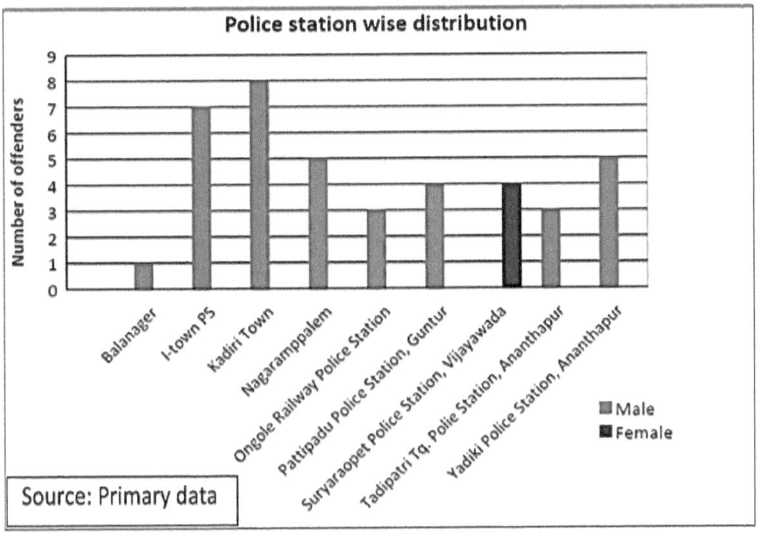

Figure 3.4: Police Station-wise Distribution of the Accused (policemen)

Table 3.4 and Figure 3.4 indicate that, over approximately three years, more police officers from Kadiri Town Police Station, Anantapur, and I-Town Police Station, Vijayawada, were involved in custodial deaths.

One possible, though premature, explanation is poor police management, where senior officials instruct or sanction juniors to use violence and aggression during interrogations.

It's worth noting that, similar to how suicides can be contagious, aggressive interrogation methods might also spread, leading junior officers to imitate the behaviors of senior officers in their treatment of victims.

To address custodial deaths in the country, various acts and policies have been proposed by police, political figures, human rights groups, and other organizations.

Research into organizational, psychological, and medical factors has grown significantly, helping to understand the human elements behind wrongful or irresponsible actions in workplaces, industries, or hospitals.

A substantial amount of research aims to identify errors and implement strategies to minimize or eliminate these deviations, thereby maintaining a positive organizational environment and protecting the organization's reputation.

Due to the lack of research in police management, understanding the problems and issues faced by its workforce has been a serious concern. Custodial deaths are always seen as a damaging aspect of a police station, which the public considers an unpardonable offense by those who are protectors of law and order. The very individuals who safeguard and maintain order in society when it becomes chaotic make it a critical issue that must be addressed through scientific investigation or research to identify the contributing factors to such disorder.

Risk factors

Risk factors are described as personal characteristics that increase the probability of adverse outcomes for individuals. However, the risk factors do not directly cause problems (Cole et al., 2008; Cole et al., 2011).

In the present context, risk factors may be described as an individual's characteristics that may contribute to the custodial death of inmates. For example, smoking is considered one of the risk factors contributing to cancer, but smoking alone may not lead to cancer or death.

Cognitive Styles and Custodial Deaths

A cognitive style test, the Matching Familiar Figures Test (MFFT), was used to identify individuals' typical information processing and problem-solving approaches. It assesses two styles: Reflective and Impulsive. Reflective individuals tend to be cautious, carefully analyzing details, which generally leads to more accurate responses.

Their tendency to pause and consider their reactions often enhances accuracy. Conversely, impulsive individuals respond quickly with the first answer that comes to mind without considering other options, often resulting in errors. In problem-solving, they may omit steps, provide incorrect responses, or skip activities, thereby reducing the accuracy of their solutions. Therefore, an impulsive style is a risk factor.

Figure 3.5 displays the test results and custodial deaths.

During interrogations, reflective police officers take time to think, understand, and frame questions logically using appropriate techniques.

In contrast, impulsive officers may lose their temper, jump to conclusions, and become aggressive when their expectations do not match the report's information.

<table>
<tr><th>Cognitive styles – Custodial deaths police</th><th>Cognitive styles – Normal Police</th></tr>
<tr><td>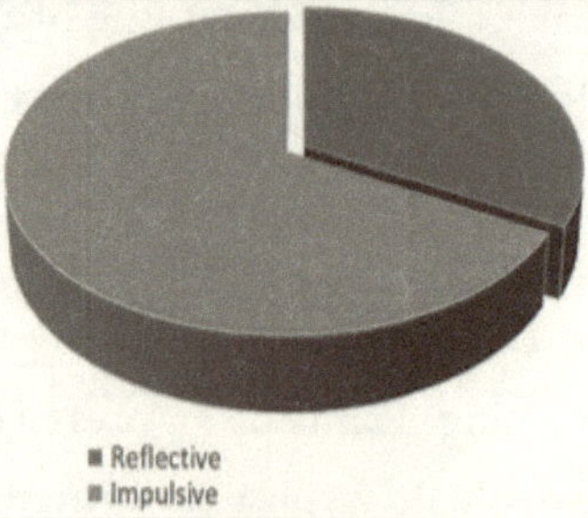
</td><td>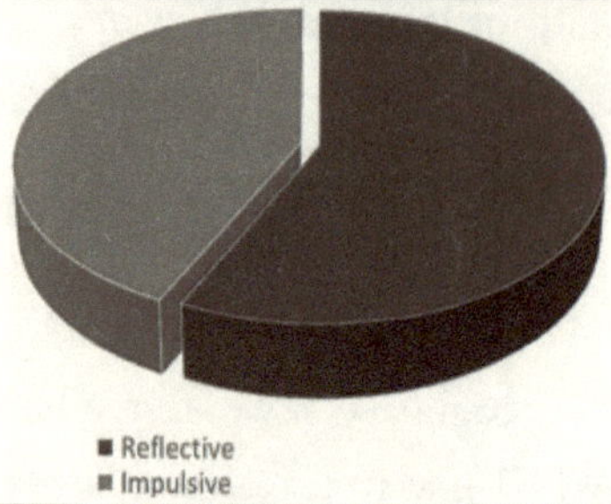
</td></tr>
<tr><td>Reflective (33%)
Impulsive (67%)</td><td>Reflective (57%)
Impulsive(43%)</td></tr>
</table>

Figure 3.5: Cognitive styles in custodial death cases and Normal police

Source: Primary data

The figure above indicates that 67% of police officers involved in custodial inmate deaths exhibit an Impulsive cognitive style, while 33% show a reflective manner. This data suggests that individuals with impulsive tendencies are more likely to be involved in such incidents compared to those with reflective tendencies. Since an impulsive approach is generally unfavorable in problem-solving situations—especially those requiring precision and efficiency—such impulsivity may be discouraged as being inappropriate. Additionally, the assessment of the Normal Police model reveals that 57% of the sample possess Reflective cognitive styles, whereas 43% have an impulsive style.

Tolerance of Ambiguity and Custodial Deaths

The Tolerance of Ambiguity test was used to measure how individuals cope with ambiguous situations. Ambiguity can occur when multiple interpretations are possible.

People with a high tolerance for ambiguity view such situations as positive and do not feel anxious, showing flexibility and making appropriate decisions across various scenarios (Mark, 1994). Conversely, those with Low Tolerance of Ambiguity tend to see ambiguous situations as threatening, resulting in anxiety and discomfort. In cases of custodial deaths, a low tolerance to ambiguity appears to be a risk factor. Table 3.5 presents the findings related to Tolerance-Intolerance of Ambiguity and custodial deaths.

TOA	N	Number of custodial deaths involved
Tolerant	1	1
Intolerant [RF]	29	1

Table 3.5: Tolerance - Intolerance of ambiguity and custodial deaths

Source: Primary data

The table shows that 97% of the sample exhibits Intolerance of Ambiguity, while only 3% demonstrate Tolerance of Ambiguity.

Data further suggests that individuals with an Intolerance of Ambiguity are more likely to be involved in custodial deaths compared to those with tolerance.

This may be because those intolerant of ambiguity struggle to handle even minor vagueness or unclear stimuli.

They often react with heightened anxiety, impatience, and anger, which can lead to custodial deaths. Proper preparation for job demands is essential, as prolonged intolerance of ambiguity could lead to undesirable behaviors. Additionally, anxiety plays a role; persistent high anxiety due to intolerance not only hampers work efficiency but can also negatively impact overall quality of life.

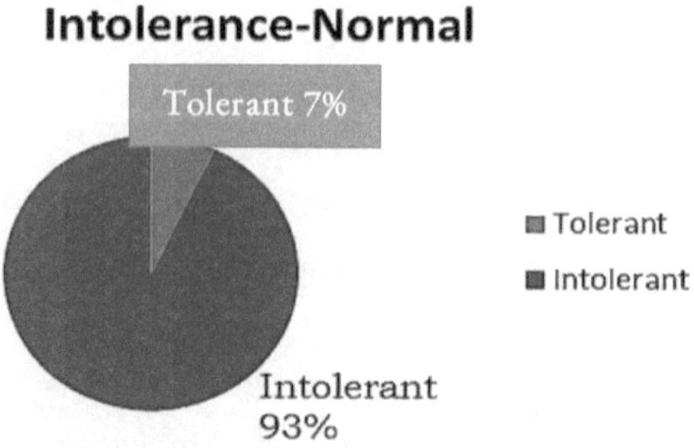

Figure 3.6 Intolerance of ambiguity

Source: Primary data

Figure 3.6 illustrates that 93% of the sample exhibits Intolerance of Ambiguity, while only 7% show tolerance of Ambiguity. This suggests that individuals with an Intolerance of Ambiguity may struggle with even slight vagueness or lack of clarity in stimuli. They often respond with high anxiety, which can manifest as impatience and anger, potentially resulting in custodial death.

Individuals need to be prepared for the job's demands. In the long run, such intolerance of ambiguity may lead to undesirable behavior. Yet another condition involved is anxiety. Constant high anxiety as a reaction to discrimination may not only hinder work efficiency but also affect the quality of life in general.

Personality Factors and Custodial Deaths

Personality factors for each sample member were assessed using the MAP (Multi-Dimensional Assessment of Personality) Series questionnaire.

This test measures 20 personality factors. Each factor has two dimensions: High and Low. A high score is a risk factor for some personality factors, while for others, a low score is a risk factor. Personality dimensions that are undesirable or harmful, considered risk factors, are listed in Table 3.6. Undesirable or harmful personality dimensions are regarded as risk factors.

S.No	Dimension	Rating	Behaviour
1	Adaptability	Low	Inappropriate responses to changing circumstances
2	Achievement Motivation	Low	Low level of aspiration to achieve the set Motivation coals
3	Boldness	Low	Has stage fright, non-energetic, lack of Insight
4	Competition	High & Low	Unrealistic, dominant/ withdrawn
5	Enthusiasm	Low	Dull & unenthusiastic
6	General ability	Low	Slow learning, intellectually low in adaptation
7	Guilt Proneness	High	Over fatigued, remorseful, shows phobias & anxiety
8	Imagination	High	Intense subjectivity, high internal anxiety, appears irresponsible
9	Innovation	Low	Low on analytical ability
10	Leadership	High	Control actions of others, tries to influence group
11	Maturity	Low	High anxiety, inappropriate responses
12	Mental Health	Low	Not well adjusted, lack zest for living, and self-development
13	Morality	Low	Low on moral standards, egoistic
14	Self-control	Low	Low control over emotional life, disturbed interpersonal relationships
15	Sensitivity	High	Tender-minded, over-protected, fidgety, clinging, and insecure

16	Shrewdness	High	Diplomatic in handling people. Prefer to keep problems to themselves.
17	Self sufficiency	Low	Always need the support of a group, incapable of working alone, overly dependent.
18	Suspiciousness	High	An individual tends to be suspicious, jealous, dogmatic, and irritable
19	Social warmth	Low	Difficult to get along, less likely to be friendly, and share feelings & positive emotions
20	Tension	High	Individuals annoyed by little issues, irascible, and suffer from insomnia

Table 3.6: Personality dimensions and behaviour
Source: MAP Series Questionnaire

S. No	Dimension	Rating	Behaviour
1	Adaptability	Low	Inappropriate responses to changing circumstances
2	Achievement Motivation	Low	Low level of aspiration to achieve the set Motivation coals
3	Boldness	Low	Has stage fright, non-energetic, lack of Insight
4	Competition	High & Low	Unrealistic, dominant/ withdrawn
5	Enthusiasm	Low	Dull & unenthusiastic
6	General ability	Low	Slow learning, intellectually low in adaptation
7	Guilt Proneness	High	Over fatigued, remorseful, shows phobias & anxiety

8	Imagination	High	Intense subjectivity, high internal anxiety, appears irresponsible
9	Innovation	Low	Low on analytical ability
10	Leadership	High	Control actions of others, tries to influence group
11	Maturity	Low	High anxiety, inappropriate responses
12	Mental Health	Low	Not well adjusted, lack zest for living, and self-development
13	Morality	Low	Low on moral standards, egoistic
14	Self-control	Low	Low control over emotional life, disturbed interpersonal relationships
15	Sensitivity	High	Tender-minded, over-protected, fidgety, clinging, and insecure
16	Shrewdness	High	Diplomatic in handling people. Prefer to keep problems to themselves.
17	Self sufficiency	Low	Always need the support of a group, incapable of working alone, overly dependent.
18	Suspiciousness	High	An individual tends to be suspicious, jealous, dogmatic, and irritable
19	Social warmth	Low	Difficult to get along, less likely to be friendly, and share feelings & positive emotions
20	Tension	High	Individuals annoyed by little issues, irascible, and suffer from insomnia

Table 3.7 Personality risk factors

Source: Primary data

Table 3.7 shows the following:

In the dimension of Adaptability, 33% of the sample has a risk factor.

1. In Achievement Motivation, 50% have a risk factor.
2. Boldness shows a 16.7% risk factor.
3. Competition has 23.3% at risk. Enthusiasm is at 50%.
4. General Ability figures indicate 76% with a risk factor. Guilt proneness affects 53.3% of the sample.
5. Imagination shows a 56.7% risk factor.
6. Innovation is at 73.3%.
7. Leadership has 43.3%.
8. Maturity involves 40%.
9. Mental Health concerns 50%.
10. Morality is at 50%.
11. Self-control is affected in 56%.
12. Sensitivity shows 43%.
13. Shrewdness has the highest at 86.7%.
14. Self-sufficiency involves 60%.
15. Suspicion affects 33%.
16. Social Warmth is at 53%. Tension affects 73%.

This indicates that a higher number of personality risk factors may increase the likelihood of being involved in custodial deaths of inmates.

The police officers involved generally had lower ability, higher guilt-proneness, reduced self-control, and lower self-sufficiency and social warmth. As a result, they are not handling the suspect professionally.

Organizational Factors that Contribute to Custodial Deaths

The Organizational Climate Inventory was used to evaluate individuals' perceptions of their workplace. These perceptions often stem from their experiences within the organization.

Those who perceive the organization's climate as conducive generally do not feel anxious, are adaptable, and make informed decisions in various situations. Conversely, individuals who perceive the organization as Non-Conducive view situations as threatening, leading to feelings of anxiety and discomfort.

Figure 3.7 reveals that 57% of the sample involved in custodial deaths see the organization's environment as Non-Conducive. The data suggest that employees in non-conducive climates are more likely to be involved in custodial deaths compared to those working in conducive environments.

This could be because a non-conducive climate heightens anxiety, resulting in impatience and anger, which may contribute to custodial deaths. Additionally, within the standard group, 57% perceive the organizational climate as conducive.

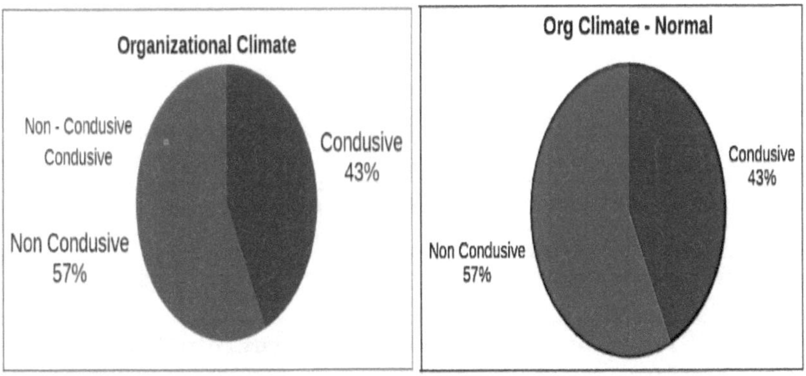

Figure 3.7 Organizational climate

Source: Primary data

Psychological Stress Factors

The psychological stress experienced by the sample was evaluated using six stress scales. These included frustration, Type-A behavior, self-perception, anxious reactions, deprivation stress, and overload. Each factor was categorized into three levels—High, Moderate, and Low—based on the scores. Risk factors were identified when factors such as high frustration, Type A behavior, and High overload were present, while moderate and low scores were considered non-risk. Those with risk factors are more susceptible to psychological stress, which can impact various types of performance, such as academic, technical, professional, and non-technical.

Research indicates that psychological stress can negatively influence performance across all task complexities.

Stress factors		Sample	%
Frustration	High & Moderate Frustration RF	16	53.33
Type-A–Behaviour	Type–A RF	8	26.67
Overload	High Overload RF Moderate /Low overload	30 0	100 0
		30	100
Self-perception	Low Self Perception	3	10
Anxious Reaction	High & Moderate Anxious Reaction RF	12	40
Deprivation	High	0	0

Table 3.8: Stress factors involved in custodial deaths

Source: Primary data, RF –Risk Factor

Table 3.8 indicates that individuals involved in custodial deaths had high levels of stress-related risk factors.

Factors such as intense frustration, excessive workload, low self-esteem, and anxious reactions may be linked to these incidents.

Stress factors for the standard Sample		Sample	%
Frustration	High &Moderate Frustration RF	22	73
Type-A Behaviour	Type–A RF	11	37
Overload	High Overload RF	30	100
	Moderate /Low overload	0	0
Self-perception	Low Self Perception	15	50
Anxious Reaction	High & Moderate Anxious Reaction RF	15	50
Deprivation	High	0	0

Table 3.9: Stress factors involved in the standard sample

Source: Primary data, RF –Risk Factor

Table 3.9 indicates that even for the standard group, the stress-related risk factors are high. This suggests that when placed in a situation of overload, frustration tends to react negatively to the problem. Generally, there is pressure for case detection (excess), resulting in a net increase (blind cases), which leads to frustration and anxiety. Thus, they resort to custodial torture for quick results, leading to custodial deaths.

Organizational vulnerability

Table 3.10 presents the details of organizational vulnerability in custodial deaths. The data covers 40 accused officers from nine police stations. Since all 40 cases are from these nine police stations, the results may be repeated if more than one accused officer is from the same station.

S.No	Guidelines	Complied	Not Complied
1	Annual Inspection by Seniors for Interrogation Instruments and Lockup Conditions	0	40
2	Training on Interrogation Skills	0	40
3	Conducive Lockup Condition -Bars for Hanging - Open Attached toilet	0	40
4	Access to case property - Phenyl - Pesticide/ -Ropes - Bottles -Alcohol -Diazepam	0	40
5	Feeding Charges guise or not/Claimed	0	40
6	Workload of P.S., reported crime, P.S. Strength	0	40
7	Infrastructure and support system, Toilets, Money, Transport	0	40
8	Pressure on detection and Recovery	0	40

Table 3.10 Organizational vulnerability

Source: Primary Data

Organizational climate assessment involves evaluating factors such as decision-making, responsibility, identity, support, and organizational environment, which are assessed through the organizational climate tool.

It is worth noting that the scale measures the factors mentioned above; however, a single score is ultimately arrived at by combining scores on all these factors.

The assessment shows that 57.5% of the sample perceives their work environment as non-conducive. Since the organizational climate is an interaction with the variables such as the social system within the organization, the social system within the culture, and management, when members feel that their organization lacks in supporting/nurturing them they will perceive it as a non-congenial and non-conducive climate which will eventually made them unhappy and unproductive and even emerge as a deviant in the work behavior.

Psychological Factors that Contribute to Custodial Deaths

Psychological factors							
	TOA		Cognitive Styles		Frustration		
Range	Tolerant	Non Tolerant	Reflective	Impulsive	Low	Moderate	High
Frequency	1	39	24	16	15	13	12
Percentage	2.5	97.5	60	40	37.5	32.5	30.5

Table 3.11 Psychological factors of the accused

Source: Primary Data

Regarding a factor linked to cognitive style, 40% of the sample exhibited an impulsive cognitive functioning style. When intolerance merges with impulsiveness, it can prompt the individual to act quickly, potentially leading to aggression in certain situations. Under critical conditions, a reflective approach would always aid in making more precise decisions than an impulsive one.

The sub-scale measuring stress caused by work overload appears to be at 100%.

Additionally, 62% of the sample appears to be experiencing frustration, and they fall into the category of experiencing stress due to frustration at high and moderate levels.

Individual factors and their significance: Verification of Hypothesis – Ho1

Ho1: Individual factors of the police personnel do not have a significant influence on custodial deaths.

Test Applied: Chi-Square Test Result:

The Chi-square test results indicate that most of the proposed sub-hypotheses, Ho1(a) to Ho1(f), were rejected at the 0.05 level of significance. Therefore, the proposed Null Hypothesis, Ho1, was rejected. It can be concluded that individual factors of police personnel significantly influence custodial deaths.

To verify the above Null hypothesis – Ho1, the following sub-hypotheses (Ho1 (a) to Ho1 (f)) were proposed and verified for their statistical significance.

In the following sections, the chi-square test of independence was used to analyze the factors related to custodial deaths. The level of significance is tested at 0.05.

1. Verification of Sub-Hypothesis -Ho1 (a)

Test of anxiety (intolerance) among police personnel does not significantly affect custodial death.

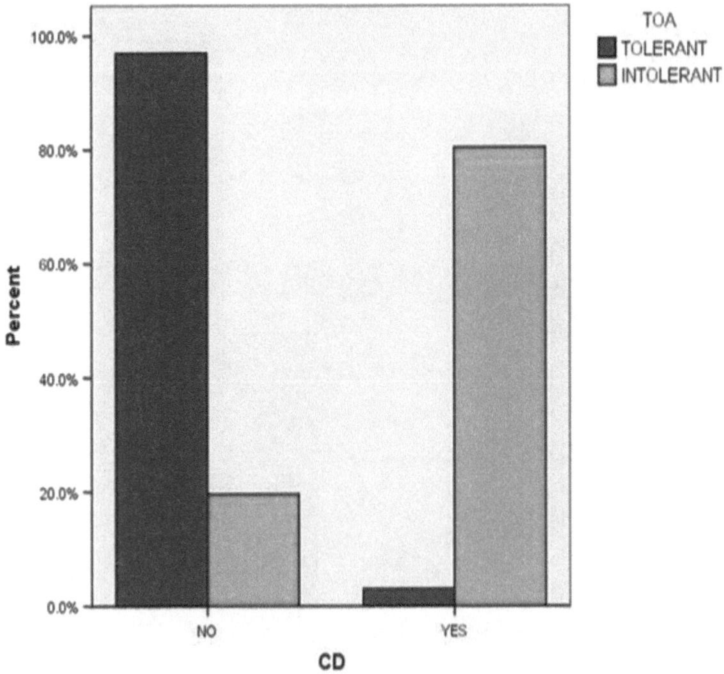

Figure 3.8: Test of anxiety vs. custodial death

Source: Primary Data

The test of anxiety vs. custodial deaths is shown in Figure 3.8. The Chi-square Test of Independence was used to analyze the data, with Test of Anxiety as the first variable and Custodial Death as the second variable. There was a significant effect, $\chi 2(1, N = 40) = 46.117$, $p = 0.000$ ($< .05$), such that most of the officers among the accused in custodial deaths are intolerant. Hence, the proposed sub-hypothesis Ho1 (a) is rejected.

2. Verification of Sub-Hypothesis -Ho1 (b)

Cognitive style (impulsive behavior) among police personnel does not significantly affect custodial death.

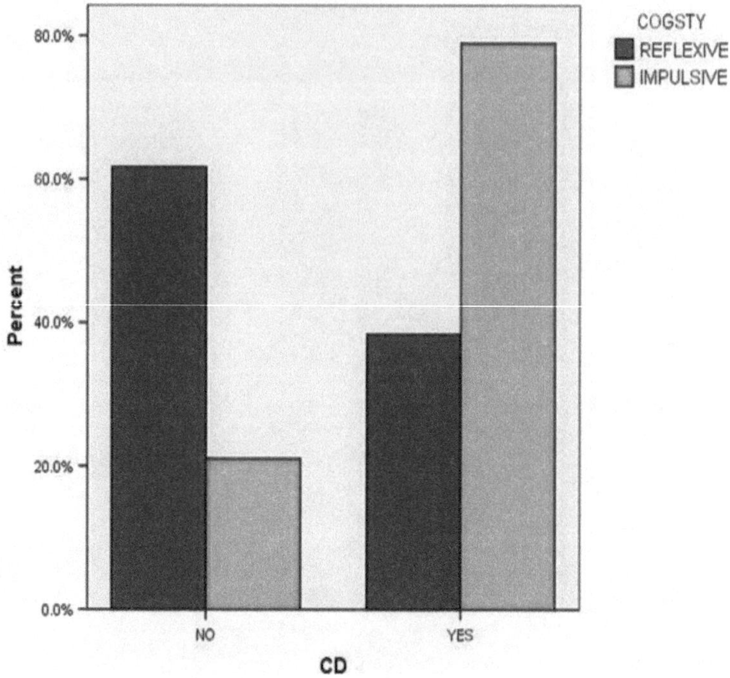

Figure 3.9: Cognitive style vs. custodial death

Source: Primary Data

The relationship between cognitive style and custodial death is illustrated in Figure 3.9. A Chi-square Test of Independence was conducted with cognitive style and the occurrence of custodial death as variables.

The results showed a significant association, $\chi 2$ (1, N=40) = 9.535, p = 0.002, indicating that officers with impulsive behavior are more likely to be involved in custodial deaths compared to those with a reflective nature. As a result, the sub-hypothesis Ho1 (b) is rejected.

3. Diabetes vs. custodial death Verification of Sub-Hypothesis -Ho1 (c)

Police personnel with diabetes are less likely to be involved in custodial deaths.

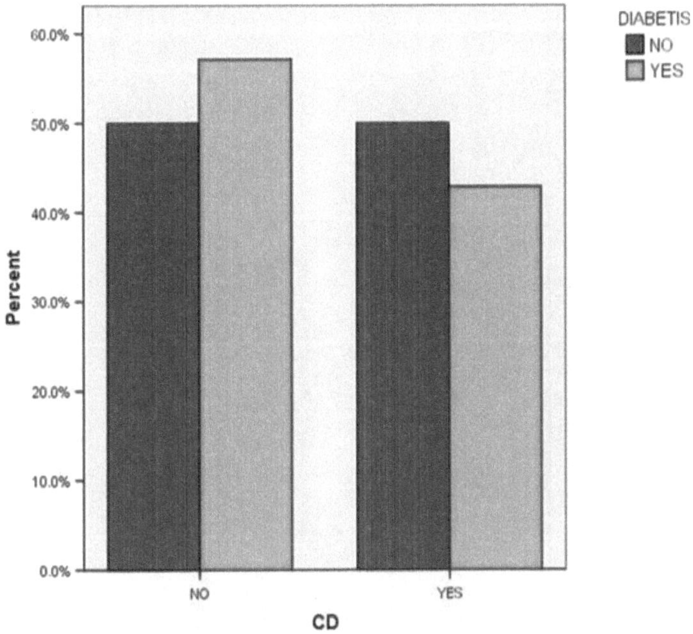

Figure 3.10: Test of diabetes vs. custodial death

Source: Primary Data

Figure 3.10 illustrates the comparison between diabetes and custodial death. The chi-square test shows no significant relationship, $\chi 2$ (1, N=40) =.315, p =.575, indicating there is no evidence that officers exhibiting diabetic behavior are more involved in custodial death than those without such complaints. Therefore, the sub-hypothesis Ho1 (c) is accepted.

The alternative Hypothesis states: Police personnel with diabetic behavior tend to be more involved in custodial deaths.

4. **Verification of Sub-Hypothesis -Ho1 (d):**
   Police personnel with peptic ulcers do not tend to be more involved in custodial deaths.

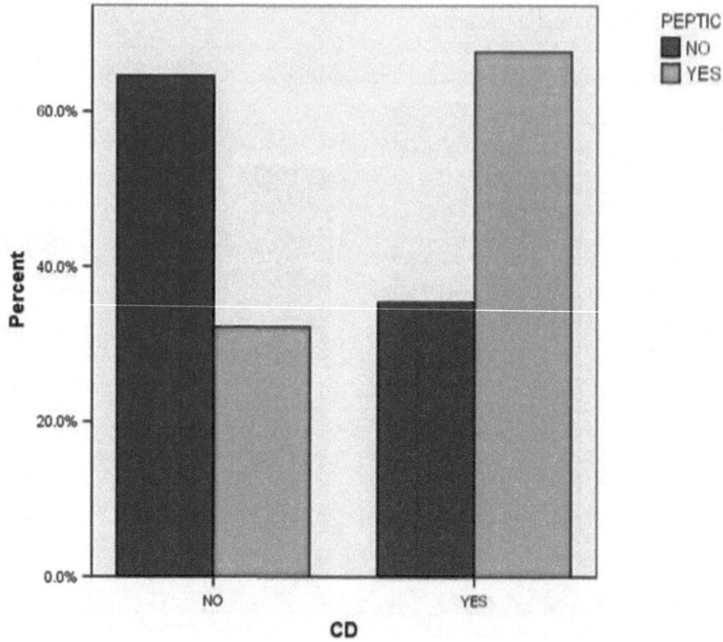

Figure 3.11: Test of peptic ulcer vs. custodial death

Source: Primary Data

The test of peptic ulcer vs. custodial death is shown in Figure 3.11. The test, $\chi 2$ (1, N= 40) = 7.88, p =0.005, indicates that the officers with Peptic Ulcer tend to be more involved in custodial deaths than the officers who do not have the complaint. The proposed sub-hypothesis Ho1 (d) is rejected.

Alternative Hypotheses: Police personnel with peptic ulcers tend to be more likely to be involved in custodial deaths.

5. **Verification of Sub-Hypothesis -Ho1 (e)**

Police Personnel with family problems do not tend to be more involved in custodial deaths.

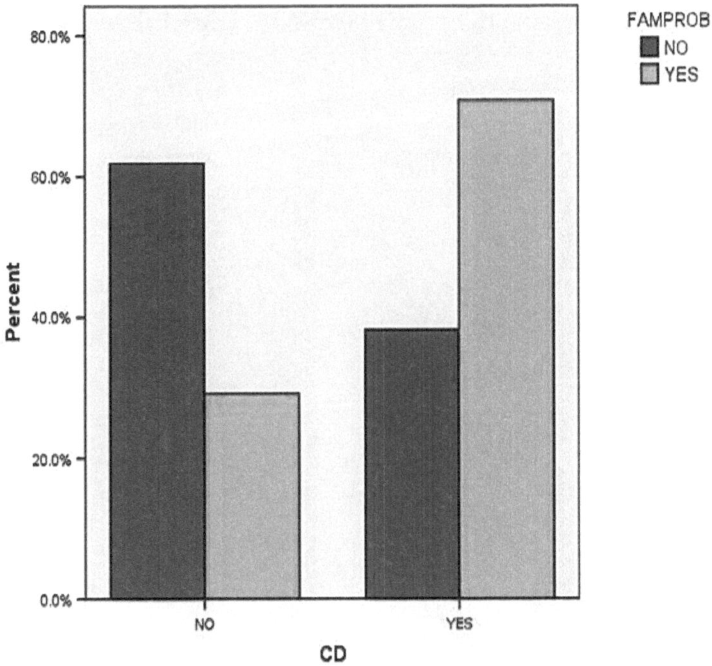

Figure 3.12: Test of family problems vs. custodial death

Source: Primary Data

The test of family problems vs. custodial death is shown in Figure 3.12. The Chi-Square test, $\chi 2$ (1, N = 40) = 7.1, p = 0.008, indicates that officers with Family Problems tend to be involved more in custodial deaths than those who do not. The proposed sub-hypothesis Ho1 (e) is rejected.

Alternative Hypotheses: Police personnel with family problems tend to be more involved in custodial deaths.

6. Hypertension vs. custodial death Verification of Sub-Hypothesis -Ho1 (f)

Police Personnel with high Blood Pressure (hypertension) do not tend to be more involved in custodial deaths.

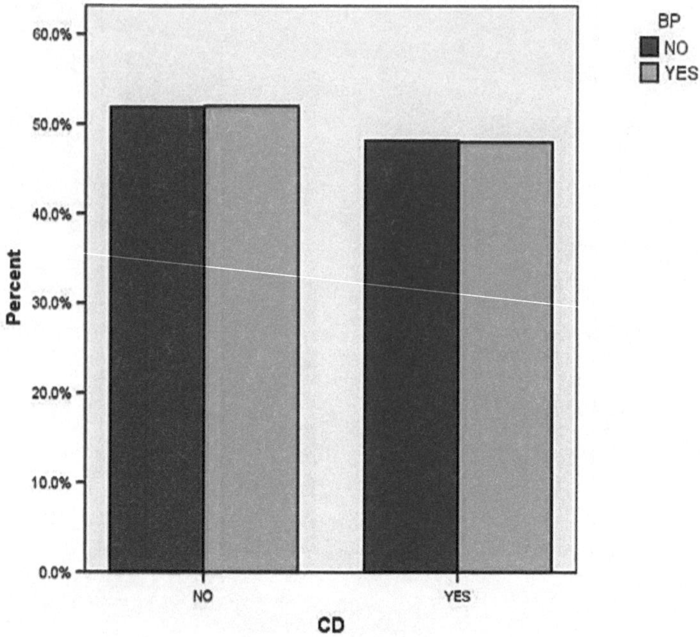

Figure 3.13: Test of hypertension (blood pressure) vs. custodial death

Source: Primary Data

The test of hypertension vs. custodial death is shown in Figure 3.13. The Chi-Square test, $\chi 2$ (1, N = 40) = 0, p = .99, provides no evidence that officers with high Blood Pressure tend to be more involved in custodial deaths than officers who do not have high Blood Pressure. The proposed sub-hypothesis Ho1 (f) is accepted.

Alternative Hypotheses: Police personnel with high blood pressure tend to be more involved in custodial deaths.

From the above analysis, the individual factors that influenced Custodial Death are Test of anxiety, Cognitive style, Family problem, and Peptic ulcer.

Medical Factors that Contribute to Custodial Deaths

Medical Factors												
	Blood Pressure			Pulse Rate			Diabetes		Peptic Ulcer		Heart Ailment	
Range	Low	Normal	High	Low	Normal	High	Diabetic	Non Diabetic	Have ulcers	No ulcers	Have ailment	No ailment
Frequency	0	16	24	0	26	14	6	34	25	15	5	35
Percentage	0	40	60	0	65	35	15	85	62.5	37.5	12.5	87.5

Table 3.12: Medical profiles of the sample accused (Frequencies in the given range from normal to deviance from normal)

Source: Primary data

	Alcohol		Tobacco	
Range	Alcoholic	Non-Alcoholic	Smokers	Non-Smokers
Frequency	20	20	11	29
percentage	50	50	27.5	72.5

Table 3.13: Substance addiction of the accused

Source: Primary data

The investigator included the range frequencies and mean values in Tables 3.12 and 3.13 to provide readers with an immediate overview of the sample's status regarding various human factors involved in this study. Moving forward, the investigator will concentrate on the risk factors that contributed to custodial deaths.

It is noted from the table that the number of police officers who are high on Blood pressure is 60%, and Peptic ulcers are 62.5% and 15% are diabetic, and 12.5% have heart ailments, which are coincidental findings that are generally associated with stress.

Closely connected to medical and psychological factors, it was also felt necessary to assess substance addiction in the sample members. The data shows 50% are addicted to alcohol, and 27.5% are addicted to Tobacco. Alcohol consumption among police officers is also an indirect indicator of stress buster, which further leads to many health issues, coupled with family problems. Each of these problems and findings affects the behavior in the approach to crime solving.

Sl. No.	Cr.No / PS	District	Date	Significant injuries		Cause of Death		Witnesses			Charge Sheet	Name of deceased	Caste	Profession	Name of Investigator	Name of Accused	Designation	Criminal History
				Post mortem Report	Inquest Report	Post mortem Report	Inquest Report	Relatives	Independent	Police								
1	211/96 Dhone	Kurnool	10-Sep 96	2	0	3	3	6	Nil	10	Yes	Ediga Venkateswarlu	BC	Shepe rd	DV. Ramana Murthy	P.Ramanjaneyulu, S.Ravinder, S.Manohar	APS constable Excise constable Excise constable	Yes
2	201/96 Ongole	Prakasham	22-Nov 96	Nil	Nil	1	1	Nil	17	24	Yes	Gaddam Yedukondalu	Dalit	Petty Elecl. works	K. Padmanaba Goud	Rama rao Srinivas	HC PC	No
3	224/98 Kodimal	Karimnagar	15-Oct 98	2	6	4	3	2	19	8	Yes	Boga Laxmi pathi	SC	Reporter	A. Sanjeeva Rao	K. Venu	S.I	Nil
4	126/99 Vijayawada	Krishna District	6-May 99	5	5	1	1	Nil	31	18	Yes	Kona Krishna Kumari	BC	Barber	B.V. Rangaraju	Smt.Kyothi Rayudu, Smt.P.Santhoshamma Smt.P.Raghava Rani, Smt.P.V.Ragini	SI, Head Constable Constable Constable	Nil
5	158/98 Mahabubabad	Warangal	11-Oct 98	Nil	Nil	2	2	10	17	12	Yes	B.Srisailam goud, P.Lingaiah Kore Devender	BC	Petty thefts	K.Padmanbha Goud	K.Venkata Rao Gopi Raju	HC PC PC	Nil
6	126/93 Yellandu	Khammam	21-Sep 93	Nil	Nil	4	4	11	10	5	Yes	Padma Ashalu	SC	RMP doctor	Koka Govinda rao	P.Apparao Venkateswarlu	ASI HC	Nil
7	136/93 Khammam	Khammam	18-Sep 93	Yes, 8	Yes, 18	4	1	9	19	10	Yes	Shaik Khadar Baba	BC	Preparing cotton beds	Koka Govinda rao	Rama Narsimha Reddy, Prabhakar Reddy, Venkanna, Srinivas	SI, ConstableConstable, Constable	Nil
8	Khammam	9-Sep 96	Nil	Nil	Yes, 2	4	4	2	1	6	Yes	Dugyala Venkulu	SC	Cooli	DV.Ramana Murthy	Koteswara Rao	SI	Nil
9	74/86 Bellampally	23-Aug 2086	Yes	Yes	Yes	1	1	2	11	7	Yes	M. Srinivas	OC	Student	P.Ramakrishna	Balaiah, Muttaiah, Shyamsunder Reddy, Siva Prasad, Laxman	CI, ASI, PC, PC, PC	Yes, 2 cases
10	Mar-93 Iragavaram	30-Jan 93	Yes	Yes	Yes	1	1	4	45	6	Yes	Birada Prasad	Kapu	Daily wage	A. Sanjeeva Rao	T.Gangaraju, B.Ramakrishna, R.Mohan Singh, T.Subrahmanyam, Sharif	PC, PC, PC, PC, PC	Yes, 2 cases
11	Dharmavaram	31-Aug 92	No	No	No	5	5	10	14	Nil	Yes	Mondi Venkatesu	OC	Electrical work	K.Padmanaba Goud	K.Venkateswarlu B. Rama krishna	SI HC	Yes
12	18/91 Amruthaluru	9-Mar 91	Yes	Yes	Yes	1	1	2	25	9	Yes	Kaavuri Vinaybabu	Kamma	Thefts	A. Sanjeeva Rao	N.Balaraju	ASI	Nil
13	24/90 Husnabad	9-Mar 90	Yes, 6	Yes, 6	Yes, 6	4	1	4	5	12	Yes	Uppuleti Chandraiah	BC	Cooli	C. Jacob	Mogellaiah	CI	Yes
14	176/86 Banswada	10-Sep 86	Yes	Yes	No	4	1	3	18	8	Yes	Yerra Sailu	SC	Agricultural Labour	EL. Bhageeratha Rao	Hyder Ali Prasad Rao	HC PC	Nil
15	190/86 Vijayawada	3-Oct 86	Yes, 13	Yes, 13	Yes, 11	4	1	Nil	69	30	Yes	T.Muralidharan	BC	Sea man-I	K.Sriranga Nayakulu	PRK. Prasad, N.Chandra Rao, Y.Nageshwer Rao, M.Babu Rao, J. Babu Rao	SI, SI, HC, PC, PC	Nil
16	121/86 Macherla	15-Sep 86	Nil	Nil	Nil	Semi starvation diet, torture	5	3	12	2	Yes	Dasari Venkateshwerlu	OC	Agricultural labour	PV.Ranga Reddy	N. Prasad, Srinivasa Rao,	SI Macherla, HC, Right Bank	Nil

Sl. No.	Cr.No / PS	District	Date	Significant Injuries		Cause of Death		Witnesses			Charge Sheet	Name of deceased	Caste	Profession	Name of Investigator	Name of Accused	Designation	Criminal History
				Post mortem Report	Inquest Report	Post mortem Report	Inquest Report	Relatives	Independent	Police								
17	243/88 Vijayawada	Krishna	2-oct-88	Yes, 8	Nil	4	5	Nil	4	25	Yes	Peetla Narsimha Rao	OC	Lorry Driver	G.J. Stephen	Chinnababu Subba Rao	ASI PC	Nl
18	59/87 Vallur	Cuddappah	26-Nov-87	Yes, 8	Yes	4	4	1	10	3	Yes	Bala Veera Reddy	BC	Labour	PL. Subbaiah	K.Janardhar Bali reddy Saidulu	SI HC PC	Nil
19	37/87 Bellampally	Adilabad	9-may-87	Yes, 2	Yes, 4	4	4	2	14	10	Yes	B. Rajaiah	ST	Colliery worker	ADV. Reddy	S. Sayana Rao, K. Balanna, N.Ramachendra Singh, Mir Wahid Ali Baig, K. Narsinga Rao	PC, PC, PC, PC, ARPC	Nil
20	252/88 Osmana University	Rang a Reddy	6-oct-88	Yes, 10	Yes, 2	3	TB	7	13	6	Yes	Vemula Venkatesh	BC	Employees in Alwyn Factory	PV. Ranga Reddy	Mallesh Goud Sadiq Babu	HC PC	Yes
21	83/88 Sringavrapu Kota	Vizayanagaram	6-Oct-88	Yes	Yes	1	Suicide	2	25	8	Yes	Penuganti Sadhu	BC	Thefts	C.Veerabhadra Rao	Annam Naidu Subbayya	SI PC	Yes
22	52/88 Yenkur	Khammam	20-Dec-88	No	No	4	Heart failure	Nil	12	4	Yes	Rentapalli Nagulu	SC	Thefts	C.Veerabhadra Rao	P.Narayana, Mohd.Admed, P.Narayana Rao,	SI, PC, PC	Yes
23	33/89 Alur	Kurnool	25-Jun 89	Yes, 4	Yes, 4	1	hanging	Nil	8	5	Yes	Harijana Chennappa	SC	Thefts	C.Narsimhulu	Mohan reddy	SI	Yes
24	50/89 Mahanandi	Kurnool	24-Jul-86	Yes, 4	Nil	1	suicide	3	11	9	Yes	Chenchu china papanna	OC	Thefts	B. Narsinga Rao	B.Obulesu P.Penchalayya	ASI HC	Nil
25	Khammam	Khammam	22-sep-86	Yes, 11	Yes, 5	3	1	2	5	7	Yes	Devid Raju	BC	Thefts	B.Rama Rao	N.Somaiah	ASI	Yes
26	61/89 Godavari Khani	Karimnagar	11-sep-89	Yes 3	Yes 3	2	1	5	6	4	Yes	Maruthi Ramesh	SC	Naxalite	VV.Ramanandam	M.Bala Naik K.Kalesha vali	CI HC	Nil

Table 2.14: Analysis on differences between injuries in inquest and Post Mortem reports

Source: Primary Data

Sl. No.	Cr.No/ PS	District	Date	Significant injuries		Cause of Death		Witnesses			Charge Sheet	Name of deceased	Compensation (Lakhs)				Cril. List	Date of Judgement		
													State		Police					
				Postmortem Report	Inquest Report	Postmortem Report	Inquest Report	Relatives	Independent	Police			SHRC	COI	SHRC	COI		SHRC	COI	District Sessions Court
1	211/96 Dhone	Kurnool	10-Sep 96	2	0	3	3	6	Nil	10	Yes	Ediga Venkateswarlu	-	0.5	-	0.5	-	-	12/2/2002	38154
2	201/96 Ongole	Prakasham	22-Nov-96	Nil	Nil	1	1	Nil	17	24	Yes	Gaddam Yedukondalu	-	1	-	0.53	-	-	30/9/1997	36661
3	224/98 Kodimal	Karimnagar	15-Oct 98	2	6	4	3	2	19	8	Yes	Boga Laxmipathi	-	2	-	-	-	-	30/11/1999	37365
4	126/99 Vijayawada	Krishna	6-May 99	5	5	1	1	Nil	31	18	Yes	Kona Krishna Kumari	-	-		0.5	-	-	31/12/1999	36971
5	158/98 Mahabuabad	Warangal	11-Oct 98	Nil	Nil	2	2	10	17	12	Yes	B.Srisailam goud, P.Lingaiah Kore Devender	-	1 1 1	-	-	-	-	10/9/1999	37607
6	126/93 Yellandu	Khammam	21-Sep-93	Nil	Nil	4	4	11	10	5	Yes	Padma Ashalu	-	-	-	0.6	Nil	-	19/3/1994	35234
7	136/93 Khammam	Khammam	18-Sep 93	Yes, 8	Yes, 18	4	1	9	19	10	Yes	Shaik Khadar Baba	-	-	-	-	-	-	30/6/1994	35482
8	Khammam	Khammam	9-Sep 96	Nil	Yes, 2	4	4	2	1	6	Yes	Dugyala Venkulu	-	-	-	0.5	Nil	-	36561	37235
9	74/86 Bellampally	Adilabad	23-Aug-86	Yes	Yes	1	1	2	11	7	Yes	M. Srinivas	-	1	-	-	Nil	-	30/6/1987	33162
10	Mar-93 Iragavaram	West Godavari	30-Jan 93	Yes	Yes	1	1	4	45	6	Yes	Birada Prasad	-	-	-	0.5	-	-	13/4/1994	35607
11	Dharmavaram	Anantapur	31 Aug 92	No	No	5	5	10	14	Nil	Yes	Mondi Venkatesu	-	-	-	0.4	-	-	30/6/1993	13/Mar/1996
12	18/91 Amruthaluru	Guntur	9-Mar 91	Yes	Yes	1	1	2	25	9	Yes	Kaavuri Vinaybabu	-	0.55	-	-	-	-	31/10/1991	34719
13	24/90 Husnabad	Karimnagar	9-Mar 90	Yes, 6	Yes, 6	4	1	4	5	12	Yes	Uppuleti Chandraiah	-	-	-	1	-	-	20/11/1990	34065

Sl. No.	Cr.No/ PS	District	Date	Significant injuries		Cause of Death		Witnesses			Charge Sheet	Name of deceased	Compensation (Lakhs)				Cril . List	Date of Judgement		
													State		Police					
				Postmortem Report	Inquest Report	Postmortem Report	Inquest Report	Relatives	Independent	Police			SH RC	COI	SH RC	COI		SH RC	COI	District Sessions Court
14	176/86 Banswada	Nizamabad	10-Sep-86	Yes	No	4	1	3	18	8	Yes	Yerra Sailu	-	0.45	-	-	-	-	22/04/1987	26-Nov 1990
15	190/86 Vijayawada	Krishna	3-Oct 86	Yes, 13	Yes, 11	4	1	Nil	69	30	Yes	T.Murali dharan	-	-	-	1	Nil	-	4/11/1987	22-May 1991
16	121/86 Macherla	Guntur	15-Sep-86	Nil	Nil	Semi starvation diet, torture	5	3	12	2	Yes	Dasari Venkateshwerlu	-	1	-	-	Nil	-	28/05/1987	9-Aug 1989
17	243/88 Vijayawada	Krishna	2-Oct 88	Yes, 8	Nil	4	5	Nil	4	25	Yes	Peetla Narsimha Rao	-	0.8	-	-	Nil	Nil	31/5/1989	14-Jan 1992
18	59/87 Vallur	Cuddappah	26-Nov-87	Yes, 8	Yes	4	4	1	10	3	Yes	Bala Veera Reddy	-	-	-	1	Nil	Nil	27/6/1988	29-Oct 1991
19	37/87 Bellampally	Adilabad	9-May 87	Yes, 2	Yes, 4	4	4	2	14	10	Yes	B. Rajaiah	-	0.1	-	-	Nil	Nil	15/10/1987	19-Feb 1990
20	252/88 Osmania University	Ranga Reddy	2-Oct 88	Yes, 10	Yes, 2	3	TB	7	13	6	Yes	Vemula Venkatesh	-	0.5	-	0.05	Nil	Nil	1/7/1989	12-Mar 1992
21	83/88 Sringavrapu Kota	Vizayanagaram	6-Oct 88	Yes	Yes	1	Suicide	2	25	8	Yes	Penuganti Sadhu	-	-	-	0.6	Nil	Nil	31/3/1989	20-Nov 1991
22	52/88 Yenkur	Khammam	20-Dec-88	No	No	4	Heart failure	Nil	12	4	Yes	Rentapalli Nagulu	-	1	-	-	Nil	Nil	31/8/1989	11-Feb 1991
23	33/89 Alur	Kurnool	25-Jun 89	Yes, 4	Yes, 4	1	hanging	Nil	8	5	Yes	Harijana Chennappa	-	-	-	0.8	Nil	Nil	30/12/1989	6-Apr 1992
24	50/89 Mahanandi	Kurnool	24-Jul 86	Yes, 4	Nil	1	suicide	3	11	9	Yes	Chenchu china papanna	-	0.55	-	-	Nil	Nil	31/8/1990	08-Sept 1993
25	Khammam	Khammam	23-Sep-86	Yes, 11	Yes, 5	3	1	2	5	7	Yes	Devid Raju	-	1	-	-	Nil	Nil	1/6/1987	04-July 1990
26	61/89 Godavari Khani	Karimnagar	11-Sep-89	Yes 3	Yes 3	2	1	5	6	4	Yes	Maruthi Ramesh	-	-	-	1	Nil	Nil	30/12/1989	5-Oct 1992

Table 3.14: Analysis on differences between injuries in inquest and Compensation Plan for Deceased detainees

Source: Primary Data

Here is a variation in Table 3.14, which shows the cause of death as observed in the inquest and post-mortem reports. Only in 7 cases do the causes of death mentioned in both reports agree with each other, and in 19 cases, they vary, which will provide ample opportunity for the defense counsel to divert the court's attention to the contradiction in the two reports, thereby potentially allowing his client to go scot-free.

When we observe the table above, containing 26 cases, in 13 cases, the injuries are replicated in both the inquest reports and the Post Mortem report; in the other 13 cases, there are many variations between the number of injuries reported in the inquest report and the number of injuries reported in the Post Mortem report. This will allow the defense counsel to benefit from the doubt for the accused Police Officer.

The Investigating Officer should be very cautious when examining the body during the inquest.

Taking the assistance of a medical officer to assess the external appearance of injuries during the inquest may also be considered. So that there will be any chance left to punish the guilty.

The post-mortem report is provided by an expert who has technical knowledge on the subject. In contrast, the Investigating Officer may need to gain more knowledge in describing the injuries. There is a need to include a training program in the basic training of Investigating Officers on examining the appearance of external injuries. Eg. The Executive Magistrate may report the Artifacts on the body as injuries that arise due to shifting the body from one place to another, which is postmortem and not antemortem, leading to a miscarriage of justice and interpretation.

Analysis of the evidence of various categories of witnesses in the inquest

In the same Table 3.14, we observe the relationship between the witnesses. In 20 cases, witnesses are related to the deceased. In 6 cases, there are no witnesses from relatives. In 23 cases, there are independent witnesses. In 24 cases, there are Police witnesses.

Evidence from independent witnesses is considered more credible than that from the deceased's relatives or the police.

When evaluating evidence, the court primarily relies on independent witnesses because statements from relatives are often viewed with skepticism, as they may testify in favor of the deceased or against the accused due to their familial relationship. In the 26 cases reviewed, no charge sheet has been filed against any police officer, suggesting that no culprits were identified in these cases.

Summary of Data		
	Treatments	
	1	2
N	24	24
df	23	23
Mean	3.77	1.85
SS	582.62	143.38
s2	23.3	5.74

Table 3.15: One-tailed t-test data to check for significant injuries in the postmortem report (Treatment 1) and inquest report (Treatment 2) on the dead bodies of the victims

Source: Primary Data

Postmortem and inquest reports have been collected to examine significant injuries on the victims' bodies (Table 3.15).

A statistical analysis of these reports was performed using a one-tailed t-test. The t-test results showed that the t-value was 1.81964, and the p-value was 0.037402. The results were significant at $p < 0.05$.

It can be concluded that there is no significant difference in the evidence from postmortem and inquest reports regarding the injuries to the deceased individuals in custodial deaths.

Summary of Data		
	Treatments	
	1	2
N	24	24
df	23	23
Mean	2.8	2.16
SS	48	59.36
s2	2	2.47

Table 3.16: One-tailed t-test data to check for the cause of death of the victims in the postmortem report (Treatment 1) and inquest report (Treatment 2)

Source: Primary Data

Postmortem and inquest reports have been obtained to examine the victims' causes of death (Table 3.16). A statistical analysis of these reports was conducted using a one-tailed t-test. The t-test results indicated that the t-value was 1.51298 and the p-value was 0.04842. The results were significant at $p < 0.05$. It can be concluded that there is a substantial difference in the evidence provided by postmortem and inquest reports regarding the cause of death in custodial death cases.

	Summary of Data			
	Treatments			
	1	2	3	Total
N	24	24	24	69
ΣX	81	409	231	721
Mean	3.375	17.0417	10.0435	10.449
ΣX^2	567	12017	3567	16151
Std.Dev.	3.573	14.8133	7.5286	11.2571
	Result Details			

Source	SS	df		MS	
Between-treatments	2344.4638	2		1172.2319	F = 12.33415
Within-treatments	6272.6087	66		95.0395	
Total	8617.0725	68			

Table 3.17: One-way ANOVA regarding postmortem reports of the witnesses (Relatives-1, Independent-2, and Police-3)

Source: Primary Data

Postmortem reports from witnesses, such as relatives of the victims, as well as independent and police personnel, provided their statements (Table 3.17). Statistical analysis of their opinions using one-way ANOVA was conducted. The ANOVA test results show that the F-value was 12.33415, which was found to be significant at the 0.05 significance level. It can be concluded that there is a substantial difference among the statements given by different witnesses regarding postmortem reports in cases of custodial death.

Compliance with Legal Provisions and D K Basu Guidelines about Custodial Deaths

Compliance with arrest and interrogation procedures, as per D.K. Basu's Guidelines, was evaluated and summarized in Table 3.18.

Sl. No	Name	CrimeNo.	Name of P.S	Interrogators list Register Maintained or not	Spot Arrest Memo & Signature taken or not	Friend was informed of Arrest or not	Within 8-12 hrs Time, Place of arrest and Place of Custody notified or not	Was he Informed about his Rightto inform someone of his arrest	Personal Diary entry of friend and name of police officers at spot	Injuries, inspection memos signed copy given to arrestee or not	Did Medical Doctor examine every 48 hrs or not	Was FIR, Arrest Memo sent to Magistrate or not	Was Lawyer allowed which interrogation or not	Was PCR informed of arrest by police within 12 hrs	SCORE OUT OF 11
				1	2	3	4	5	6	7	8	9	10	11	
1	Rama Rao P, CI	334/2000	I-town PS Vijayawada	No	No	Yes	No	Yes	Yes	No	No	Yes	No	No	4
2	Krishna Chaitanya,	-do -	-do-	No	No	Yes	No	Yes	Yes	No	No	Yes	No	No	4
3	Raghava Rani K, WPC-564	148/1999	Suryaraopet PS Vijayawada	No	No	Yes	No	No	Yes	No	No	Yes	No	No	3
4	Jyothi Rayudu, SI	-do-	-do -	No	No	Yes	No	No	Yes	No	No	Yes	No	No	3
5	Santhoshamma, WHC-1192	-do-	-do-	No	No	Yes	No	No	Yes	No	No	Yes	No	No	3
6	Ragini, WPC-295	-do-	-do-	No	No	Yes	No	No	Yes	No	No	Yes	No	No	3
7	Narasimha Rao P, PC-792	334/2000	I-town PS Vijayawada	No	No	No	No	No	Yes	No	No	Yes	No	No	2
8	Ranga Rao, PC-1333	-do-	-do-	No	No	No	No	No	Yes	No	No	Yes	No	No	2
9	Venkateswer Rao B, ASI-137	-do-	-do-	No	No	No	No	No	Yes	No	No	Yes	No	No	2
10	Prem Kumar G, PC-143	-do-	-do-	No	No	No	No	No	Yes	No	No	Yes	No	No	2
11	Venkateswer Rao K, PC 846	-do-	-do-	No	No	No	No	No	Yes	No	No	Yes	No	No	2
12	Purshotham, PC-1982	70/1997	Ongole Railway PS	No	No	No	No	No	Yes	No	No	Yes	No	No	2
13	Balu K, PC-1483	10/2003	Balanagar PS, R.R. Dist	No	No	No	No	No	Yes	No	No	Yes	No	No	2
14	Rambabu, PC-445	18/1996	Nagaramppalem PS, Guntur	No	No	No	No	No	Yes	No	No	Yes	No	No	2
15	Laxmaiah, PC-2530	70/1997	Ongole Railway PS	No	No	No	No	No	Yes	No	No	Yes	No	No	2
16	Jeelani, HC-2275	18/1996	Nagaramppalem PS, Guntur	No	No	No	No	No	Yes	No	No	Yes	No	No	2
17	Azeez, PC-2509	90/1991	Pattipadu PS Guntur	No	No	No	No	No	Yes	No	No	Yes	No	No	2
18	Sambasiva Rao G, PC-1243	-do-	-do-	No	No	No	No	No	Yes	No	No	Yes	No	No	2

19	Samabasiva Rao T, PC-1466	-do-	-do-	No	No	No	No	No	Yes	No	No	Yes	No	No	2
20	Narayana	-do-	-do-	No	No	No	No	No	Yes	No	No	Yes	No	No	2
21	Subba Rao, PC-1211	18/1996	Nagarampalem PS, Guntur	No	No	No	No	No	Yes	No	No	Yes	No	No	2
22	Papa Rao, PC-1495	-do-	-do-	No	No	No	No	No	Yes	No	No	Yes	No	No	2
23	Venkata Ramappa	-do-	-do-	No	No	No	No	No	Yes	No	No	Yes	No	No	2
24	Narayana Swamy, PC-134	95/1998	Kadiri Town PS, Ananthapur	No	No	No	No	No	Yes	No	No	Yes	No	No	2
25	Gowri Shankar , PC-107	-do-	-do-	No	No	No	No	No	Yes	No	No	Yes	No	No	2
26	Raja Vardhan Raj, HC-1595	54/2003	Yadiki PS, Ananthapur	No	No	No	No	No	Yes	No	No	Yes	No	No	2
27	Kishore Reddy, PC-2079	-do-	-do-	No	No	No	No	No	Yes	No	No	Yes	No	No	2
28	Srinivasulu, HC-717	104/1997	Tadipatri Tq. PS, Ananthapur	No	No	No	No	No	Yes	No	No	Yes	No	No	2
29	Chandra Mouli, PC-723	-do-	-do-	No	No	No	No	No	Yes	No	No	Yes	No	No	2
30	Rafi, PC-120	95/1998	Kadiri Town PS, Ananthapur	No	No	No	No	No	Yes	No	No	Yes	No	No	2
31	Y.Ramchandra Reddy, CI	-do-	-do-	No	No	No	No	No	Yes	No	No	Yes	No	No	2
32	Mahboob Vali, HC-30	-do-	-do-	No	No	No	No	No	Yes	No	No	Yes	No	No	2
33	Raja Gopal	-do-	-do-	No	No	No	No	No	Yes	No	No	Yes	No	No	2
34	Dastagiri, SI	95/1998	Kadiri Town PS, Ananthapur	No	No	No	No	No	Yes	No	No	Yes	No	No	2
35	Chalma Reddy, SI	-do-	-do-	No	No	No	No	No	Yes	No	No	Yes	No	No	2
36	Nagendrudu, SI	104/1997	Tadipatri Tq.PS, Ananthapur	No	No	No	No	No	Yes	No	No	Yes	No	No	2
37	Tejeswer Rao , SI	54/2003	Yadiki PS, Ananthapur	No	No	No	No	No	Yes	No	No	Yes	No	No	2
38	Ramachendra Reddy	-do-	-do-	No	No	No	No	No	Yes	No	No	Yes	No	No	2
39	Prabhakar Reddy	-do-	-do-	No	No	No	No	No	Yes	No	No	Yes	No	No	2
40	Balu Naik , PC-1595	70/1997	Ongole Railway PS	No	No	No	No	No	Yes	No	No	Yes	No	No	2

SCORE SHEET							
5	Fully Complied	9-11/11		2	Just	3-5	**Yes - 1**
4	Nearly Complied	7-9/11		1	Attempted	1-3	
3	Partially Complied	5-7		0	0, Not complied	0	**No - 0**

Table 3.18: Compliance status of D.K. Basu guidelines Source: Primary Data

Legal issues

Only guidelines 6 and 9 are adhered to in the case of the accused's arrest. Compliance with guidelines 3 and 5 is insignificant. Other guidelines must be followed accordingly. The submission of the D K Basu guidelines is presented in Table 3.18 and Figure 3.14.

S.No	Guidelines	Complied	Not Complied
1	Interrogation Register	0	40
2	Spot arrest memo and Signature	0	40
3	The friend was informed of the arrest	6	34
4	Within 8-12 Hrs, the Time, Place of arrest, and Place of custody are notified	0	40
5	Was he informed about his right to inform someone of his arrest	2	38
6	Personal Diary entry of a friend and the name of the police officers at the spot	0	40
7	Injuries, Inspection memos signed copy given to the arrestee	0	40
8	A Medical Doctor examined every 48 hrs	0	40
9	FIR, Arrest memo sent to Magistrate	40	0
10	The lawyer allowed the interrogation	0	40
11	PCR informed of arrest by police within 12 hrs.	0	40

Table 3.19: D K Basu guidelines

Source: Primary Data

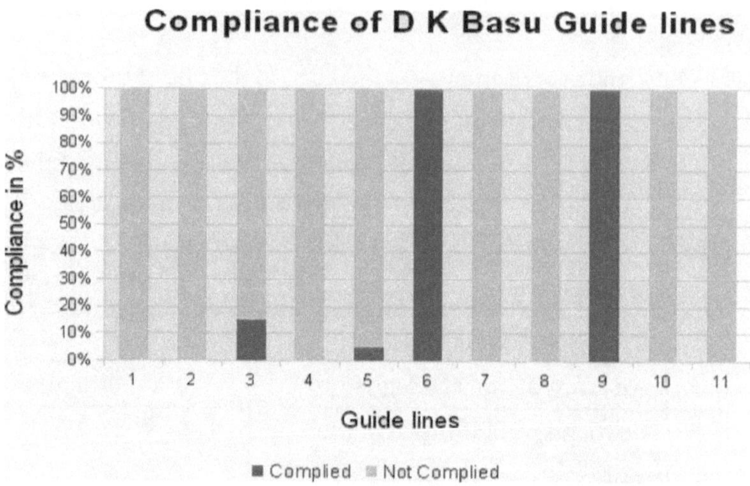

Figure 3.14 Compliance of DK Basu guidelines

Source: Primary Data

Magnitude of Risk (Sign of Risk or Vulnerability)

Profile of the Deceased (Victims of Custodial Deaths)

The profiles of the deceased are studied to know whether there are any standard features among victims of custodial deaths, and the results are summarized in Table 3.20 and Figure 3.15.

	Years	Frequency	Percent
Age Group	Up to 20	2	6.7
	21 to 30	7	23.3
	31 to 40	11	36.7
	Above 40	10	33.3
	Total	30	100.0

Table 3.20: Age Group-wise distribution of the deceased

Source: Primary Data

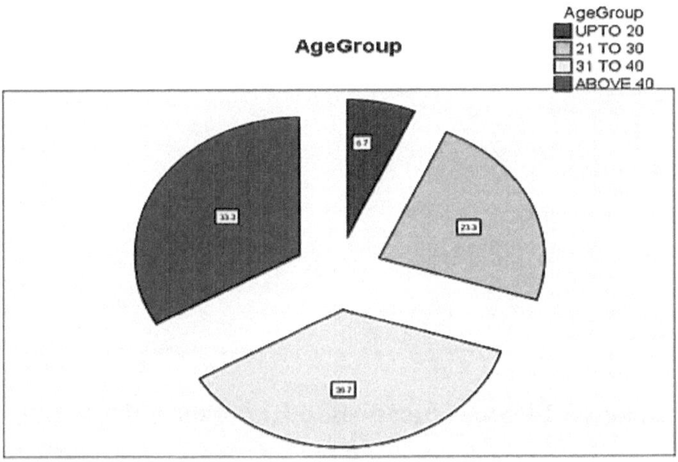

Figure 3.15: Profiles of deceased in custodial deaths

Source: Primary Data

The age group most affected among the deceased is 31 to 40 years, accounting for 36.7%. Approximately 70% of the victims are above 30 years old. The majority of victims are in the 31-40 age bracket, followed by 33.3% above 40, while 23.3% are between 21 and 30 years old. The distribution of the deceased by social status is depicted in Table 3.21 and Figure 3.16.

		Frequency	Percent	Valid Percent	Cumulative Percent
Social status	**OC**	1	3.3	3.3	3.3
	BC	17	56.7	56.7	60.0
	SC	10	33.3	33.3	93.3
	ST	2	6.7	6.7	100.0
	Total	30	100.0	100.0	

Table 3.21: Social status-wise distribution of the deceased (N=30)

Source: Primary Data

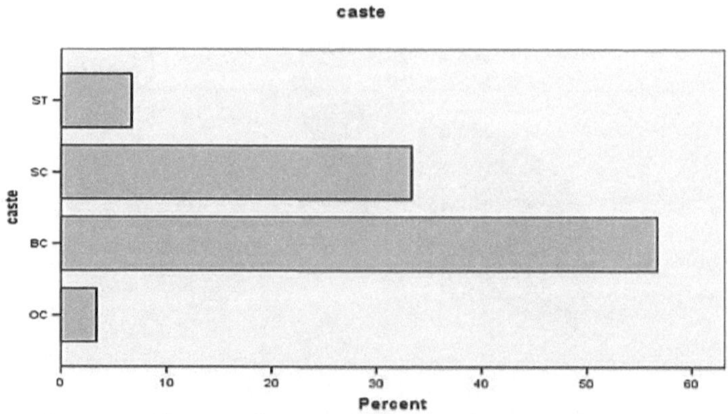

Figure 3.16: Social status-wise distribution of the deceased

The sample clearly shows that socially backward classes, specifically BCs and SCs, are most vulnerable to violence compared to other societal groups. The proportion of deceased SCs (33%) is notably high relative to their representation in the population. The majority of victims belong to the BC community, accounting for 56.7%, followed by 33.3% from the SC community and 6.7% from the ST community. The OC group has the lowest victim count.

	Type	Frequency	Percent
Type of Employment	Student	1	3.3
	Unemployed	20	66.7
	Govt Employee	1	3.3
	Private Employee	3	10.0
	Laborer	1	3.3
	Self Employed	2	6.7
	Total	28	93.3
Missing	System	2	6.7
	Total	30	100.0

Table 3.22: Employment status of the Deceased (N=30)

Source: Primary Data

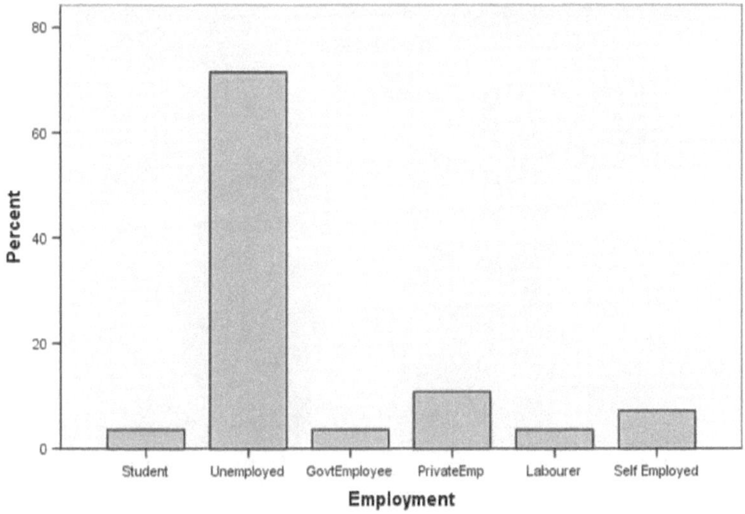

Figure 3.17: Employment status of the Deceased

Source: Primary Data

Among the deceased, approximately 70% are either unemployed or students. The group also includes self-employed individuals, private employees, and laborers. As shown in Table 3.22 and Figure 3.17, 66.7% of all victims were unemployed at the time of the incident. Additionally, three victims belonged to BC/SC/ST communities. This suggests a possible bias in police treatment towards suspects in these cases.

		Frequency	Percent
Criminal History	Yes	13	43.3
	No	15	50.0
	Total	28	93.3
Missing	System	2	6.7
	Total	30	100.0

Table 3.23: Criminal history of the deceased (N=30)

Source: Primary Data

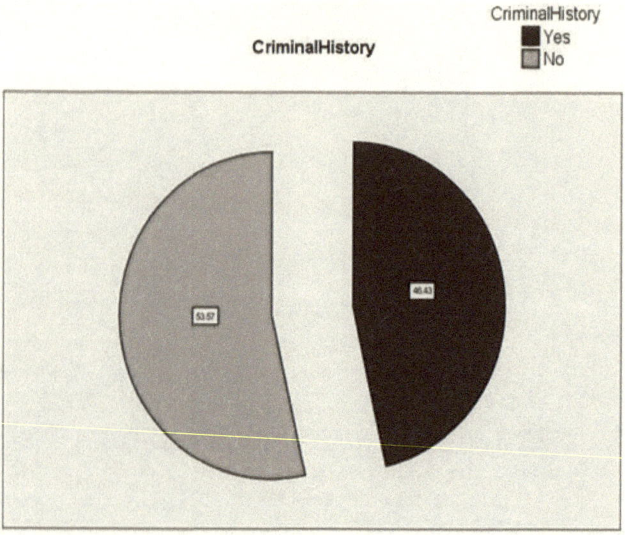

Figure 3.18: Criminal history of the deceased

Source: Primary Data

Out of the 30 victims, 53.6% of those who died had no prior criminal record or negative background. Eighteen were linked to property crimes. Four were involved in other types of crimes, such as nuisance, assault, murder, and illegal liquor cases. Sixteen victims had no previous criminal involvement and were first-time visitors to the police station. These findings are detailed in Table 3.23 and Figure 3.18.

Category	Accused (%)	Deceased (%)
OC	20.0	3.3
BC	55.0	56.7
SC	7.5	33.3
ST	2.5	6.7
Minority	15.0	0

Table 3.24: Social status of accused vs. deceased

Source: Primary Data

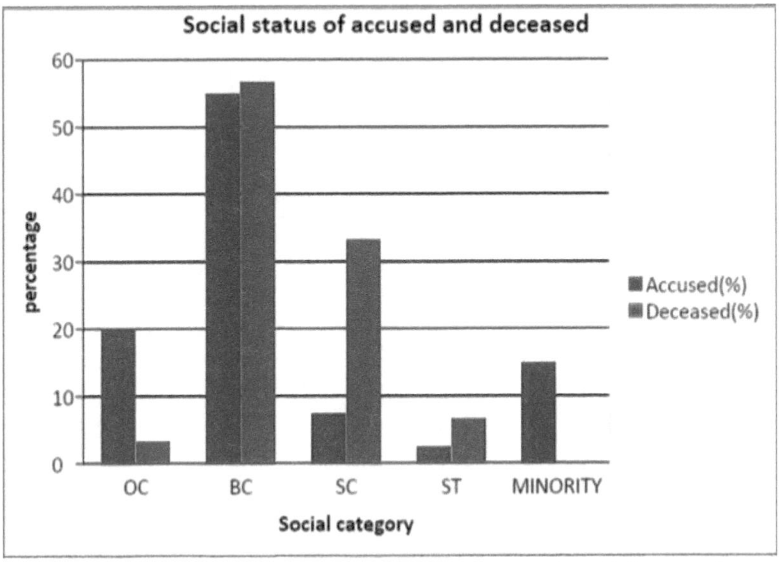

Figure 3.19: Social status of the accused and deceased

Source: Primary Data

Table 3.24 and Figure 3.19 illustrate the ratio of social categories among the accused and the deceased in the sample. The differences are particularly evident in the OC and SC groups. In the OC category, 20% are accused, compared to 3.3% who are deceased. In the SC category, 33.3% are deceased, compared to 7.5% who are accused. No significant difference exists between the accused and deceased in the BC and ST groups.

Minorities constitute 15% of the accused, with no deceased appearances in this group. A chi-square test for a 2×5 contingency table was conducted to assess the significance of differences between accused and deceased categories regarding causes of death in custody. The chi-square value was $\chi 2 = 41.6948$, with a p-value of 0.00001, indicating significance at $p < 0.01$. This suggests a notable difference in social status between the accused and deceased in the BC and ST categories.

Sl. No.	Cr.No.	PS	District	Date	Name of deceased	Caste	Profession	Criminal History	Significant injuries		Cause of Death	
									Postmortem Report	Inquest Report	Postmortem Report	Inquest Report
1	2	3	4	5	6	7	8	9	10	11	12	13
1	14/2003	Kotabommali	W.G.	2.3.2003	Mylapalli Satyanarayana	Vedabalija	Nil	Yes	Yes, 8	Nil	hanging	suicide
2	112/98	Kothapet	Guntur	28.3.1998	Reddy David	Mala	Nil	Yes	Nil	Nil	Ill-Health	Ill-Health
3	131/98	Kothapet	Guntur	15.4.1998	Barireddy Seshareddy	Nil	Nil	Yes	Nil	Nil	Lung decease	Ill-Health
4	439/99	Ongole	Ongole	4.11.1999	Gurram Ramaiah	Mala	Painting	Nil	Nil	Yes, 5	Acute left Ventricular fail	beating
5	50/1997	Macherla	Guntur	10.4.1997	Bathula Koteswararao	Vaddera	Nil	Yes	Yes, 10	Yes, 9	Alcohol intoxication	beating
6	238/1996	Guntur	Guntur	26.12.1996	Routhu Kodandam	Gouda	Nil	Nil	Yes, 1	Nil	Massive Myocardial infraction	heart attack
7	72/97	Kanigiri	Prakasam	16.6.1997	Gandham Anandarao	Madiga	Nil	Yes	Yes, 1	Nil	Hanging	Suicide by hanging

Table continued as follows:

Sl. No.	Cr.No.	Witnesses			Name of Accused	Designation
		Relatives	Independent	Police		
	12	13	14	15	16	17
1	14/2003	Nil	5	Nil	Nil	Nil
2	112/98	2	Nil	5	Nil	Nil
3	131/98	3	Nil	Nil	Nil	Nil
4	439/99	3	Nil	Nil	Nil	Nil
5	50/1997	3	1	1	Nil	Nil
6	238/1996	2	1	Nil	Nil	Nil
7	72/97	2	5	3	Nil	Nil

Table 3.25: Criminal history of the deceased

In Table 3.25, when we examine the criminal history of the deceased, out of seven cases, only four persons have a criminal history, whereas three have no past Criminal History. When the caste profile of the dead is examined, most of them are BC/ST, but no upper caste person is found in the list of the deceased. Furthermore, when we verified the details of compensation paid to the state or by the Police based on the orders of the SHRC Commissioner of Enquiries/NHRC, etc., the amount was found to Be Nil. This shows the pathetic stage of justice caused to victims by the Government and regulatory systems.

Interrogation Procedures

Verification of Hypothesis – Ho5

Ho5: There is no significant difference between the police justification and the established cause of death in custody.

Test applied: Chi-Square Test.

Established cause		Police Justification				
		Hanging	Suicide	Natural	Torture	Unknown
Hanging	Police	100.00	0.00	0.00	0.00	0.00
	PM	33.33%	0.00%	0.00%	0.00%	0.00%
Suicide	Police	0.00	10.00	0.00	0.00	0.00
	PM	0.00%	3.33%	0.00%	0.00%	0.00%
Natural	Police	0.00	0.00	90.00	0.00	0.00
	PM	0.00%	0.00%	300.00%	0.00%	0.00%
Torture	Police	40.00	10.00	10.00	10.00	20.00
	PM	13.33%	3.33%	3.33%	3.33%	6.67%
Unknown	Police	0.00	0.00	10.00	0.00	0.00
	PM	0.00%	0.00%	3.33%	0.00%	0.00%

Table 3.27: Cause of death: Police Justification vs. established cause

Source: Primary Data

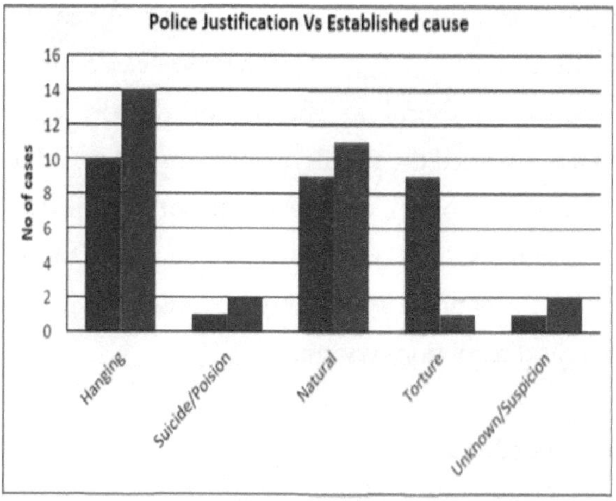

Figure 3.20: Cause of death-Police Justification vs. established cause

Source: Primary Data

A chi-square calculator for a 2 × 5 contingency table was used to assess the significance of differences between Police justification and the established causes of death in custody.

The chi-square test indicated a significant effect, with $\chi2 = 7.9333$, and the p-value was 0.094051. The results were significant at $p < 0.10$.

The Chi-square test clearly shows a significant difference between the established cause and police justification, with 9 cases differing. Notably, Table 3.26 and Figure 3.20 reveal that the police identified only one case as torture, while nine cases were established as such. The test results indicate a p-value of 0.094 and a chi-square value of 7.933, both of which are significant at the 0.01 level. This suggests a substantial difference between police justification and the confirmed cause of death in custody.

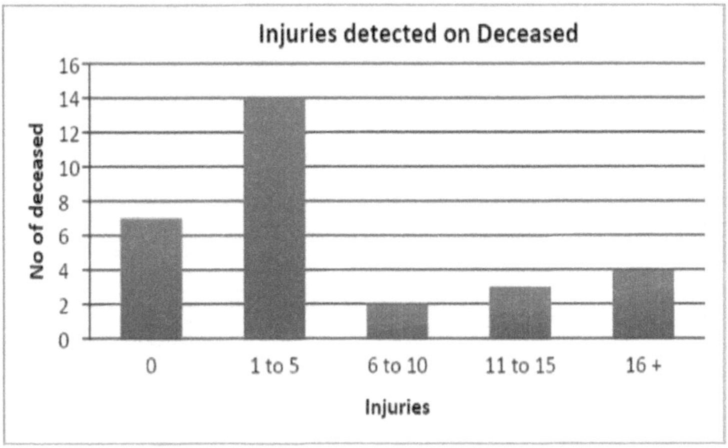

Figure 3.21: Injuries detected on the deceased victims

Source: Primary Data

The above figure shows the injuries detected on the deceased victims in custodial death cases. The average number of injuries was found to be 5. Four cases have more than 16 injuries (Figure 3.21).

Verification of Hypothesis – Ho6

Ho6: There is no significant difference in the pattern of injuries and the cause of death shown in the police justification.

The test applied: Chi-Square Test.

Police justification	No Injuries	Injuries	Total Injuries
Hanging	2	12	14
	6.67%	400.00%	46.67%
Suicide	1	1	2
	3.33%	3.33%	6.67%
Natural	4	7	11
	13.33%	23.33%	36.67%
Torture	0	1	1
	00.00%	3.33%	3.33%
Unknown	0	2	2
	00.00%	6.67%	6.67%
Total	7	23	30
	23.33%	76.67%	1000.00%

Table 3.28: Police justification and injuries

Source: Primary Data

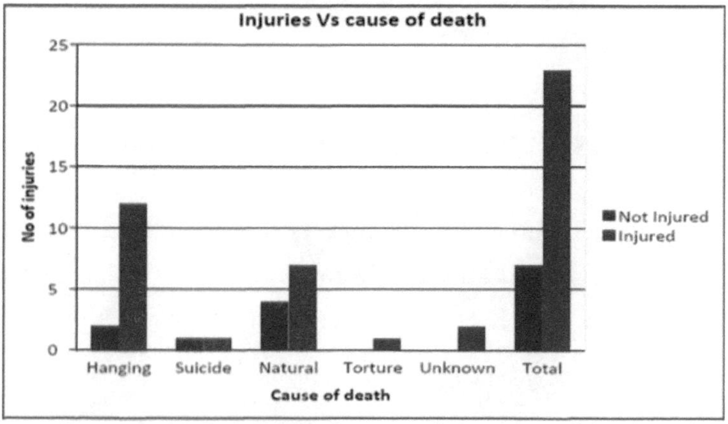

Figure 3.22: Police justification of the cause of death and injuries to the victims

Table 3.28 and Figure 3.22 illustrate the injury patterns related to the cause of death as per police reports. Many of the deceased (77%) sustained injuries regardless of their cause of death. For example, 12 out of 14 individuals who died by hanging had injuries.

Similarly, in natural death cases, 7 out of 11 had injuries. This contradicts the police's justification.

A chi-square test for a simple 2 × 5 contingency table was conducted to analyze the injury pattern concerning the cause of death indicated in police reports. The analysis assessed the significance of differences between 'Not injured' and 'Injured' cases regarding the cause of death in custody. The chi-square test showed no significant effect, with $\chi 2 = 2.267$, and the p-value was 0.686785. The findings were not significant at $p < 0.10$.

The test results indicated a p-value of 0.686, with a chi-square statistic of 2.267, which is not significant at the 0.01 level. Therefore, it can be concluded that there is no significant difference in injury patterns relative to the cause of death as described in the police justification.

Enquiries and Compensation

Only ten deceased were given compensation out of 30. The average time taken for final judgment was 11.17 months. Four cases took nearly four years. In one case, only Rs. 5,000 was given as compensation.

The above analysis clearly shows that:

1. The cause of death given by the Police or Executive Magistrate differs significantly from the cause determined after the postmortem examination.
2. Regardless of the declared cause, many deceased individuals had injuries, with some cases exhibiting more

than 16 injuries. These injuries are noteworthy because some artifacts may occur on the body during shifting for postmortem, so the variations should be interpreted with caution.

3. The final judgment took about a year on average from various inquiry authorities.
4. Only about one-third of the deceased (based on the sample) received compensation.

Table 3.29 summarizes key monthly statistics of cases registered by NHRC in October 2019. Out of the total cases, the NHRC disposed of only 4,973, leaving 18,637 cases pending. The compensation awarded for six cases disposed of in December amounts to approximately 16 lakhs.

Table 3.30 presents the budget and expenditures of NHRC from 1994-95 to 2019-20. The NHRC's annual budget for the financial year ending in 2018-2019 was 46.57 crores. The yearly expenditure by NHRC remains nearly constant. Each intervention by SHRC/NHRC requires a budget allocation for travel expenses and related costs.

NATIONAL HUMAN RIGHTS COMMISSION
(ACCOUNTS DIVISION)

Rupees in Lakhs

YEAR	BUDGET ESTIMATES		REVISED ESTIMATES		EXPENDITURE	
	Non-Plan	Plan	Non-Plan	Plan	Non-Plan	Plan
1994-1995			210.00		187.07	
1995-1996	220.00		225.00		215.64	
1996-1997	300.00		381.00		329.43	
1997-1998	450.00		450.00		381.36	
1998-1999	500.00		650.00		536.66	
1999-2000	616.00		600.00		490.63	
2000-2001	655.00		620.00		566.08	
2001-2002	620.00		720.00		693.05	
2002-2003	732.00		860.00 MEA 10.00		817.63	
2003-2004	938.00	50.00	1033.00	100.00	961.15	100.00
2004-2005	1070.00	400.00	1135.00	188.00	1063.51	188.00
2005-2006	1234.00	400.00	1228.00	*	1119.82	Nil
2006-2007	1174.00	400.00	1348.00	*	1317.59	Nil
2007-2008	1461.00	100.00	1651.00	100.00	1612.37	100.00
2008-2009	1661.00	50-MAB@ 100-CHMS#	1894.00	50-MAB 100-CHMS	1854.49	50-MAB 100-CHMS
2009-2010	1911.00	2868-MAB 300-CHMS	1911.00	2295.00 67.00	1910.13	2295-MAB .33-CHMS
2010-2011	1800.00	50-MAB 200-CHMS	2489.00	823.00-MAB 50.00-CHMS	2388.15	823-MAB 48.27-CHM
2011-2012	2832.00	100-MAB 200-CHMS	2575.00	200.00 MAB 1.00 CHMS	2543.76	200-MAB NIL CHMS
2012-2013	2700.00	200-MAB	2717.00	625.00 MAB 1.00 CHMS	2625.51	625-MAB NIL CHMS
2013-2014	3151.00	50-MAB 1-CHMS	3073.75	64.00 MAB 1.00 CHMS	3058.80	64 - MAB NIL CHMS
2014-2015	3193.00	40-MAB 1-CHMS	3510.00	71.00 MAB 1.00 CHMS	3384.12	71 - MAB NIL CHMS
2015-2016	3755.00	1-MAB 1-CHMS	3754.54	1.00 MAB 1.00 CHMS	3467.47	NIL- MAB NIL CHMS
2016-2017	4404.00	1-MAB 1-CHMS	4404.00	1.00 MAB 1.00 CHMS	4044.24	NIL- MAB NIL CHMS
2017-18	4890.00*	1 - MAB+	4648.20*	1.00 MAB+	4403.11	NIL-MAB
2018-19	4872.00*	1 - MAB+	4872.00*	1.00 MAB+	4657.83	NIL-MAB
2019-20	5080.00*	-	##5510.00*	-	++	-

*Surrendered @ MAB - Manav Adhikar Bhawan # CHMS - Complaint Handling Management System
+Capital Section * Revenue Section
Tentative

++ information will be provided after closing of FY 2019-20 i.e. 31st March, 2020.

Table 3.29: Monthly salient statistics of cases registered by NHRC during October 2019

Source: NHRC Human Rights Case Statistics

MONTHLY SALIENT STATISTICS OF CASES REGISTERED / DISPOSED BY NHRC DURING OCTOBER 2019
(data as on 07.11.2019)

Nature of incident	No. of cases registered	No. of cases disposed	Pendency as on date
CUSTODIAL DEATH (POLICE) (Inc. Code 807)	7	8	367
CUSTODIAL DEATH (JUDICIAL) (Inc. Code 301)	135	161	3041
DEATH IN POLICE ENCOUNTER (POLICE) (Inc. Code 812)	10	4	807
BONDED LABOUR (Inc. Code 601)	27	22	1125
CHILDREN (Inc. Code 100-117)	93	64	746
WOMEN (Inc. Code 1300-1316)	578	390	3065
SC/ST/OBC (Inc. Code 1900-1909)	199	117	888
OTHERS	4771	3421	12761
TOTAL	**5820**	**4187**	**22800**

SUO-MOTU Cognizance / Human Rights Defenders Cases registered during the month of October 2019

	No. of cases registered	No. of cases disposed	Pendency as on date
SUO-MOTU Cognizance	2	3	171
Human Rights Defenders	12	6	141

Cases where NHRC recommended Monetary relief during the month of October 2019

Nature of incident	No of Cases	Amount recommended (in Rs.)
MALFUNCTIONING OF MEDICAL PROFESSIONALS	1	300000
MEDICAL NEGLIGENCE	1	100000
CUSTODIAL DEATH (Judicial)	7	1700000
EXPLOITATION OF LABOUR	1	200000
ABUSE OF POWER	1	300000
CUSTODIAL DEATH (Police)	1	300000
FAILURE IN TAKING LAWFUL ACTION	2	320000
UNLAWFUL DETENTION	1	50000
NON-PAYMENT OF PENSION/COMPENSATION	1	100000
EXPLOITATION OF WOMEN	1	100000
GANG RAPE	1	100000
INACTION BY THE STATE GOVERNMENT/CENTRAL GOVT.OFFICIALS	2	300000
TOTAL	**20**	**3870000**

Table 3.30: Budget and expenditure of NHRC from 1994-95 to 2019-20

Source: NHRC Human Rights Case Statistics

NCRB Data on custodial deaths from 2013 (Andhra Pradesh)

Year 2013					
Sl. No	**State**	**Custodial Deaths**	**Cases registered**	**Police Charge Sheet**	**Police Convicted**
1.	Maharashtra	35	2	0	0
2.	Tamil Nadu	15	15	0	0
3.	Uttar Pradesh	15	15	0	0
4.	Gujarat	13	2	1	0
5.	Andhra Pradesh	6	5	0	0
Year 2014					
Sl. No	**State**	**Custodial Deaths**	**Cases registered**	**Police Charge Sheet**	**Police Convicted**
1.	Maharashtra	21	4	8	0
2.	Andhra Pradesh	18	0	0	0
3.	Gujarat	8	1	0	0
4.	Uttar Pradesh	8	8	2	0
5.	Tamil Nadu	7	7	0	0
Year 2015					
Sl. No	**State**	**Custodial Deaths**	**Cases registered**	**Police Charge Sheet**	**Police Convicted**
1.	Maharashtra	19	1	6	0
2.	Gujarat	9	2	0	0
3.	Uttar Pradesh	9	9	2	0
4.	Andhra Pradesh	8	1	0	0
5.	Assam	7	5	3	0

Year 2016					
Sl. No	State	Custodial Deaths	Cases registered	Police Charge Sheet	Police Convicted
1.	Andhra Pradesh	6	0	0	0
2.	Madhya Pradesh	6	1	10	0
3.	Maharashtra	4	0	0	0
4.	Assam	2	0	0	0
5.	Gujarat	2	0	0	0
Year 2017					
Sl. No	State	Custodial Deaths	Cases registered	Police Charge Sheet	Police Convicted
1.	Maharashtra	10	2	1	0
2.	Andhra Pradesh	7	7	0	0
3.	Uttar Pradesh	4	4	1	0
4.	Madhya Pradesh	4	0	0	0
5.	Madhya Pradesh	4	0	0	0
6.	Punjab	3	1	0	0
Year 2018					
Sl. No	State	Custodial Deaths	Cases registered	Police Charge Sheet	Police Convicted
1.	Andhra Pradesh	9	9	0	0
2.	Madhya Pradesh	4	0	0	0
3.	Maharashtra	2	0	0	0
4.	Odissa	2	1	0	0
5.	Assam	1	1	0	0

Year 2019					
Sl. No	**State**	**Custodial Deaths**	**Cases registered**	**Police Charge Sheet**	**Police Convicted**
1.	Madhya Pradesh	6	1	0	0
2.	Telangana	6	3	0	0
3.	Chhattisgarh	5	2	1	0
4.	Himachal Pradesh	3	0	0	0
5.	Andhra Pradesh	3	3	0	0
Year 2020					
Sl. No	**State**	**Custodial Deaths**	**Cases registered**	**Police Charge Sheet**	**Police Convicted**
1.	Andhra Pradesh	6	6	0	0
2.	Madhya Pradesh	5	1	0	0
3.	Rajasthan	4	1	0	0
4.	Kerala	3	3	0	0
5.	Tamil Nadu	2	2	0	0
Year 2021					
Sl. No	**State**	**Custodial Deaths**	**Cases registered**	**Police Charge Sheet**	**Police Convicted**
1.	Madhya Pradesh	6	3	0	0
2.	Maharashtra	6	1	1	0
3.	Andhra Pradesh	5	5	0	0
4.	Uttar Pradesh	4	3	0	0
5.	Karnataka	2	2	0	0

Examining the above tables shows that Andhra Pradesh topped the list for custodial deaths in 2016, 2018, and 2020. It ranked second in 2014 and 2017, third in 2021, fourth in 2015, and fifth in 2013 and 2019.

Magnitude of Risk

Table 3.31 displays the risk factors identified for each police officer in the sample, including the total number and percentage of risk factors. All risk factors are considered equally important, reflecting the vulnerability associated with handing a suspect over to police officers.

Since custodial death often results from multiple factors, the table assesses and categorizes medical, organizational, psychological, and legal aspects according to established norms. The investigator identified these risk factors based on prevalent undesirable or abnormal indicators, which are used for various purposes within the police organization.

For example, when management approves extended leave or extra allowances, they review medical reports that indicate deviations, such as high blood pressure or diabetes.

These criteria ensure that police officers with the right attitude, skills, and an organizational climate conducive to effective crime detection are assigned, rather than by routine.

One-way ANOVA tests the significance of these risk factors across four categories: Medical (5 RFs), Organizational (8 RFs), Legal (11 RFs), and Psychological (8 RFs). The study involved 40 accused police personnel in each category. The cumulative used police personnel in each category. The cumulative percentage of risk factors in this sample is very high, exceeding permissible limits for any organization considering its roles.

Name	Police Station (occasions)	Police station Code	Age	Sex	Medical (5 RFs)	Organizational (8 RFs)	Legal (11RFs)	Psychological (8 RFs)	Total Risk Factors (32)	Percentage
Rama Rao P	I-town PS Vijayawada	2	32	M	3	7	7	2	19	59.38
Krishna Chaitanya	I-town PS Vijayawada	2	26	M	3	7	7	2	16	50.00
Raghava Rani K	Suryapet PS Vijayawada	7	30	F	3	8	8	3	19	59.38
Raghava Rani K	Suryapet PS Vijayawada	7	32	F	4	7	8	4	19	59.38
Santhoshamma	Suryapet PS Vijayawada	7	36	F	1	8	8	3	19	59.38
Ragini	Suryapet PS Vijayawada	7	28	F	2	7	8	2	17	53.13
Narasimha Rao P	I-town PS Vijayawada	2	34	M	4	8	8	4	20	62.50
Ranga Rao	I-town PS Vijayawada	2	36	M	4	8	8	4	20	62.50
Venkateswara Rao B	I-town PS Vijayawada	2	40	M	1	7	8	2	17	53.13
Prem Kumar G	I-town PS Vijayawada	2	33	M	4	8	8	3	19	59.38
Venkateswara Rao K	I-town PS Vijayawada	2	37	M	3	8	8	4	20	62.50
Purushotham	Ongole Railway PS	5	25	M	5	8	8	4	20	62.50
Balu K	Balanagar PS RR	1	26	M	3	7	8	4	19	59.38
Rambabu	Nagarampalem PS Guntur	4	36	M	5	8	8	4	20	62.50
Laxmaiah	Ongole Railway PS	5	36	M	4	7	8	3	18	56.25

Jeelani	Nagarampalem PS Guntur	4	34	M	3	7	8	1	16	500.00
Azeez	Prattipadu PS Guntur	6	28	M	4	8	8	4	20	62.50
Sambasiva Rao G	Prattipadu PS Guntur	6	38	M	3	8	8	6	22	68.75
Sambasiva Rao T	Prattipadu PS Guntur	6	36	M	2	8	8	2	18	56.25
Narayana	Prattipadu PSGuntur	6	24	M	3	8	8	2	18	56.25
Subba Rao	Nagarampalem PS Guntur	4	32	M	3	8	8	4	20	62.50
Papa Rao	Nagarampalem PS Guntur	4	42	M	0	7	8	2	17	53.13
Venkat Ramappa	Nagarampalem PS Guntur	4	40	M	2	8	8	5	21	65.63
Narayana Swamy	Kadiri Town PS Ananthapur	3	38	M	3	7	8	4	19	59.38
Gowri Shankar	Kadiri Town PS Ananthapur	3	32	M	3	7	8	4	19	59.38
Raja Vardhan Raj	Yadiki PS Ananthapur	9	40	M	3	7	8	4	19	59.38
Kishore Reddy	Yadiki PS Ananthapur	9	42	M	1	8	8	3	19	59.38
Srinivasulu	Tadipatri Tq PS Ananthapur	8	36	M	3	7	8	3	18	56.25

Chandra Mouli	Tadipatri Tq PS Ananthapur	8	34	M	5	8	8	5	21	65.63
Rafi	Kadiri Town PS Ananthapur	3	36	M	4	7	8	5	20	62.50
YRamachandra Reddy	Kadiri Town PS Ananthapur	3	42	M	2	8	8	3	19	59.38
Mahboob Vali	Kadiri Town PS Ananthapur	3	40	M	2	7	8	4	19	59.38
Raja Gopal	Kadiri Town PS Ananthapur	3	28	M	3	8	8	4	20	62.50
Dastagiri	Kadiri Town PS Ananthapur	3	43	M	4	8	8	5	21	65.63
Chalma Reddy	Kadiri Town PS Ananthapur	3	42	M	4	8	8	3	19	59.38
Nagendrudu	Tadipatri Tq PS Ananthapur	8	44	M	3	7	8	5	20	62.50
Rejeswara Rao	Yadiki PS Ananthapur	9	28	M	3	7	8	2	17	53.13
Ramachendra Reddy	Yadiki PS Ananthapur	9	37	M	4	8	8	7	23	71.88
Prabhakar Reddy	Yadiki PS Ananthapur	9	40	M	3	8	8	5	21	65.63
Balu Naik	Ongole Railway PS	5	42	M	3	8	8	7	23	71.88

Table 3.31: Risk factors of the accused

Source: Primary Data

Verification of Hypothesis – Ho7

Ho7: There exists no significant effect of organizational, psychological, medical, and legal factors in the assessment of risk factors for custodial deaths.

Test Applied: ANOVA

Summary of Data					
	Treatments				
	M1 (Medical)	M2 (Organizational)	M3 (Legal)	M4 (Psycho logical)	Total
N	40	40	40	40	160
ΣX	122	303	318	147	890
Mean	3.05	7.575	7.95	3.675	5.563
ΣX^2	420	2305	2530	613	5868
Std.Dev.	1.1082	0.5006	0.2207	1.366	2.402

Result Details

Source	SS	df	MS	
Between-treatments	785.025	3	261.675	$F = 308.43445$
Within-treatments	132.35	156	0.8484	
Total	917.375	159		

Table 3.32: Summary data of one-way ANOVA

Source: Computed

The one-way ANOVA test results indicate an F-value of 308.43445 and a p-value of $< .00001$ (Table 3.32). The findings are significant at $p < .05$. This suggests that organizational, psychological, medical, and legal factors significantly influence the assessment of risk factors regarding.

Tukey HSD Test:

Tukey's range test, also known as Tukey's honestly significant difference (HSD) test, is a one-step multiple comparison procedure and statistical test. It can analyze raw data or be used in conjunction with an ANOVA to identify means that differ significantly. The test compares all possible pairs of groups and relies on a studentized range distribution (q), similar to the t-distribution used in t-tests. Tukey's test evaluates the means of each treatment against all others, applying simultaneously to all pairwise comparisons. The results are shown below.

Tukey's HSD compares the means of every treatment to every other treatment, simultaneously for all pairwise comparisons. The results are as follows: HSD[05]=0.54; HSD[01]=0.65; M1 vs. M2 P<.01; M1 vs. M3 P<.01; M1 vs M4 P<.05; M2 vs. M3 non-significant; M2 vs. M4 P<.01; M3 vs. M4 P<.01; where M1 = mean of Sample 1, M2 = mean of Sample 2, etc. HSD is the minimum absolute difference between two means needed for significance at the specified level. HSD[.05] for the .05 level; HSD[.01] for the .01 level.

Tukey's HSD test showed significant differences between most pairs of means. However, M2 versus M3 showed no significant difference, indicating that Organizational and Legal factors have an equal effect on the assessment.

	N	Minimum	Maximum	Mean	Std. Dev.
High	2	72.97	76.72	74.8484	2.65163
Moderate	7	63.49	69.74	67.1694	2.36095
Total	9	63.49	76.72	68.8759	4.06513

Table 3.33: One-way mean risk factors (high & moderate)

Source: Computed

Table 3.33 shows that the composite mean risk factor is 68.88, which is above 50%. Descriptive statistics of various risk factors, including Medical, Legal, Organizational, and Psychological, among personnel with different designations are summarized in Tables 3.34 and 2.35, as well as Figures 3.23 to 3.26.

Verification of Hypothesis – H08

Ho8: There is no significant difference among the genders of the police personnel in the percentage of risk factors in custodial deaths.

Test Applied: t-Test

	Gender	N	Mean	Std. Dev.	Mean	T	Sig
Medical Risk Percentage	Male	36	62.2222	21.79267	3.63211	1.048	.301
	Female	4	50.0000	25.81989	12.90994		
Organizatio-nal Risk Percentage	Male	36	94.7917	6.25000	1.04167	.312	.757
	Female	4	93.7500	7.21688	3.60844		
Legal Risk Percentage	Male	36	72.2222	2.11192	.35199	.473	.639
	Female	4	72.7273	.00000	.00000		
Psychological Risk percentage	Male	36	46.8750	17.51912	2.91985	1.043	.304
	Female	4	37.5000	10.20621	5.10310		

Table 3.34: Group Statistics and T-Test (Guntur Dist.)

Source: Computed

The t-test indicates no significant difference between male and female police personnel involved in custodial deaths. The results show that the mean medical risk percentage for males is 3.63211, while for females it is 12.90994, with a t-value of 1.048, which is not statistically significant. Similarly, the mean organizational risk is 1.04167 for males and 3.608844 for females, with a t-value of 0.312, also not significant. For legal risk, males have a mean of 0.35199, and females have a mean of 0.00000, with a t-value of 0.473, indicating no significant difference. Lastly, the mean psychological risk percentage is 2.91985 for males and 5.10310 for females, with a t-value of 1.043, which is not statistically significant.

The t-test result shows that the derived values were not significant at a 0.05 level of significance. It can be inferred that there is no significant difference among the genders of the police personnel regarding the risk factor in custodial deaths.

One-way (Designations)

Warnings: Post hoc tests are not performed because at least one group has fewer than two cases.

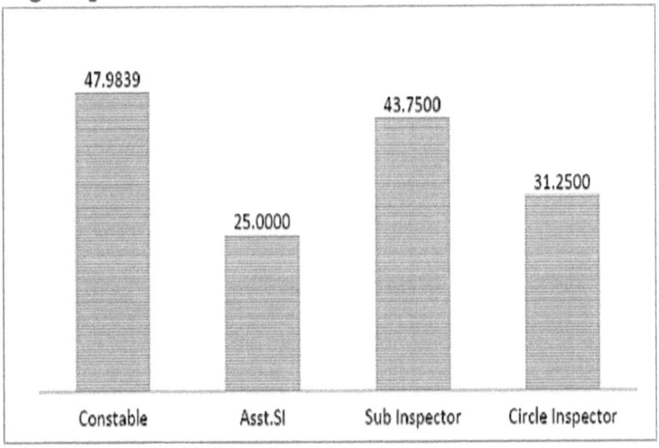

Figure 3.23 Risk Factors-Medical

Source: Computed

		N	Mean	SD	SE
Medical Risk percentage	Constable	31	61.2903	23.05673	4.14111
	Asst.SI	1	20.0000		
	Sub-Inspector	6	70.0000	10.95445	4.47214
	Circle Inspector	2	50.0000	14.14214	10.00000
	Total	40	61.0000	22.16488	3.50458
Organizational Risk percentage	Constable	31	95.5645	6.07967	1.09194
	Asst.SI	1	87.5000		
	Sub-Inspector	6	91.6667	6.45497	2.63523
	Circle Inspector	2	93.7500	8.83883	6.25000
	Total	40	94.6875	6.25801	.98948
Legal Risk percentage	Constable	31	72.7273	.00000	.0000
	Asst.SI	1	72.7273		
	Sub-Inspector	6	71.2121	3.71135	1.51515
	Circle Inspector	2	68.1818	6.42824	4.54545
	Total	40	72.2727	2.00656	.31726
Psychological Risk Percentage	Constable	31	47.9839	17.10774	3.07264
	Asst.SI	1	25.0000		
	Sub-Inspector	6	43.7500	17.23006	7.03414
	Circle Inspector	2	31.2500	8.83883	6.25000
	Total	40	45.9375	17.07532	2.69984

Table 3.35: Descriptive statistics of various risk factors

Source: Computed

A one-way ANOVA was conducted to examine the significant differences in mean scores of various risk factors (Medical, Legal, Organizational, and Psychological) among personnel with different designations.

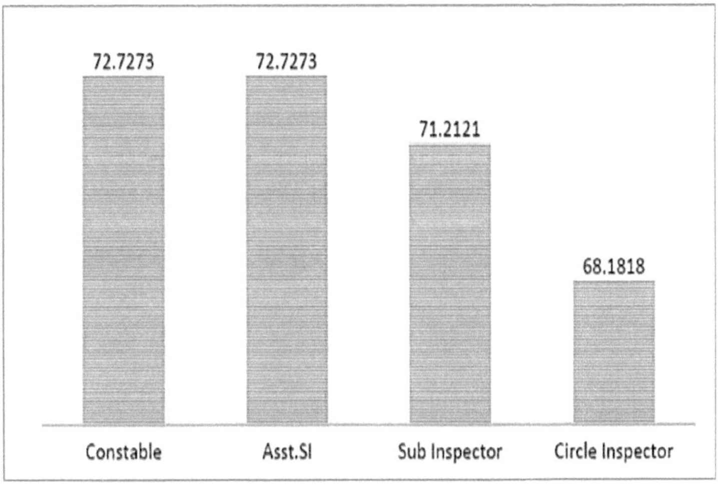

Figure 3.24: Risk factors-Organizational

Source: Computed

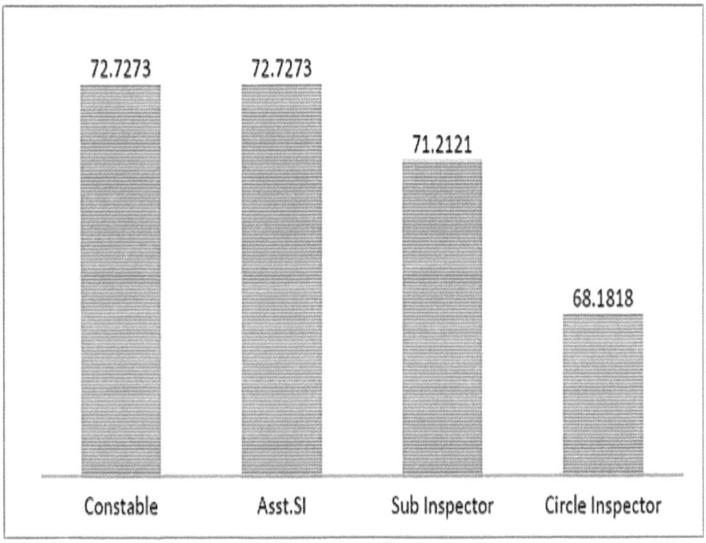

Figure 3.25: Risk factors-Psychological

Source: Computed

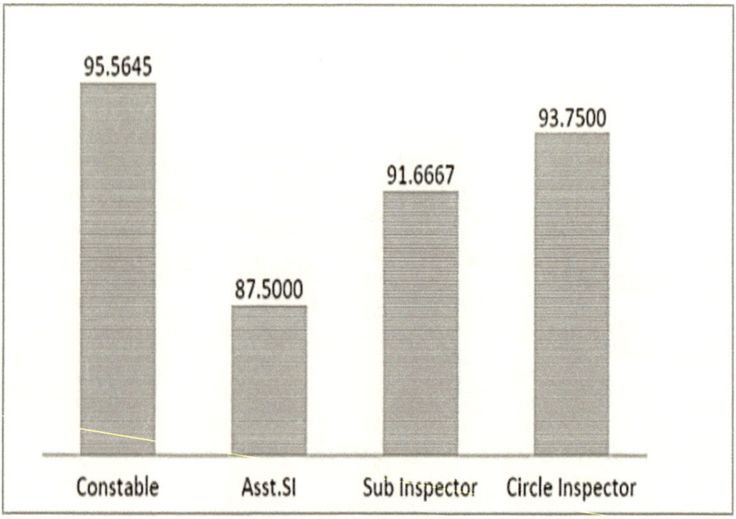

Figure 3.26 Risk factors-Legal

Source: Computed

Verification of Hypothesis – H09

Ho9: There is no significant difference among the designations of the police personnel about the risk factor percentage in custodial deaths

Test applied: ANOVA

		Sum of Squares	df	Mean Square	F	Sig	Result
Medical Risk percentage	Between Groups	2411.613	3	803.871	1.728	.179	NS
	Within Groups	16748.387	36	465.233			
	Total	19160.000	39				
Organizational Risk Percentage	Between Groups	132.014	3	44.005	1.135	.348	NS
	Within Groups	1395.329	36	38.759			

	Total	1527.344	39				
Legal Risk percentage	Between Groups	46.832	3	15.611	5.100	.005	Sig
	Within Groups	110.193	36	3.061			
	Total	157.025	39				
Psychological Risk percentage	Between Groups	1028.352	3	342.784	1.193	.326	NS
	Within Groups	10342.742	36	287.298			
	Total	11371.094	39				

Table 3.36 One-way ANOVA for risk factors involved

Source: Computed

The only significant risk factor is legal risk (P<0.01); the other risk factors are not significant. Table 3.36 presents the results of a one-way ANOVA examining the percentage of each risk factor among police personnel's designations concerning custodial deaths. The F-value for medical risk percentage versus police designation is 1.728, which is not significant. The F-value for organizational risk percentage is 1.135, indicating it is negligible.

The F-value for legal risk percentage is 5.100, demonstrating significance. The F-value for psychological risk percentage is 1.193, which is also insignificant. The ANOVA results indicate that the F-values were not statistically significant at the 0.01 level of significance. This suggests that there are no meaningful differences among police personnel designations regarding the risk factor percentage in custodial deaths. The descriptive statistics of various risk factors associated with selected police stations are summarized in Tables 3.35 and 3.36.

Risk Factor	N	Minimum	Maximum	Mean
Medical Risk percentage	1	60.00	60.00	60.0000
Organizational Risk Percentage	1	87.50	87.50	87.5000
Legal Risk percentage	1	72.73	72.73	72.7273
Psychological Risk percentage	1	50.00	50.00	50.0000
Valid N (list-wise)	1			

Police Station = Balanagar Police Station

Table 3.37: Descriptive statistics of risk factors

Source: Computed

(This is one individual; we merged it with the non-constable category for some tables.)

Risk Factor	N	Minimum	Maximum	Mean	Std. Dev.
Medical Risk percentage	7	20.00	80.00	62.8571	21.38090
Organizational Risk Percentage	7	87.50	100.00	94.6429	6.68153
Legal Risk percentage	7	63.64	72.73	70.1299	4.43591
Psychological Risk percentage	7	25.00	50.00	37.5000	12.50000
Valid N (list-wise)	7				

Table 3.38: Descriptive statistics (I Town Police Station, Vijayawada) Police Station =I Town Police Station

Source: Computed

Risk Factor	N	Minimum	Maximum	Mean	Std. Dev.
Medical Risk percentage	8	40.00	80.00	62.5000	16.69046
Organizational Risk Percentage	8	87.50	100.00	93.7500	6.68153
Legal Risk percentage	8	72.73	72.73	72.7273	.0000
Psychological Risk percentage	8	37.50	62.50	50.0000	9.44911
Valid N (list-wise)	8				

Table 3.39: Descriptive statistics (Kadiri Town Police Station, Ananthapur) Police Station = Kadiri Town

Source: Computed

Risk Factor	N	Minimum	Maximum	Mean	Std. Dev.
Medical Risk percentage	5	.00	100.00	52.0000	36.33180
Organizational Risk Percentage	5	87.50	100.00	95.0000	6.84653
Legal Risk percentage	5	72.73	72.73	72.7273	.0000
Psychological Risk percentage	5	12.50	62.50	40.0000	20.53960
Valid N (list-wise)	5				

Table 3.40: Descriptive Statistics (Nagarampalem Police Station, Guntur) Police Station = Nagarampalem

Source: Computed

Risk Factor	N	Minimum	Maximum	Mean	Std. Dev.
Medical Risk percentage	3	60.00	100.00	80.0000	20.00000
Organizational Risk Percentage	3	87.50	100.00	95.8333	7.21688
Legal Risk percentage	3	72.73	72.73	72.7273	.00000
Psychological Risk percentage	3	37.50	87.50	56.3333	26.02082
Valid N (list-wise)	3				

Table 3.41: Descriptive Statistics (Ongole Railway Police Station) Police Station = Ongole Railway Police Station

Source: Computed

Risk Factor	N	Minimum	Maximum	Mean	Std. Dev.
Medical Risk percentage	4	40.00	80.00	60.0000	16.32993
Organizational Risk Percentage	4	100.00	100.00	100.0000	.00000
Legal Risk percentage	4	72.73	72.73	72.7273	.00000
Psychological Risk percentage	4	25.00	75.00	43.7500	23.93568
Valid N (list-wise)	4				

Table 3.42: Descriptive Statistics (Prattipadu Police Station, Guntur) Police Station = Prattipadu Police Station, Guntur

Source: Computed

Risk Factor	N	Minimum	Maximum	Mean	Std. Dev.
Medical Risk percentage	4	20.00	80.00	50.0000	25.81989
Organizational Risk Percentage	4	87.50	100.00	93.7500	7.21688
Legal Risk percentage	4	72.73	72.73	72.7273	.00000
Psychological Risk percentage	4	25.00	50.00	37.5000	10.20621
Valid N (list-wise)	4				

Table 3.43: Descriptive Statistics (Suryaraopet Police Station, Vijayawada) Police Station = Suryaraopet Police Station

Source: Computed

Risk Factor	N	Minimum	Maximum	Mean	Std. Dev.
Medical Risk percentage	3	60.00	100.00	73.3333	23.09401
Organizational Risk Percentage	3	87.50	100.00	91.6667	7.21688
Legal Risk percentage	3	72.73	72.73	72.7273	.00000
Psychological Risk percentage	3	37.50	62.50	54.1667	14.43376
Valid N (list-wise)	3				

Table 3.44: Descriptive Statisticsa (Tadipatri TQ Police Station, Ananthapur) Police Station = Tadipatri Tq Police Station

Source: Computed

Risk Factor	N	Minimum	Maximum	Mean	Std. Dev.
Medical Risk percentage	5	20.00	80.00	56.0000	21.90890
Organizational Risk Percentage	5	87.50	100.00	95.0000	6.84653
Legal Risk percentage	5	72.73	72.73	72.7273	.00000
Psychological Risk percentage	5	25.00	87.50	52.5000	24.04423
Valid N (list-wise)	5				

Table 3.45: Descriptive Statisticsa (Yadiki Police Station, Ananthapur) Police Station = Yadiki Police Station, Ananthapur

Source: Computed

Vulnerability Scores, Vulnerability Index, and Custody Quotient of Custodial Deaths

Tables 3.46 to 3.48 and Figures 3.27 to 3.31 provide detailed explanations of vulnerability scores based on individual, legal, and organizational factors, as well as the vulnerability index of police officers and cops.

		Individual, weightage 20																		
		Medical			30			Psychological							60		Other			10	100
Sl. No.	Name	B.P	P.R	Diabeties	Peptic Alcer	Heart Ailments	score	TOA	COG.STY	SAF	SASP	SA1	SADS	SAAR	SAOL	score	Alcohol	Tobacco Smoking	Training on Interrogation skills	score	Weighted score Individual
	Weightages	**20**	**20**	**20**	**20**	**20**	**100**	**20**	**20**	**10**	**10**	**10**	**10**	**10**	**10**	**100**	**20**	**20**	**60**	**100**	
1	Rama Rao P	0	0	0	0	0	**0**	1	0	0	1	0	0	0	1	**40**	1	0	1	**80**	***32***
2	Krishna Chaitanya	0	0	0	0	0	**0**	1	0	0	1	0	0	0	1	**40**	1	1	1	**100**	***34***
3	Raghava Rani K	0	0	0	1	0	**20**	1	0	0	0	0	0	0	1	**30**	0	0	1	**60**	***30***
4	Jyothi R	1	0	0	1	0	**40**	1	0	1.	0	0	0	0	1	**40**	0	0	1	**60**	***42***
5	Santhoshamma	0	0	1	1	1	**60**	1	0	0	0	0	0	0	1	**30**	0	0	1	**60**	***42***
6	Ragini	0	0	0	1	0	**20**	1	0	0	1	0	0	0	1	**40**	0	0	1	**60**	***36***
7	Narasimha Rao P	0	0	0	1	0	**20**	1	0	1	1	1	0	0	1	**60**	1	1	1	**100**	***52***
8	Ranga Rao	1	1	0	1	0	**60**	1	1	0	1	0	0	0	1	**60**	1	1	1	**100**	***64***
9	Venkateswer Rao B	0	0	1	1	0	**40**	1	0	0	1	0	0	0	1	**40**	1	1	1	**100**	***46***
10	Prem Kumar G	1	0	0	1	0	**20**	1	1	0	0	0	0	0	1	**50**	1	1	1	**100**	***46***
11	Venkateswer Rao K	0	0	0	0	0	**0**	1	0	0	0	0	0	0	1	**30**	0	0	1	**60**	***24***
12	Purshotham	1	1	0	0	0	**40**	1	1	1	0	0	0	0	1	**60**	0	0	1	**60**	***54***
13	Balu K	0	0	0	0	0	**0**	1	0	1	1	0	0	1	1	**60**	0	0	1	**60**	***42***
14	Rambabu	0	1	0	1	0	**40**	1	1	0	1	0	0	0	1	**60**	1	0	1	**80**	***56***
15	Laxmaiah	1	0	0	1	0	**40**	1	1	0	1	0	0	0	1	**60**	1	0	1	**80**	***56***
16	Jeelani	0	0	0	0	0	**0**	0	0	0	1	0	0	0	1	**20**	0	0	1	**60**	***18***
17	Azeez	0	0	0	0	0	**0**	1	1	0	0	1	0	0	1	**60**	0	0	1	**60**	***42***
18	Sambasiva Rao G	1	0	1	1	0	**60**	1	1	0	1	1	0	1	1	**80**	1	0	1	**80**	***74***
19	Samabasiva Rao T	0	0	0	1	0	**20**	1	0	0	1	0	0	0	1	**40**	1	1	1	**100**	***40***
20	Narayana	0	0	0	0	0	**0**	1	0	0	1	0	0	0	1	**40**	0	0	1	**60**	***30***

21	Subba Rao	0	0	0	1	0	**20**	1	1	1	0	0	0	0	1	**60**	1	1	1	**100**	*52*
22	Papa Rao	0	0	1	1	1	**60**	1	0	0	1	0	0	0	1	**40**	1	1	1	**100**	*52*
23	Venkata Ramappa	1	0	1	1	0	**60**	1	0	1	1	1	0	1	1	**70**	1	0	1	**80**	*68*
24	Narayana Swamy	0	0	0	0	0	**0**	1	0	1	1	1	0	0	1	**60**	0	0	1	**60**	*42*
25	Gowri Shankar	0	0	0	0	0	**0**	1	0	0	1	1	0	0	1	**50**	0	0	1	**60**	*36*
26	Raja Vardhan Raj	1	0	1	1	0	**60**	1	1	0	0	0	0	0	1	**50**	1	1	1	**100**	*58*
27	Kishore Reddy	0	0	0	1	1	**40**	1	0	0	0	1	0	0	1	**40**	0	0	1	**60**	*42*
28	Srinivasulu	0	0	0	1	0	**20**	1	1	0	0	0	0	0	1	**50**	0	0	1	**60**	*42*
29	Chandra Mouli	0	0	0	0	0	**0**	1	1	1	1	0	0	1	1	**80**	1	0	1	**80**	*56*
30	Rafi	1	0	0	1	0	**40**	1	1	0	1	1	0	0	1	**70**	0	0	1	**60**	*60*
31	Y.Ramchandra Reddy	0	0	0	1	1	**40**	1	0	0	1	0	0	0	1	**40**	1	0	1	**80**	*44*
32	Mahboob Vali	0	0	0	1	0	**20**	1	1	0	1	0	0	0	1	**60**	0	0	1	**60**	*48*
33	Raja Gopal	0	0	0	1	0	**20**	1	0	0	0	0	0	0	1	**30**	0	0	1	**60**	*30*
34	Dastagiri	1	0	0	1	0	**40**	1	1	1	0	0	0	1	1	**70**	1	0	1	**80**	*62*
35	Chalma Reddy	0	0	0	0	0	**0**	1	0	0	0	0	0	0	1	**30**	0	0	1	**60**	*24*
36	Nagendrudu	0	0	0	1	0	**20**	1	0	1	0	1	0	1	1	**60**	0	0	1	**60**	*48*
37	Tejeswer Rao	0	0	0	0	0	**0**	1	0	0	1	0	0	0	1	**40**	0	0	1	**60**	*30*
38	Ramachendra Reddy	1	0	0	1	0	**40**	1	1	1	0	1	0	1	1	**80**	1	1	1	**100**	*70*
39	Prabhakar Reddy	0	0	0	0	0	**0**	1	0	0	0	0	0	1	1	**40**	1	0	1	**80**	*32*
40	Balu Naik	1	0	0	1	0	**40**	1	1	1	0	1	0	1	1	**80**	1	0	1	**80**	*68*
	No. found positive	**11**	**3**	**6**	**26**	**4**		**39**	**16**	**12**	**22**	**11**	**0**	**9**	**40**		**20**	**10**	**40**		

SCORE SHEET

0	Not Vulnerable	0		Vulnerable	4-6
1	Just Vulnerable	0-2	4	Mostly Vulnerable	6-8
2	Partly	2-4	5	Highly Vulnerable	8-10

Table 3.46: Cops medical vulnerability index

Sl. No	Name of the Accused Police Officer	Age	Sex	B.P	P.R	H/o Family Problem	Away From Family	Diabetes	Peptic Ulcer	Heart Ailments	Alcohol	Tobacco Smoking	Medical Checkup done or not
1	Rama Rao P	54	Male	120/80	78	No	Yes	No	No	No	Yes	No	No
2	Krishna Chaitanya	33	Male	120/80	72	No	No	No	No	No	Yes	Yes	No
3	Raghava Rani K	34	Female	130/90	76	Yes	Yes	No	Y	No	No	No	No
4	Raghava Rani K	42	Female	140/90	82	Yes	Yes	No	Yes	No	No	No	Yes
5	Santhoshamma	45	Female	130/90	80	Yes	Yes	Yes	Yes	Yes	No	No	Yes
6	Ragini	29	Female	120/80	76	Yes	Yes	No	Yes	No	No	No	Yes
7	Narasimha Rao P	34	Male	130/90	88	Yes	Yes	No	Yes	No	Yes	Yes	No
8	Ranga Rao	36	Male	140/90	92	Yes	Yes	No	Yes	No	Yes	Yes	No
9	Venkateswer Rao B	40	Male	120/80	76	No	Yes	Yes	Yes	No	Yes	Yes	Yes
10	Prem Kumar G	33	Male	140/90	90	Yes	Yes	No	Yes	No	Yes	Yes	No
11	Venkateswer Rao K	37	Male	120/80	80	No	No	No	No	No	No	No	No
12	Purshotham	25	Male	140/90	92	Yes	Yes	No	No	No	No	No	No
13	Balu K	26	Male	120/80	70	No	Yes	No	No	No	No	No	No
14	Rambabu	36	Male	130/90	90	Yes	Yes	No	Yes	No	Yes	No	No
15	Laxmaiah	36	Male	140/90	88	Yes	Yes	No	Yes	No	Yes	No	No
16	Jeelani	34	Male	120/80	70	No	No	No	No	No	No	No	No
17	Azeez	28	Male	130/80	76	No	No	No	No	No	No	No	No
18	Sambasiva Rao G	38	Male	140/90	82	Yes	Yes	Yes	Yes	No	Yes	No	Yes
19	Samabasiva Rao T	36	Male	120/80	76	No	No	No	Yes	No	Yes	Yes	No
20	Narayana	24	Male	120/80	74	No	No	No	No	No	No	No	No

Sl. No	Name of the Accused Police Officer	Age	Sex	B.P	P.R	H/o Family Problem	Away From Family	Diabetes	Peptic Ulcer	Heart Ailments	Alcohol	Tobacco Smoking	Medical Checkup done or not
21	Subba Rao	32	Male	130/90	78	Yes	Yes	No	Yes	No	Yes	Yes	No
22	Papa Rao	42	Male	120/80	76	Yes	No	Yes	Yes	Yes	Yes	Yes	Yes
23	Venkata Ramappa	40	Male	140/90	72	No	No	Yes	Yes	No	Yes	No	Yes
24	Narayana Swamy	38	Male	120/80	74	No	No	No	No	No	No	No	No
25	Gowri Shankar	32	Male	120/80	74	No	No	No	No	No	No	No	No
26	Raja Vardhan Raj	40	Male	140/90	82	Yes	Yes	Yes	Yes	No	Yes	Yes	Yes
27	Kishore Reddy	42	Male	120/80	76	No	No	No	Yes	Yes	No	No	No
28	Srinivasulu	36	Male	130/90	80	Yes	Yes	No	Yes	No	No	No	No
29	Chandra Mouli	34	Male	130/90	84	Yes	Yes	No	No	No	Yes	No	No
30	Rafi	36	Male	140/90	82	No	Yes	No	Yes	No	No	No	No
31	Y.RamchandraReddy	42	Male	130/80	78	No	Yes	No	Yes	Yes	Yes	No	Yes
32	Mahboob Vali	40	Male	130/80	76	Yes	Yes	No	Yes	Yes	No	No	No
33	Raja Gopal	28	Male	120/80	74	No	No	No	No	No	No	No	No
34	Dastagiri	43	Male	140/90	88	Yes	Yes	No	Yes	No	Yes	Yes	No
35	Chalma Reddy	42	Male	140/90	80	Yes	Yes	No	No	No	Yes	No	No
36	Nagendrudu	44	Male	130/90	74	No	Yes	No	Yes	No	No	No	No
37	Tejeswer Rao	28	Male	120/80	72	No	Yes	No	No	No	No	No	No
38	Ramachendra Reddy	37	Male	130/90	82	No	Yes	No	Yes	No	No	No	No
39	Prabhakar Reddy	40	Male	130/90	80	No	Yes	No	Yes	No	Yes	No	No
40	Balu Naik	42	Male	120/80	82	No	Yes	No	Yes	No	Yes	Yes	No

Table 3.47: Police officers' medical vulnerability index

Source: Computed

Sl.No	Name	Rank	Age	Sex	Caste	Crime No.	Police Station	E.L.availed/ Not	B.P	P.R	H/o Family Problem	Away From Family	Diabetes	Peptic Ulcer	Alcohol	Tobacco Smoking	Medical Checkup done	Name of Disease
1	Rama Rao P, CI	CI	54	Male	Kapu	334/2000	I-town PS Vijayawada	No	140/90	80	Yes	Yes	Yes	Yes	Yes	No	No	B.P
2	Krishna Chaitanya,	SI	33	Male	Kamma	-do -	-do-	No	120/80	72	No	No	No	No	Yes	Yes	No	No
3	Raghava Rani K,WPC-564	WPC	34	Female	Setti Balij	148/1999	Suryaraopet PS Vijayawada	No	120/80	76	Yes	No	No	Yes	No	No	No	No
4	Jyothi Rayudu, SI	WSI	42	Female	B.C	-do-	-do -	No	120/90	84	Yes	Yes	Yes	Yes	No	No	Yes	No
5	Santhoshamma, WHC-1192	WHC	45	Female	Christian	-do-	-do-	No	130/80	80	Yes	Yes	Yes	Yes	No	No	Yes	No
6	Ragini, WPC-295	WPC	29	Female	Rajaka	-do-	-do-	No	120/80	80	Yes	No	No	No	No	No	Yes	No
7	Narasimha Rao P,PC-792	PC	36	Male	Telga	334/2000	I-town PS Vijayawada	Yes	110/70	82	No	Yes	No	No	Yes	Yes	No	No
8	Ranga Rao, PC-1333	PC	38	Male	Gouda	-do-	-do-	Yes	130/90	80	Yes	No	No	Yes	Yes	Yes	No	1. Ca. stomach chemotherapy, 2. RecurrentCa. stomach
9	Venkateswer Rao B,ASI-137	ASI	47	Male	Gouda	-do-	-do-	No	130/90	86	No	Yes	No	Yes	Yes	Yes	Yes	No
10	Prem Kumar G, PC-143	PC	27	Male	SC (Christian)	-do-	-do-	Yes	120/80	72	Yes	No	No	Yes	Yes	Yes	No	No
11	Venkateswer Rao K, PC 846	PC	38	Male	Rajaka	-do-	-do-	Yes	120/80	76	Yes	Yes	No	No	No	No	No	No
12	Purshotham, PC-1982	PC	40	Male	Kapu	70/1997	Ongole Railway PS	No	130/80	74	Yes	No	No	Yes	No	No	No	No

13	Balu K, PC-1483	PC	34	Male	Kapu	10/2003	Balanagar PS, R.R. Dist	No	110/80	72	Yes	No	No	No	No	No	No	No
14	Rambabu, PC-445	PC	34	Male	Telaga	18/1996	Nagaramppalem PS, Guntur	No	110/70	74	Yes	Yes	No	Yes	Yes	No	No	No
15	Laxmaiah, PC-2530	PC	36	Male	S.C	70/1997	Ongole Railway PS	Yes	110/70	72	Yes	Yes	No	YES	Yes	No	No	No
16	Jeelani, HC-2275	HC	39	Male	Muslim	18/1996	Nagaramppalem PS, Guntur	Yes	130/90	80	No	No	No	No	No	No	No	No
17	Azeez, PC-2509	PC	35	Male	Muslim	90/1991	Pattipadu PS Guntur	No	160/90	76	No	Yes	No	Yes	No	No	No	IHD, CAD, PTCA + Stent to Mid RCA
18	Sambasiva RaoG, PC-1243	PC	36	Male	Telga	-do-	-do-	No	130/90	72	Yes	No	No	Yes	Yes	No	Yes	Nonunion rt. Subtrochautic facture with ill,
19	Samabasiva Rao T, PC-466	PC	33	Male	Telga	-do-	-do-	No	120/80	76	No	No	No	No	Yes	Yes	No	No
20	Narayana	PC	40	Male	Kapu	-do-	-do-	No	140/90	80	Yes	Yes	No	Yes	No	No	No	No
21	Subba Rao, PC-1211	PC	36	Male	Yerukulas	18/1996	Nagarampalem PS, Guntur	Yes	120/80	72	No	No	No	No	Yes	Yes	No	No
22	Papa Rao, PC-1495	PC	41	Male	Muthurasi	-do-	-do-	Yes	120/80	76	No	No	No	No	Yes	Yes	Yes	No
23	Venkata Ramappa	PC	48	Male	B.C	-do-	-do-	No	110/80	82	Yes	Yes	No	Yes	Yes	No	Yes	No
24	Narayana Swamy, PC-134	PC	40	Male	Kamma	95/1998	Kadiri Town PS, Ananthapur	No	110/80	84	No	No	No	No	No	No	No	No
25	Gowri Shankar PC-107	PC	42	Male	Kapu	-do-	-do-	No	120/80	86	No	Yes	No	No	No	No	No	No
26	Raja Vardhan Raj, HC-1595	HC	50	Male	Kamma	54/2003	Yadiki PS, Ananthapur	Yes	140/90	86	Yes	Yes	No	Yes	Yes	Yes	Yes	No
27	Kishore Reddy, PC-2079	PC	32	Male	Kapu	-do-	-do-	No	120/80	72	No	No	No	No	No	No	No	No

28	Srinivasulu, HC-717	HC	52	Male	Balija	104/1997	Tadipatri Tq. PS, Ananthapur	No	140/90	84	Yes	Yes	No	Yes	No	No	No	No
29	Chandra Mouli, PC-723	PC	36	Male	Balija	-do-	-do-	No	140/90	70	No	No	No	No	Yes	No	No	No
30	Rafi, PC-120	PC	32	Male	Muslim	95/1998	Kadiri Town PS, Ananthapur	No	120/80	76	No	No	No	No	No	No	No	No
31	Y.Ramchandra Reddy, CI	CI	38	Male	Reddy	-do-	-do-	No	130/90	78	Yes	No	No	No	Yes	No	Yes	No
32	Mahboob Vali, HC-30	HC	54	Male	Muslim	-do-	-do-	No	150/90	80	Yes	Yes	No	Yes	No	No	No	No
33	Raja Gopal PC	PC	42	Male	Kapu	-do-	-do-	No	130/90	76	Yes	No	No	Yes	No	No	No	No
34	Dastagiri, SI	SI	42	Male	Muslim	95/1998	Kadiri Town PS, Ananthapur	No	130/90	72	No	No	No	Yes	Yes	Yes	No	No
35	Chalma Reddy, SI	SI	40	Male	Reddy	-do-	-do-	No	140/80	80	No	Yes	No	No	Yes	No	No	No
36	Nagendrudu, SI	SI	36	Male	Kapu	104/1997	Tadipatri Tq. PS, Ananthapur	No	130/80	80	No	No	No	No	No	No	No	No
37	Tejeswer Rao, SI	SI	40	Male	Kamma	54/2003	Yadiki PS, Ananthapur	No	120/80	76	No	No	No	Yes	No	No	No	No
38	Ramachendra Reddy	PC	40	Male	Reddy	-do-	-do-	No	140/90	84	No	No	No	No	No	No	No	No
39	Prabhakar Reddy	PC	36	Male	Reddy	-do-	-do-	No	130/90	72	Yes	No	No	No	Yes	No	No	No
40	Balu Naik, PC-1595	PC	34	Male	S.T	70/1997	Ongole Railway PS	No	120/80	74	Yes	No	No	No	Yes	Yes	No	No

Table 3.48: Cops' medical vulnerability index

Source: Computed

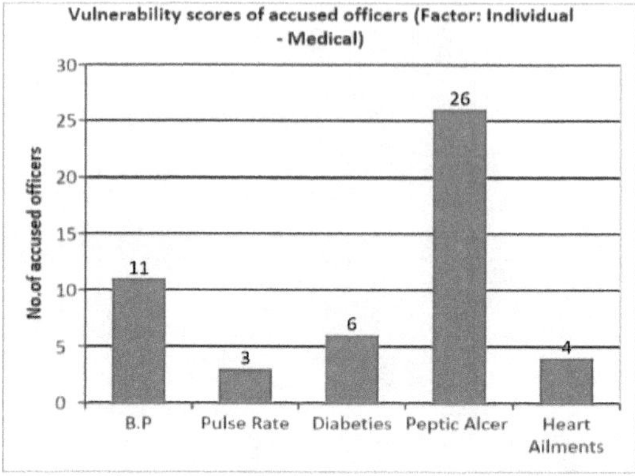

Figure 3.27: Vulnerability scores of accused officers (Factor: Individual-Medical)
Source: Computed

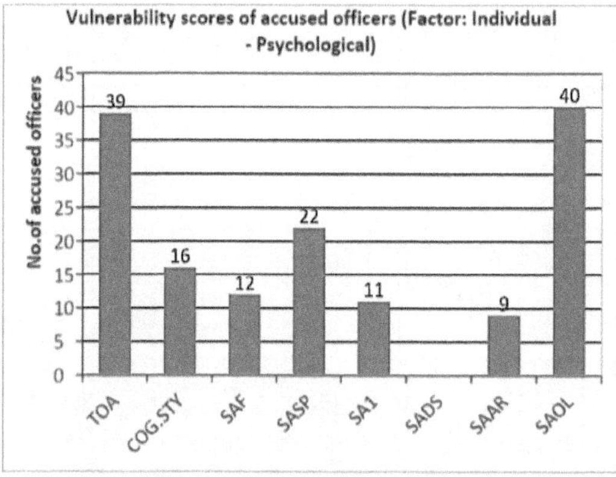

Figure 3.28: Vulnerability scores of accused officers (Factor: Individual - Psychological)
Source: Computed

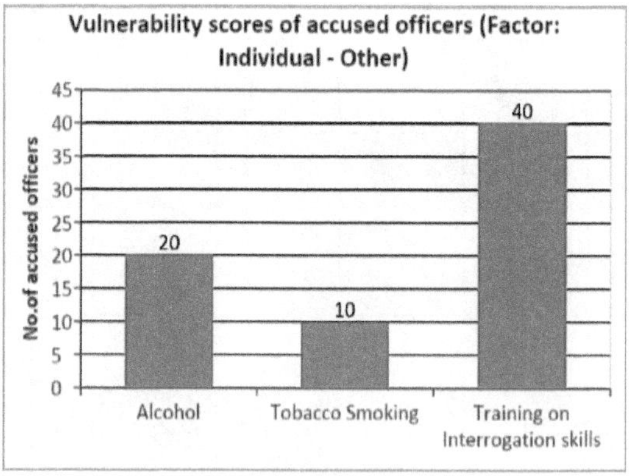

Figure 3.29: Vulnerability scores of accused officers (Factor: Individual - Other)
Source: Computed

		Legal, Weightage 40											
Sl. No.	Name	Interro gators list Register Maintained or not	Spot Arrest Memo & Signature taken or 1t	Friend was informed of Arrest or not	Within 8-12 hrs Time, Place of arrest and Place of Custody 1tified or1t	Was he Informed about his Right to inform someone of his arrest	Personal Diary entry of friend and name of police officers at spot	Injuries, inspection memos signed copy given to arrestee or 1t	Did Medical Doctor examine every 48 hrs or 1t	Was FIR, Arrest Memo sent to Magistrate or 1t	Was Lawyer allowed which interrogation or 1t	Was PCR informed of arrest by police within 12hrs	Weighted score Legal
	Weightages	5	10	5	10	10	10	10	10	10	10	10	100
1	Rama Rao P	0	0	0	0	0	0	0	0	1	0	0	*10*
2	Krishna Chaitanya	0	0	0	0	0	0	0	0	1	0	0	*10*
3	Raghava Rani K	0	0	0	0	1	0	0	1	1	0	0	*30*
4	Jyothi R	0	0	0	0	1	0	0	1	0	0	0	*20*
5	Santhoshamma	0	0	0	0	1	0	0	0	0	0	0	*10*
6	Ragini	0	0	0	0	1	0	0	0	1	0	0	*20*
7	Narasimha Rao P	0	0	1	0	1	0	0	0	1	0	0	*25*
8	Ranga Rao	0	0	1	0	1	0	0	0	1	0	0	*25*
9	Venkateswer Rao B	0	0	1	0	1	0	0	1	1	0	0	*35*
10	Prem Kumar G	0	0	1	0	1	0	0	1	1	0	0	*35*
11	Venkateswer Rao K	0	0	1	0	1	0	0	1	1	0	0	*35*
12	Purshotham	0	0	1	0	1	0	0	1	1	0	0	*35*
13	Balu K	0	0	1	0	1	0	0	1	1	0	0	*35*
14	Rambabu	0	0	1	0	1	0	0	0	1	0	0	*25*
15	Laxmaiah	0	0	1	0	1	0	0	0	1	0	0	*25*
16	Jeelani	0	0	1	0	1	0	0	0	0	0	0	*15*
17	Azeez	0	0	1	0	1	0	0	1	0	0	0	*25*
18	Sambasiva Rao G	0	0	1	0	1	0	0	1	0	0	0	*25*
19	Samabasiva Rao T	0	0	1	0	1	0	0	1	1	0	0	*35*

20	Narayana	0	0	1	0	1	0	0	1	1	0	0	*35*
21	Subba Rao	0	0	1	0	1	0	0	0	1	0	0	*25*
22	Papa Rao	0	0	1	0	1	0	0	1	1	0	0	*35*
23	Venkata Ramappa	0	0	1	0	1	0	0	1	0	0	0	*25*
24	Narayana Swamy	0	0	1	0	1	0	0	1	1	0	0	*35*
25	Gowri Shankar	0	0	1	0	1	0	0	1	1	0	0	*35*
26	Raja Vardhan Raj	0	0	1	0	1	0	0	1	0	0	0	*25*
27	Kishore Reddy	0	0	1	0	1	0	0	1	0	0	0	*25*
28	Srinivasulu	0	0	1	0	1	0	0	1	1	0	0	*35*
29	Chandra Mouli	0	0	1	0	1	0	0	1	1	0	0	*35*
30	Rafi	0	0	1	0	1	0	0	1	1	0	0	*35*
31	Y.Ramch. Reddy	0	0	1	0	1	0	0	1	1	0	0	*35*
32	Mahboob Vali	0	0	1	0	1	0	0	1	1	0	0	*35*
33	Raja Gopal	0	0	1	0	1	0	0	1	1	0	0	*35*
34	Dastagiri	0	0	1	0	1	0	0	1	1	0	0	*35*
35	Chalma Reddy	0	0	1	0	1	0	0	1	1	0	0	*35*
36	Nagendrudu	0	0	1	0	1	0	0	1	1	0	0	*35*
37	Tejeswer Rao	0	0	1	0	1	0	0	1	1	0	0	*35*
38	Ramachendra Reddy	0	0	1	0	1	0	0	1	1	0	0	*35*
39	Prabhakar Reddy	0	0	1	0	1	0	0	1	1	0	0	*35*
40	Balu Naik	0	0	1	0	1	0	0	1	1	0	0	*35*
	found positive	0	0	34	0	38	0	0	30	32	0	0	

Table 3.49: Vulnerability scores of accused officers (Factor: Legal, weightage 40%)

Source: Computed

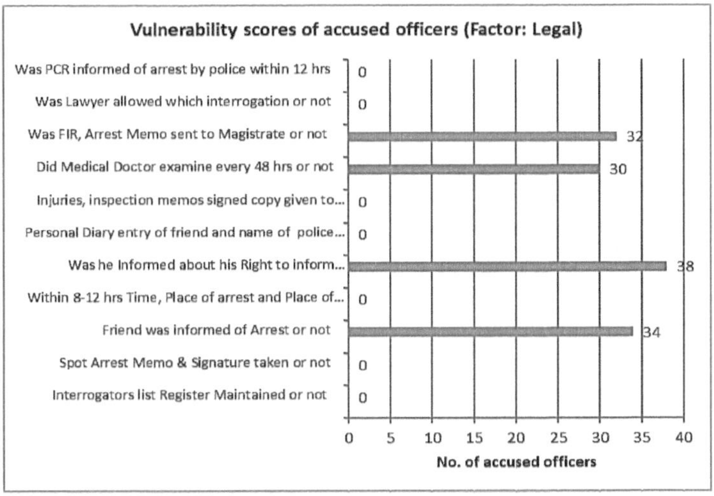

Figure 3.30: Vulnerability scores of accused officers (Factor: Legal)

Source: Primary Data

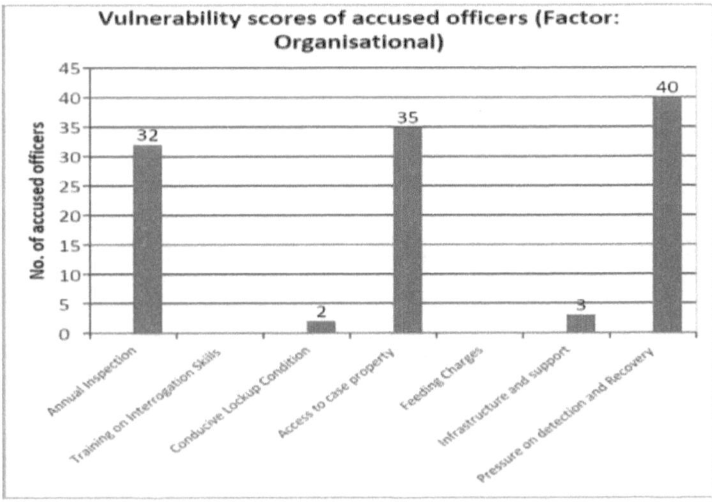

Figure 3.31: Vulnerability scores of accused officers (Factor: Organizational)

Source: Primary Data

Sl. No.	Name	Organisational 40								Overall score (Individual +Legal +Organizational)
		Annual Inspection	Training on Interrogation Skills	Conducive Lockup Condition	Access to case property	Feeding Charges	Infrastructure and support	Pressure on detection and Recovery	Weighted score Organisational	
	Weightages	15	15	15	10	10	15	20	*100*	*100*
1	Rama Rao P	0	0	0	1	0	0	1	*30*	*22*
2	Krishna Chaitanya	0	0	0	1	0	0	1	*30*	*23*
3	Raghava Rani K	1	0	0	1	0	1	1	*60*	*42*
4	Jyothi R	1	0	0	1	0	0	1	*45*	*34*
5	Santhoshamma	0	0	1	1	0	0	1	*45*	*30*
6	Ragini	0	0	0	1	0	0	1	*30*	*27*
7	Narasimha Rao P	1	0	0	1	0	0	1	*45*	*38*
8	Ranga Rao	0	0	0	1	0	0	1	*30*	*35*
9	Venkateswer Rao B	0	0	0	0	0	1	1	*35*	*37*
10	Prem Kumar G	0	0	0	1	0	0	1	*30*	*35*
11	Venkateswer Rao K	1	0	0	1	0	0	1	*45*	*37*
12	Purshotham	1	0	0	1	0	0	1	*45*	*43*
13	Balu K	1	0	0	1	0	0	1	*45*	*40*
14	Rambabu	1	0	1	1	0	0	1	*60*	*45*
15	Laxmaiah	1	0	0	1	0	0	1	*45*	*39*
16	Jeelani	1	0	0	0	0	0	1	*35*	*24*
17	Azeez	1	0	0	1	0	1	1	*60*	*42*
18	Sambasiva Rao G	0	0	0	1	0	0	1	*30*	*37*

19	Samabasiva Rao T	1	0	0	1	0	0	1	*45*	*40*
20	Narayana	1	0	0	0	0	0	1	*35*	*34*
21	Subba Rao	1	0	0	1	0	0	1	*45*	*38*
22	Papa Rao	1	0	0	1	0	0	1	*45*	*42*
23	Venkata Ramappa	1	0	0	1	0	0	1	*45*	*42*
24	Narayana Swamy	1	0	0	0	0	0	1	*35*	*36*
25	Gowri Shankar	1	0	0	1	0	0	1	*45*	*39*
26	Raja Vardhan Raj	1	0	0	1	0	0	1	*45*	*40*
27	Kishore Reddy	1	0	0	0	0	0	1	*35*	*32*
28	Srinivasulu	1	0	0	1	0	0	1	*45*	*40*
29	Chandra Mouli	1	0	0	1	0	0	1	*45*	*43*
30	Rafi	1	0	0	1	0	0	1	*45*	*44*
31	Y Ramchandra Reddy	1	0	0	1	0	0	1	*45*	*41*
32	Mahboob Vali	1	0	0	1	0	0	1	*45*	*42*
33	Raja Gopal	1	0	0	1	0	0	1	*45*	*38*
34	Dastagiri	1	0	0	1	0	0	1	*45*	*44*
35	Chalma Reddy	1	0	0	1	0	0	1	*45*	*37*
36	Nagendrudu	1	0	0	1	0	0	1	*45*	*42*
37	Tejeswer Rao	1	0	0	1	0	0	1	*45*	*38*
38	Ramachendra Reddy	1	0	0	1	0	0	1	*45*	*46*
39	Prabhakar Reddy	1	0	0	1	0	0	1	*45*	*38*
40	Balu Naik	1	0	0	1	0	0	1	*45*	*46*
	No. found positive	32	0	2	35	0	3	40		

Table 3.50: Vulnerability scores of accused officers (Factor: Organizational, weightage 40%)

Source: Computed

Vulnerability scores of the custodial deaths

Sl.No.	Name of the Accused Police Officer	Individual (helath and psychological)	Legal	Organizational	Final Risk Percent	Weighted Average (Vulnerabiliyt Index)			
						Individual	Legal	Organizational	Total Vulnerability Index
	Weightages	***20***	***40***	***40***	***100***	**0.200**	**0.400**	**0.400**	**1.000**
1	Rama Rao P	32	10	30	*22.4*	0.096	0.03	0.12	0.246
2	Krishna Chaitanya	34	10	30	*22.8*	0.102	0.03	0.12	0.252
3	Raghava Rani K	30	30	60	*42*	0.09	0.09	0.24	0.420
4	Jyothi R	42	20	45	*34.4*	0.126	0.06	0.18	0.366
5	Santhoshamma	42	10	45	*30.4*	0.126	0.03	0.18	0.336
6	Ragini	36	20	30	*27.2*	0.108	0.06	0.12	0.288
7	Narasimha Rao P	52	25	45	*38.4*	0.156	0.075	0.18	0.411
8	Ranga Rao	64	25	30	*34.8*	0.192	0.075	0.12	0.387
9	Venkateswer Rao B	46	35	35	*37.2*	0.138	0.105	0.14	0.383
10	Prem Kumar G	46	35	30	*35.2*	0.138	0.105	0.12	0.363
11	Venkateswer Rao K	24	35	45	*36.8*	0.072	0.105	0.18	0.357
12	Purshotham	54	35	45	*42.8*	0.162	0.105	0.18	0.447
13	Balu K	42	35	45	*40.4*	0.126	0.105	0.18	0.411
14	Rambabu	56	25	60	*45.2*	0.168	0.075	0.24	0.483
15	Laxmaiah	56	25	45	*39.2*	0.168	0.075	0.18	0.423
16	Jeelani	18	15	35	*23.6*	0.054	0.045	0.14	0.239
17	Azeez	42	25	60	*42.4*	0.126	0.075	0.24	0.441
18	Sambasiva Rao G	74	25	30	*36.8*	0.222	0.075	0.12	0.417
19	Samabasiva Rao T	40	35	45	*40*	0.12	0.105	0.18	0.405

20	Narayana	30	35	35	*34*	0.09	0.105	0.14	0.335
21	Subba Rao	52	25	45	*38.4*	0.156	0.075	0.18	0.411
22	Papa Rao	52	35	45	*42.4*	0.156	0.105	0.18	0.441
23	Venkata Ramappa	68	25	45	*41.6*	0.204	0.075	0.18	0.459
24	Narayana Swamy	42	35	35	*36.4*	0.126	0.105	0.14	0.371
25	Gowri Shankar	36	35	45	*39.2*	0.108	0.105	0.18	0.393
26	Raja Vardhan Raj	58	25	45	*39.6*	0.174	0.075	0.18	0.429
27	Kishore Reddy	42	25	35	*32.4*	0.126	0.075	0.14	0.341
28	Srinivasulu	42	35	45	*40.4*	0.126	0.105	0.18	0.411
29	Chandra Mouli	56	35	45	*43.2*	0.168	0.105	0.18	0.453
30	Rafi	60	35	45	*44*	0.18	0.105	0.18	0.465
31	Y.Ramchandra Reddy	44	35	45	*40.8*	0.132	0.105	0.18	0.417
32	Mahboob Vali	48	35	45	*41.6*	0.144	0.105	0.18	0.429
33	Raja Gopal	30	35	45	*38*	0.09	0.105	0.18	0.375
34	Dastagiri	62	35	45	*44.4*	0.186	0.105	0.18	0.471
35	Chalma Reddy	24	35	45	*36.8*	0.072	0.105	0.18	0.357
36	Nagendrudu	48	35	45	*41.6*	0.144	0.105	0.18	0.429
37	Tejeswer Rao	30	35	45	*38*	0.09	0.105	0.18	0.375
38	Ramachendra Reddy	70	35	45	*46*	0.21	0.105	0.18	0.495
39	Prabhakar Reddy	32	35	45	*38.4*	0.096	0.105	0.18	0.381
40	Balu Naik	68	35	45	*45.6*	0.204	0.105	0.18	0.489
	Average	45.6	29.25	42.625	37.87	0.137	0.088	0.17	0.395

Table 3.51: Summary of vulnerability scores and vulnerability index of custodial deaths

Source: Computed

Vulnerability Scores of the Custodial Deaths

The risk involved in each case of the sample under study is calculated using the method explained above, and the results are shown in Table 3.51.

Sl.No.	Name	Individual	Legal	Organizational	Final Risk Percent	Vulnerability Index
	Weightages	*20*	*40*	*40*	*100*	*1.000*
1	Rama Rao P	32	65	100	*69*	0.691
2	Krishna Chaitanya	36	65	100	*70*	0.703
3	Raghava Rani K	32	75	100	*72*	0.721
4	Jyothi R	44	75	100	*76*	0.757
5	Santhoshamma	48	75	100	*77*	0.769
6	Ragini	36	75	100	*73*	0.733
7	Narasimha Rao P	52	80	100	*80*	0.796
8	Ranga Rao	68	80	100	*84*	0.844
9	Venkateswer Rao B	52	80	100	*80*	0.796
10	Prem Kumar G	48	80	100	*78*	0.784
11	Venkateswer Rao K	24	80	100	*71*	0.712
12	Purshotham	52	80	100	*80*	0.796
13	Balu K	36	80	100	*75*	0.748
14	Rambabu	56	80	100	*81*	0.808
15	Laxmaiah	56	80	100	*81*	0.808
16	Jeelani	20	80	100	*70*	0.7
17	Azeez	36	80	100	*75*	0.748
18	Sambasiva Rao G	72	80	100	*86*	0.856
19	Samabasiva Rao T	44	80	100	*77*	0.772
20	Narayana	28	80	100	*72*	0.724
21	Subba Rao	52	80	100	*80*	0.796
22	Papa Rao	60	80	100	*82*	0.82
23	Venkata Ramappa	68	80	100	*84*	0.844
24	Narayana Swamy	36	80	100	*75*	0.748
25	Gowri Shankar	32	80	100	*74*	0.736
26	Raja Vardhan Raj	64	80	100	*83*	0.832
27	Kishore Reddy	44	80	100	*77*	0.772
28	Srinivasulu	40	80	100	*76*	0.76
29	Chandra Mouli	48	80	100	*78*	0.784
30	Rafi	56	80	100	*81*	0.808

31	Y.Ramchandra Reddy	48	80	100	*78*	0.784
32	Mahboob Vali	44	80	100	*77*	0.772
33	Raja Gopal	32	80	100	*74*	0.736
34	Dastagiri	60	80	100	*82*	0.82
35	Chalma Reddy	24	80	100	*71*	0.712
36	Nagendrudu	44	80	100	*77*	0.772
37	Tejeswer Rao	28	80	100	*72*	0.724
38	Ramachendra Reddy	68	80	100	*84*	0.844
39	Prabhakar Reddy	32	80	100	*74*	0.736
40	Balu Naik	64	80	100	*83*	0.832
	Average	45	79	100	77	0.772

Table 3.52: Vulnerability scores of the custodial deaths

Source: Computed

Table 3.52 outlines the risks associated with assigning custody of expired victims during interrogation. Here, a score of zero indicates no risk or vulnerability, while a score of 100 denotes a high level of risk. A vulnerability index of 1.000 signifies the highest possible risk. The data reveal that there are more lapses in organizational and legal areas than among individuals. It is essential to assess the risk factor before assigning custody to a victim.

If the risk falls below a certain threshold, custody should only be entrusted to a specific officer or police station. To facilitate this, each police officer and station should undergo periodic vulnerability assessments—such as annually or biennially—and the same rating could be applied for this purpose.

The Investigation

The following steps should be taken as part of the investigation:

1. The scene of the death should be visited and documented photographically. Diagrams may be created if it is believed they could be of assistance.

2. A complete account of the circumstances surrounding the fatal incident should be obtained. The actions of individuals involved immediately before, at, and after the death should be determined. Police reports of the incident, including copies of interviews with the police officers involved, witnesses, and medical personnel, should be obtained.
3. Medical records of the fatal incident should be obtained. It should be determined if and when drugs were administered or medical procedures were conducted.
4. Past medical records of the deceased should be obtained.
5. If the deceased was on any medications, this information should be determined. One should determine the dosage, frequency, and length of treatment for each individual.
6. The results of any police laboratory examinations should be obtained.
7. Any blood taken on admission should be sought and obtained if the individual was hospitalized.

The material included in this list is then submitted to the office, where a detailed report is prepared for the forensic pathologist performing the autopsy.

The material should be retained for subsequent closer review by the forensic pathologist. Some information (e.g., interviews) may not be initially available. The investigation report may be supplemented by information subsequently obtained from additional witnesses, other agencies, police reports, and crime lab reports.

Autopsy

A complete autopsy should be conducted. The autopsy should be performed by or under the direct supervision of an experienced forensic pathologist board-certified in Forensic Medicine. The autopsy should include a detailed examination of the external aspects of the body for evidence of disease or trauma. Any trauma noted should be located on the body, described in detail, measured, and photographed. The deceased's clothing should also be examined for evidence of violence.

Photographs of the body should be taken even in the absence of injuries to document the absence.

The internal examination of the body should include an assessment of all three body cavities (i.e., the cranial cavity, the thoracic cavity, and the abdominal cavity). The neck organs should be removed and examined in detail. When it felt necessary, additional incisions and examinations should be made. Any trauma noted should be described in detail, measured, and photographed.

A microscopic examination of all organs, particularly the heart, should be conducted. Body fluids should be retained for toxicological analysis. Video recording should be done. Histopathological examination of relevant tissues should be done to validate the observation.

Microscopy

At the time of autopsy, tissue should be retained from all the major organs for microscopic examination. At least six heart sections should be examined, with at least one coming from the area of the conduction system.

All microscopic slides and paraffin blocks should be retained indefinitely. Tissue removed at autopsy should be retained for a minimum of five years.

Certification of Death

Following the autopsy, if there is no evidence of sufficient trauma to explain death, this information should be released to the public. No ruling of death should be made until all the investigation and testing are complete.

Two of the most essential functions of a forensic pathologist are determining the cause and manner of death. The cause of death is any injury or disease that produces a physiological derangement in the body, resulting in the individual's death. The causes of death are a gunshot wound, a stab wound to the chest, adenocarcinoma of the lung, or coronary atherosclerosis. The mechanism of death is the physiological derangement produced by the cause of death that results in death.

Examples of mechanisms of death would be hemorrhage, septicemia, and cardiac arrhythmia.

The manner of death explains how the cause of death came about. The manners of death are natural, homicide, suicide, accident, and undetermined. The manner of death is an opinion based on the known facts concerning the circumstances leading up to and surrounding the death in conjunction with the findings at autopsy and laboratory tests. A manner of death is ruled undetermined when there is insufficient information about the circumstances surrounding the death to make a ruling or when the cause of death is unknown.

4

POLICE MANAGEMENT, HUMAN RIGHTS VIOLATION ISSUES, AND PROPOSED POLICE MANAGEMENT MODEL FOR THE PREVENTION OF CUSTODIAL DEATHS

The primary purpose of this chapter is to present and interpret the findings of the study. The data collected from various sources have been systematically analyzed using appropriate statistical tools. The results obtained from this analysis have been synthesized into key findings. These findings are discussed in the following sections to draw logical and meaningful conclusions. At the end, based on the insights gained, practical suggestions are given to improve managerial and behavioral aspects of police management to prevent custodial issues that may lead to the deaths of accused individuals.

Custodial Torture And Reforms In Police Administration

Police brutality is not an alien concept to any country out there. In 2020, the USA witnessed a massive protest when George Floyd, a black man, was murdered at the hands of a white police officer. In the same year, not even a month past the death of George Floyd, India witnessed a massive outrage by the public over the custodial torture and death of a father-son duo by police officers at Sathankulam police station in Thoothukudi district, Tamil Nadu. What was even more incredulous to the public was the alleged charge against them – their shop was kept open past the permitted time. The role of the magistrate in this case was also under scrutiny, considering it was a petty offense, and the accused should have been granted bail.

This case would have been swept under the carpet if not for one media outlet posting a video about this incident. People started to show outrage, which put the limelight on Police brutality. The case is still under investigation, and the accused officers have been taken into custody. People started voicing their opinions about police reforms, anti-torture laws, and many other things that need to be changed in police administration.

India has a long way to go in this field; according to a report by the National Crime Bureau, from 2001 to 2018, there were 1727 reported custodial deaths. Out of these custodial deaths, only 26 police personnel have been convicted.

During the same period, the National Human Rights Commission has recorded 2,000 human rights violations committed by police, out of which only 34 have resulted in convictions. India has a mere 5% conviction rate in custodial torture and death. Police brutality and atrocities mainly target underprivileged and poor people.

Custodial Torture: Definition and Indian Context

Torture, in the standard dictionary, refers to the act and practice of inflicting severe pain on someone as a form of punishment or to compel them to do or say something.

Custodial torture is a form of torture that generally happens when a person is alleged to have committed any crime and is under the custody of law enforcement officials. The Supreme Court has held that Custodial torture is a naked violation of human dignity and degradation, which destroys human personality to a considerable extent. Custodial torture is a punishable offense under the existing laws, but due to various reasons, the accused do not get convicted. Specific modifications in the law are required, and more critical is the appropriate implementation of existing and newly enacted laws.

Enacting a law is not the crucial step; implementing it effectively is. India has been a signatory to the United Nations Convention against Torture and other Cruel, Inhuman or Degrading Treatment or Punishment (UNCAT) since 1997. India has yet to ratify the convention due to the absence of a detailed or complete domestic law that deals with torture. In 2017, the Law Commission proposed an anti-torture law, but the government has not taken action.

The Indian Constitution has granted rights to every person under fundamental rights enshrined in Article 21, which includes the right to life, applicable to all persons, including those convicted or arrested. The Fundamental human rights cannot be taken away; additionally, Article 22 outlines the rights of people who are arrested and detained.

Human Rights Violation And Judicial/Quasi-Judicial Remedies

The data for 1990 (7 cases), 1991 (15 cases), 1992 (21 cases), and 1993 (18 cases) were reviewed, totaling 61 cases of death in police custody. Judicial inquiries, magisterial inquiries, and other relevant investigations were conducted. The compensation paid to the victims, etc., is analyzed.

In six cases, prosecution was initiated against the responsible police officers. In 52 cases, the erring Police officers are placed under suspension by the Police Department, and the concerned officers are suspended for 1 to 2 years.

Even after a Magisterial inquiry/ Judicial inquiry, there is no solace for the victim's family. For investigating incidents of deaths in police custody, a judicial commission may be appointed.

The process of establishing such a commission and completing the inquiry involves examining witnesses, collecting documents, serving summons on witnesses or agencies, and covering expenses, including salaries for the judicial officer and staff, accommodation, and allowances, requiring substantial administrative and financial support.

The government has to spend between ₹50 lakhs and ₹2 crores, depending on the period or tenure of the commission.

When examining the data of the National Human Rights Commission (NHRC) for the year 2017-2018 as a sample, 17 cases were found in which the NHRC awarded compensation for custodial deaths. Among the 17 cases, 15 cases of Custodial deaths are in Judicial Custody. In the remaining two cases, the NHRC recommended compensation of ₹1 lakh each, which is a pittance compared to the expenditure for establishing a judicial commission.

Furthermore, even after a lengthy inquiry, justice is often not truly served, and when it is, it may not be appropriate. Usually, only a recommendation for compensation is issued, but victims' families frequently encounter significant delays in receiving it. For example, in the case of G. Yerra Sailu, who died by jumping into the well at Bhanswada Police Station, Nizamabad District, during the night of September 9/10, 1986, the Andhra Pradesh government issued G.O. Ms. No. 520 on October 15, 1986. This order appointed a commission of inquiry led by Retired E.L. Bhagiratha Rao, a former Sessions Judge. The committee conducted its investigation and submitted a report with four recommendations.

In April 1987, the Hon'ble Andhra Pradesh Chief Minister presented the report to the Legislative Assembly. The inquiry commission suggested Departmental action against the Circle Inspector of Police, Bhodhan, and the S.I. of Police for sending the dead body for autopsy without waiting for the deceased's wife and relatives, and not arranging a photo of the dead body. It is further ordered to communicate with all the police officers about the necessity of the presence of relatives of the deceased before sending the body to autopsy and photographing the dead body. Now, the NHRC and the Supreme Court have provided detailed guidelines in the event of death in Custody.

Proposed Police Management Model For The Prevention Of Custodial Deaths

1. Application of Technology in Preventing Custodial Deaths through People's Participation.

The following applications should be made mandatory, widely available, and accessible to schools, workplaces, the press, and the media. By 2017, 73 crore people had Mobile/Internet connections, of whom 34 crore used smartphones. The growth of smartphone usage is expected to reach 47 crore by 2021. One can immediately report the arrest to the Police, HRC, and the Courts with photos.

Moreover, this can also be used as evidence by the prosecution or defense in their support. The accused can use these Apps to show his place of arrest and its witnesses. Police can also request local witnesses to use mobile phones to send SMS messages (which acts as a form of prosecution evidence).

The following application software is a prime example. Pressing a designated button in these applications can trigger a specific action.

1 **Bsafe** - Sends a message to a friend/police/court/or advocate.

2 **Fight Back** - Sends the GPS location and sends an SOS email.

3 **I Follow** - Generates three to four calls to already chosen numbers within five seconds.

4 **RA (Red Alert)** - Sends SMS alerts to selected contacts.

These software applications help prevent illegal arrests, detention, and HR violations, tracking different times and Places of arrest and addressing the problems faced by witnesses.

2. Prevention of Death in police remand, transit, and escape.

1 Surveillance Cameras with Audio Visual recordings and 2-way Communication in all lock-ups and detention centers with H.C., SHRC, and PCR. Custodial violence and death issues will be checked, and Human Rights will be upheld.

2 Police vans transporting under-trial prisoners should be equipped with internal and external video cameras to record audio and video, thereby reducing the risk of escapes

and ensuring police accountability in cases of alleged fake encounters.

3 The journey from jail to court and back is to be recorded in its entirety.

4 Network chart

5 PS to NHRC

6 Police Reporting on Arrest–Format/Template

7 PS-wise–violations and detention

8 Countrywide–releases.

9 GPS on vehicles.

3. Organogram - Police Management - Remedies:

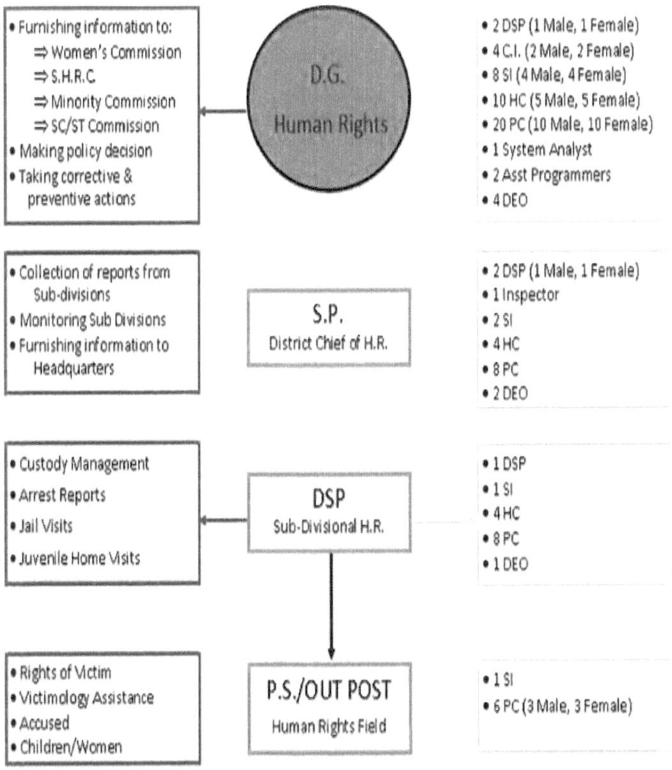

Figure 4.1 Organogram–Police Management - Remedies

Source: Proposed Model by the Researcher

Figure 4.1 shows the designed organogram of the hierarchy and responsibilities of personnel at different levels for handling and custodial management. The remedies suggested are as follows.

4. Training Activities for the Staff Members

All responsible officers must receive proper training, which includes refresher courses, specialized sessions, and periodic visits to prisons, hospitals, police stations, and courts. This training should also encompass report writing, photography, computer and mobile phone use, as well as communication skills. For example, a department administrator who deliberately fails to provide training in a specific area, thereby violating an individual's constitutional rights, is accountable. Therefore, officers should undergo regularly scheduled training that aligns with their duties, ensuring ongoing and consistent professional development.

Regular officer training fulfills the court's holding in Canton and is a viable risk management strategy. It can be instrumental in improving officer performance, increasing skill proficiency, directing officer decision-making, enhancing officer safety, reducing job risks, and defending against lawsuits.

The following areas should be considered when determining the training to provide to police officers on custodial deaths.

1. If policies and procedures are updated, officers should receive training on the changes, including any adjustments to legal responsibilities related to the use of force, relevant case law, and liability issues.
2. Training should be related to high-risk incidents such as mentally impaired cases and sudden deaths in police custody.
3. Training should also focus on officer evaluation of behaviors, including bizarre and agitated behaviors,

meaningless actions, fleeing from officers, and violent behaviors toward officers.

4. Police officers should be trained to assess the health conditions of individuals after restraining them, monitoring the subject's condition by inspecting for physical and physiological distress, which can assist the officer in making informed healthcare decisions.
5. Training should be provided on the reasonable use of force measures. The training should include verbal instructions, empty-hand soft control methods, application of restraints, limited invasive weapons and equipment, and the use of lethal force.
6. Team take-down control systems by officers should be taught in training to implement proper coordination and control strategies, as suggested by several researchers earlier (Beck et al., 2001; Siddle, 1996; Krosch et al., 1992). Many custodial deaths occur in a violent restraint, so properly using authorized restraining equipment and monitoring after a violent encounter is essential.
7. Officers should be trained in the use of appropriate methods and vehicles for transporting detainees safely and effectively. Reports suggested possible custodial deaths occurred during transport, as in the recent **Ongole incident** in August 2020.

a. The details of the Ongole incident are as follows: Dasari Malyadri, 59 years, Scheduled Caste, Nelaturu (v), Muttukuru Mandal, Nellore district, committed suicide by falling under an unknown running train and died on the spot. During the investigation, it became apparent that Mr. Narahari, a retired Additional Superintendent of

Police, had lent money to the deceased. As the deceased failed to repay the loan, Narahari influenced Inspector Lakshman of Ongole Taluka PS to recover the loan from Dasari Malyadri. Malyadri was brought to the police station and harassed for repayment of the loan to Mr. Narahari. It is a civil dispute, and the police do not need to involve themselves. Because of Police involvement, Dasari Malyadri committed suicide. The accused, Narahari, a retired Additional Superintendent of Police, was arrested and sent for judicial remand.

b. Training should be provided on the transportation policy, type of vehicle, number, and responsibilities of officers involved during transport, location, directions of the carrier, special precautions, medical facilities, and Audio-Video recording facilities.

c. Departmental investigators should also be trained on case law, techniques and equipment, departmental policies, witness interview methods, assessing officers' conduct, officer reports, and evaluating medical documents during custodial death investigations.

Training should be focused on the following issues:

1. Recruitment–Induction Training
2. Midterm Training, Refresher Courses
3. Specialized training
4. Visits to Jails, Hospitals, Police Stations, Courts
5. Report writing
6. Photography
7. Computers/Mobile Phones
8. Communication

Training that focuses on officer assessment of behaviors may include noting bizarre and agitated behaviors, purposeless actions, running from officers, violently resisting or attacking officers, shouting, exhibiting a high threshold to pain, nude, partially clothed, or disrobing, showing extreme strength, hallucinations, actions or statements of paranoia, and quickly moving from combative to tranquil behavior.

Administrators should provide training for supervisors regarding their responsibilities in responding to or directing officers while controlling and restraining an individual. Furthermore, training for departmental investigators should be conducted. Such activity may include death investigations, use-of-force techniques, equipment, applicable departmental policies, witness interview skills, use-of-force case law, officer conduct assessment, officer reports, medical documents and evaluations, and symptomologies associated with sudden custodial deaths.

Although officer training provides an essential ingredient in correctly applying force and other associated topic areas, it will not prevent all sudden custodial deaths. The health condition and drug abuse lifestyle may be the primary cause of death of those who have died after a violent struggle with officers.

The objective of the training is to equip officers with practical methods, response options, and appropriate equipment to maximize the safety of both officers and subjects, while also enhancing their skill proficiency to best respond to the unpredictable nature and rapidly evolving circumstances they may encounter. Maintaining a commitment to training in this subject matter will enable officers to make informed decisions and respond appropriately.

5. Psychological assumptions

a. **Crime Detection Course** - Before posting training in the academy on Interrogation Techniques, those who pass are added to a list and are then chosen for the assignment.

b. **Psychological assessment**

c. **Medical assessment**

d. Depending on the case's needs, intensive interviews, behavioral analysis, forensic statement analysis, layered voice analysis, Video statement analysis (micro level), Brain Fingerprinting, Polygraph, psychological evaluation, forensic hypnosis, Traditional interrogation methods, and cognitive interviewing techniques are employed.

Anything that prevents police from resorting to the third degree or conducting further investigation must be explored and documented.

6. Proposed model lock-up with a toilet attached

The Model lock-up room should be designed to be self-sufficient, with an attached toilet featuring a short privacy wall for nature calls, separating the two.

High ventilation doors with no provision for hanging should be provided. No access to the store room with clothes and wires.

Must have proper exterior illumination, with switches located outside. Once in custody, they should be in shorts and T-shirts only, which are flimsy and cannot support the detainee's weight.

No projections, grills, exposed pipes, or bars should be accessible. Bars should be covered with fine wire mesh or stretch-resistant polycarbonate glazing. Cells designated for accommodating a person at risk should be constructed to facilitate continuous observation of the occupant. Cells should have windows with a view to the outside, not to jeopardize perceptual orientation and normal thought processes.

Furniture, bedding, and other materials made available to persons should be made of fire-retardant material, which will not emit toxic fumes when ignited. Blankets and sheets should be made of material that tears under body weight to prevent their use in suicide attempts. Smoke detectors should be installed in each facility, with an audible alarm to a constantly manned control center. First Aid, resuscitation equipment, and cell keys should be readily available to custodial officers. Cells should be painted in a light pastel color with non-flammable paint.

For Women, there shall be a complete women's lock-up in each Police Station. They should be appropriately clothed. The toilet walls should be covered and have more height than the male lock-up, and be arranged so that the women detainee is not visible to outsiders while attending to nature's calls.

Although the model lock-up is designed in this manner, the custody period of any arrested accused with the Police will usually be 24 hours, as per Section 167 Cr.PC. If the investigation is not completed within 24 hours, the individual will invariably be required to appear before the court. However, when the court sanctions Police custody, the Model lock-up will be very helpful.

Risk minimization management strategies:

1. Implementing police training regarding caring for people in custody.
2. Scientific & Psychological bound graded interrogation techniques.
3. Reviewing lockup design and surroundings.

4. D.K. Basu's norms compliance and Arnesh Kumar Vs Bihar Compliance.
5. 24/7 medical checkup: list all parameters and prepare a template.
6. Transportation means are equipped with audio-visual aids and utilize video conferencing to facilitate remand extensions as mandated by law.
7. A notification should be issued in the Gazette to re-designate the Additional Director General (ADG), Legal, as the State Custody Supervising Officer—ADG (Legal and Human Rights). At the district level, officers of the rank of Deputy Superintendent of Police (DSP) should be appointed for each district, assisted by one male and one female Sub-Inspector (SI), four Police Constables (PC), four Women Police Constables (WPC), and eight Home Guards (HG).

A decision-making model for liability in custodial deaths has been designed and recommended for future action (Figure 4.2).

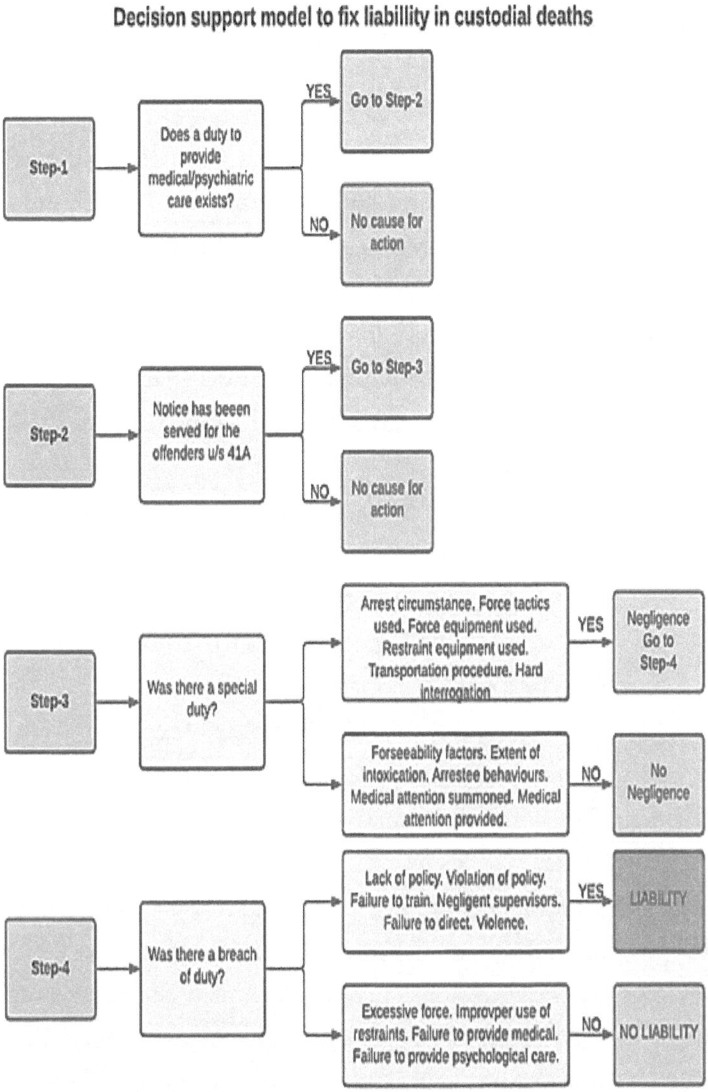

Figure 4.2: Decision-making model for liability of custodial deaths

Source: Proposed Model by the Researcher

7. Administrative implications

The complexity and importance of custodial deaths have created several administrative implications for law enforcement agencies, trainers, and officers. Deficiencies in training, policy, or lack of proper equipment result in improper handling of restraint situations.

Due to the subject's diversity and the numerous factors involved in these encounters, officers require guidance to ensure they are adhering to their agency's use-of-force training, policies, and relevant case law decisions.

This will help them make informed and justifiable decisions in determining the appropriate course of action in various situations.

8. Adopting a risk management approach to reduce custodial deaths

Generally, incidents of sudden (in-custody) deaths are based on the following broad areas:

1. The type and degree of force/ restraint measures used.
2. The medical or psychological factors associated with the death of the subject.
3. The medical care provided by police officers.
4. The method of transportation used for the accused.
5. The conducive material support and environment available

It is recommended that a risk management perspective be adopted in building a "use-of-force management system". This involves assessing previous encounters to plan and reduce future such events. Risk management encompasses fundamental managerial functions, including planning, organizing, controlling, budgeting, staffing, allocating resources, reporting, and evaluation.

Risk management is an ongoing process that involves incident investigation, job evaluation, risk exposure identification, forecasting, resource allocation, and risk mitigation. It encompasses reduction and prevention, policy development and implementation, training, operational monitoring, and assessment. While it cannot eliminate all job risks, it helps control costs, reduce losses, and defend against legal issues.

The following stages are proposed in Risk Management.

1. **Incident analysis:** Analyze case study analyses of previous incidents and case decisions involving custodial deaths, focusing on the medical factors associated with these deaths. Their systematic documentation will be helpful.
2. **Policy development:** There is a need to develop or revise a departmental policy to address the issue of the use of force. The components of policy development can include: medical care, transportation, and custody. Procedures should be developed that (a) describe the methods for performing an arrest operation and (b) identify the responsible personnel for acting. A broadly written use-of-force policy will help in decision-making and authorizing measures that will reduce allegations of excessive force, brutality, and wrongful custodial deaths---the policy guides the development of a training tool. A policy or procedure must confine to the four 'C's: Current, Comprehensive, Consistent, and Constitutional.
3. **Planning:** The investigation of the Law and Order load at the police station should be taken into account, and accordingly, the workforce budget should be planned, considering the annual calendar of events.
4. **Organizing:** The officer-in-charge should organize classes and refresher courses and assign the right personnel to the right job.

5. **Controlling:** The state and subdivision level control room should monitor every arrest and document it by all processes and procedures established by law, duly complying with the DK Basu guidelines and the Arnesh Kumar Judgment. The lockups with AV cameras must be activated, and the responses of the accused must be recorded twice daily. Similarly, audio and video must be monitored during transportation, and the accused's responses must be recorded twice daily. Additionally, when interrogating offenses and their detection, the AV facility must be used in the presence of a lawyer whom Police Officials can call upon in court to exculpate themselves or incriminate the accused. The court should give custody only to the custody-compliant police station and the team of policemen, and not to everyone.
6. **Budgeting:** An adequate budget should be allocated for the following expenses: feeding charges for suspects, men on duty, AMC for gadgets, AV and control room power backup, etc., as well as transportation facilities with fuel expenses and electrical charges.
7. **Staffing:** Well-trained staff should be assigned to monitor the control room at the Sub-Division/State Level, with a reasonable span of control, well-established alerts, and a communication system in place from PS/transport vehicles to control rooms, staffed by trained personnel. Custodial interrogation staff should be well-trained in domain knowledge and familiar with graded approaches and techniques, medically and psychologically fit, and qualified to handle individuals in custody, including those who require monitoring, handling, and interrogation.

8. Graded Approach to Interrogation Procedures.

A graded approach to interrogation is recommended, as illustrated in Figure 4.3.

Depending on the case's needs, intensive interviews, behavioral analysis, forensic statement analysis, layered voice analysis, psychological evaluation, and forensic hypnosis and cognitive interviewing techniques are employed.

1. Forensic written statement analysis.
2. Video statement analysis–micro level.
3. Brain Finger Printing.
4. Polygraph.
5. Voice analysis.
6. Traditional interrogation methods – guile and graft.

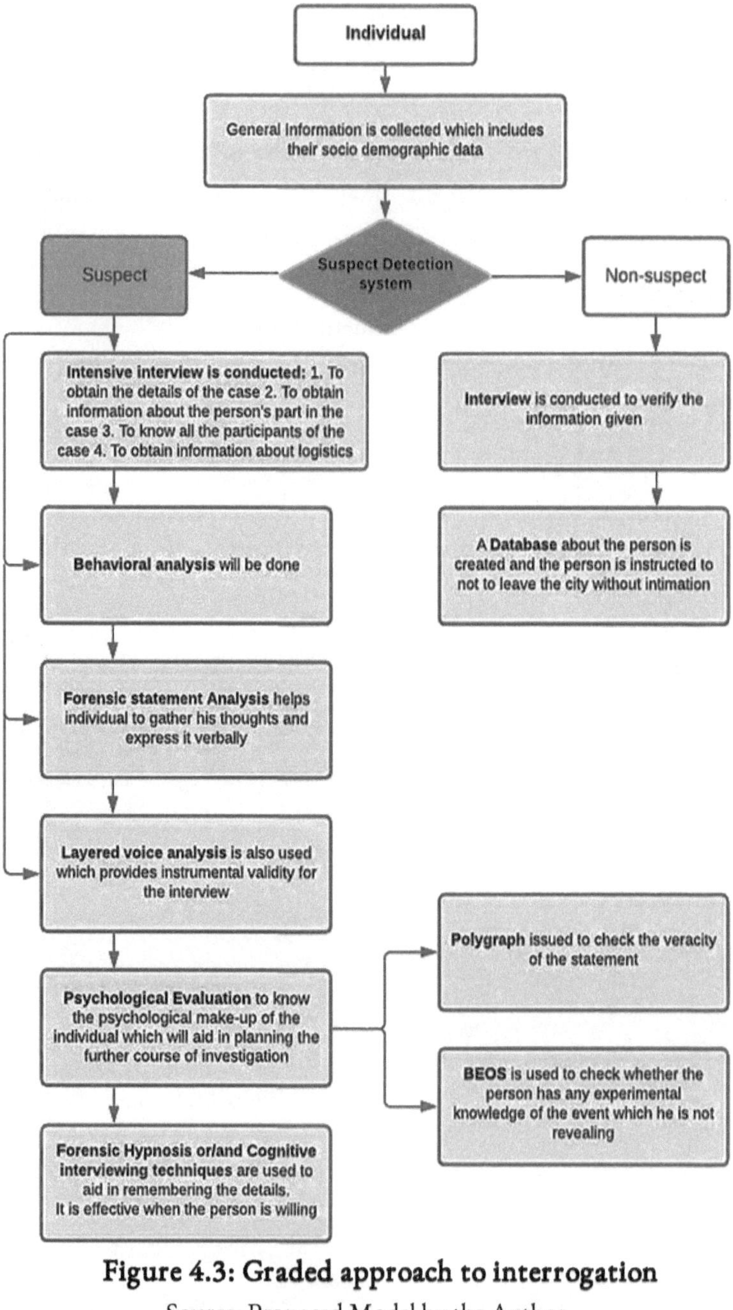

Figure 4.3: Graded approach to interrogation

Source: Proposed Model by the Author

1. Gestured D contempt, others bilateral.
2. No definitive evidence of torture marks.

Errece Meeddox, an army staff sergeant whose interrogations in Iraq ultimately led to the capture of Saddam Hussein.

Arrests: In America (756), the highest number of arrests is made, followed by China and Russia (629). India stands 5th with 33 people every 100,000 (International Centre for Prison Studies).

Technology is one of the few arms left in the arsenal of a poor investigation against the hardcore terrorists, wherein we must crack.

The Abhaya Nun case in Kerala, wherein brain mapping was done. This will wean police away from the use of 3rd degrees. Anything that keeps police away from the temptation to resort to third-degree tactics and which may reveal something on which further investigation can proceed must be explored and documented.

9. Shared leadership and police (Wuestewald, Oklahoma)

Police administration gravitated toward a military orientation during intense reform early in the 20th century. A paramilitary police model evolved in response to widespread corruption and political interference that threatened the credibility of U.S. police. In a drive to instill discipline, leaders seized the authoritarian hierarchy as a bulwark against political cooptation and low-level corruption. The scientific and bureaucratic management principles of Frederick Taylor and Max Weber were in vogue and found welcome application in the drive to professionalize law enforcement.

Even today, this management philosophy persists, perhaps understandably. After all, control-oriented supervision succeeded in bringing professionalism to police in the U.S.

Many administrators remain protective of this progress and are suspicious of calls for officer autonomy and empowerment. In the face of ongoing scandals and charges of inequity, police administrators tend to maintain an almost phobic preoccupation with accountability and conformity. However, control-oriented approaches must recognize that police work has always been highly discretionary.

10. Controlling police discretion

The fundamental paradox of police hierarchy is that discretionary authority tends to be greatest at the bottom of the police organization. This is where patrol officers apply laws, policies, and regulations to situations that require a precise fit within the rulebook. Furthermore, these discretionary choices are made in the field, removed from direct management scrutiny. It may be self-deceptive to place a great deal of faith in authoritarian management styles.

National umbrella organizations tend to advocate adversarial tactics that rely on formal, legal redress of grievances. Police unions have also become increasingly political, endorsing and actively campaigning for local, state, and federal candidates.

Researchers have found that police unions can significantly influence the role of police. Associations tend to emphasize law enforcement functions over service delivery. They have also experienced considerable success in preserving officers' discretionary authority. Some researchers and union officials emphasize that buy-in from unions is crucial to community policing initiatives, as they wield considerable veto power.

Risk control strategies:

The proposed risk-control strategies are risk avoidance, risk transfer, loss prevention, loss reduction, resource segregation, and training.

1. **Risk avoidance** involves avoiding an action. For example, the police department may provide an escort vehicle based on safety concerns, medical instability, or the absence of an arrest.
2. **Risk transfer** involves transferring a task or risk from one party to another. In policing, this may include transporting a mentally impaired arrestee to a hospital for psychiatric evaluation and health clearance before sending them to jail. E.g., Ongole incident (Cr. No.388/2020, u/s 306 IPC r/w Sec. 3(1)(r)(s) of SC and ST (Prevention of Atrocities Act of Ongole Taluka PS).
3. **Loss prevention** aims to reduce the frequency of events that cause losses. This involves establishing and implementing departmental policies and procedures, conducting in-service training, maintaining equipment and vehicles, providing vehicles with protective screens, maintaining functional observation cells and closed-circuit cameras in cells, and conducting security checks.
4. **Loss reduction** differs from loss prevention in that it aims to minimize the likelihood of a loss occurring. Examples are admission practices, screening detainees regarding medical and psychological needs, and maintaining access to health, which reduces the frequency of custodial deaths.
5. **Segregating resources** can include maintaining backup equipment, such as restraint devices, other force equipment, and backup vehicles, where possible.

Implementation of risk strategies

It should consist of supervisors managing the implementation of strategies by line officers. Supervisors should visit the field at the station level regularly and work alongside officers to protect police officers' liability.

Monitoring and assessing risk control: Supervisory officers should monitor the progress of risk-control strategies. Monitoring is achieved through several methods, including field visits, review of reports, analysis of use-of-force incidents, examination of detainee and citizen complaints, video footage, and officers' training.

Outcome

The following outcomes can be expected with the above-proposed risk management strategies.

1. Officers safety can be enhanced.
2. Enhance employee performance and agency operations.
3. Decrease citizen complaints and detainee grievances.
4. Incident analysis can enhance the performance and optimization of the police force for use in a specific restraint process.
5. This type of officer training can improve officer and detainee safety, enhance decision-making, and increase organizational effectiveness.
6. Police departments and officers can be in a defensible position against claims of liability and possible misconduct. Adopting a proper risk management strategy can minimize the risk of custodial deaths and liability, potential misconduct of police officers, and improve the efficient execution of the custodial process.

Policy development recommendations

The following actions are recommended for drafting future policy revisions: a framework to guide officers in making decisions on the use of force.

1. **Policy statement:** The first step proposed is to frame a Policy Statement that clearly describes the policy's objectives and purpose.
2. **Definitions:** This section should include various definitions, such as resistance, control, reasonable force, lethal force, vehicles as a form of force, custodial death, restraint stress, and other relevant terms.
3. **Statutory language:** This section should comprise the language of state laws and the constitution.
4. **Resistance types:** This section should identify the various types of resistance, including psychological, verbal, passive, and defensive resistance, as well as active aggression and force-based resistance.
5. **Levels of officer force/ control:** This section should consist of options for officer control and be divided into four types:
6. Less lethal force options include using verbal commands and empty hands.
7. Use of restraints, such as handcuffs, leg-restraints, flex-cuffs, and soft-restraints,
8. intermediate use of weapons, which include aerosols, rubber bullet guns, tear gas guns, water cannons, and flashlights.
9. Lethal force should be specified as the final stage.
10. **Team control system:** Three to five police officers should discuss violent restraint confrontation and define each

officer's responsibility for restraining and controlling the subject.

11. **Variables influencing the use of force:** Variables that should be evaluated include the number of subjects, reaction time, the subject's strength, age, and sex, evolving issues, backup availability, and the officer's perception. The principles of escalation and de-escalation, the totality of circumstances, and the 1+1 theory should be addressed.
12. **Response to a subject showing strange behaviors:** Based on the subject's violent or bizarre behavior, police officers should consider proper solutions for control, restraint, transportation, and medical care.
13. **Use-of-force during medical examination:** Proper force should be used during medical interventions because a detainee or prisoner exhibits self-harming behaviors and refuses to cooperate with healthcare personnel.
14. **Monitoring the restrained subject:** This section should discuss monitoring procedures of restrained subjects after a violent use-of-force encounter, which describes the subject's physical, physiological, verbal, and psychological actions/signs.
15. **Medical concerns:** This section should identify an officer responsible for summoning emergency medical care personnel to the crime scene.
16. **Transportation procedures:** These should outline how the detainee is to be transported and in what type of vehicle. The procedures to be taken during transport are to be addressed.
17. **Investigation on force incidents:** In this section, the type of incidents that prompt an internal/external

investigation, including addressing the responsibilities of officers and supervisors involved in the incident.

The above 13 sections outline the suggested policy measures that risk managers should implement when addressing the use of force and officers' responses. While developing the force policy, administrators are expected to review state standards, expert standards, model policies, input from the legal department, the training curriculum for use of force, and past literature research on custodial deaths. Risk managers for the agency and the legal department should also be consulted. There is no ideal method for addressing this topic. The primary purpose of these recommendations is to ensure that the subject matter is addressed and to provide a framework for determining an appropriate response based on the circumstances officers and supervisors face.

The policy drafts should be disseminated to all officers, and periodic training should be provided.

Considerations on sudden custodial death investigation

In the event of a custodial death investigation, the questions range from the cause of death, use of force by officers that contributed to death, and the responsible officer for the death. \As several factors are involved in custodial deaths, it is difficult to conclude on this issue. Therefore, a thorough incident investigation, which the police department should conduct, is always recommended.

Police and detention agencies should improve and revise existing policies for performing custodial death investigations.

1. The agency should evaluate the standards and laws governing the conduct of investigations.

2. An internal investigation must be conducted by the department head as required by law.
3. Proper training should be given to public relations officers to handle the press and media.
4. If a custodial death has occurred, the investigators should be advised to perform an adequate investigation and submit detailed reports as described earlier.
5. An assigned officer should attend the autopsy, as this is of utmost importance, and report the details mentioned in the recommendations.
6. Investigators should conduct an extensive background investigation of the incident reported by Lawrence (2004), such as family, employment, medical, and behavioral history.
7. The investigator should submit a thorough report of findings that includes the names of the officers involved in the incident, statements and interviews of witnesses, medical and legal reports, photographs, videos, and audio recordings.

The investigator should not suggest any recommendations on the incident. The report must be submitted to a proper department official for further review and action. The checklist for investigators is designed and summarized in Table 4.1.

Parameter	Action to be taken
On scene	• Scene briefing and walk through
	• Photographs, drawings, videos, and measurements
	• Collecting/securing evidence as per law
	• Officer and witness statements/interviews
	• Environmental conditions

Documentation	• List and storage of evidence
	• List of officers/witnesses/statements/interviews
	• Officers reports
	• Appropriate policies
	• Use-of-force training
	• List of force equipment employed
	• Drafting time-line of events
	• Emergency medical and Autopsy reports (on scene/athospital)
	• Toxicology, histology, and serology reports
	• Press and Media coverage
	• Communication tapes, incident/video produced
	• Duty shift records for officers involved
	• Prosecutor's report
	• Proper documentation of investigation
Decedent History	• Family
	• Residential
	• Employment
	• Employment
	• Arrest/convictions/imprisonment
Police Intervention	• Nature of contact
	• Behaviors/statements of the decedent
	• Actions of the decedent
	• Officers verbal instructions
	• Officers use of empty-hand control techniques
	• Officers use of aerosols
	• Officers use of intermediate weapons
	• Officers use of restraints
	• Officers use of lethal force
	• Officers summon supervisors/investigators

	• Position of decedent after restraint
	• Behaviors of decedent after restraint
	• Decontaminate procedures used
	• First aid rendered by officers
	• Officers summon emergency medical care
	• Monitoring restrained subject by officers
	• How summoned to scene
	• Time stamps of emergency medical on scene
Medical Care intervention	• Medical care assessment
	• Actions of emergency medical on scene
	• Police vehicle
	• Medical vehicle/Medical care
Transport	• Location/duration of transport
	• Transported in restraints
	• Position in vehicle
	• Number of officers in police transport
	• Officers monitor subject during transport
	• Decedent behaviors/statements during transport
	• Behaviors and statements at hospital
	• Medical care given
Hospital Care	• Attending health care personnel
	• Length of stay at hospital
	• Interview/statements/reports of health care people
	• Time stamp, performed by whom
	• Photos taken
Autopsy	• Autopsy report
	• Toxicology, Histology, Serology reports
	• Cause and manner of death

Table 4.1: Checklist for investigators on custodial deaths

Source: Primary Data

Transportation procedures

This section addresses the transportation of the restrained subject and the type of vehicle to be used. Each case will present different variables for officers to consider, and the policy should allow for discretion in officer and supervisor decision-making. If emergency medical care is required during transportation to the hospital, an officer should accompany the subject, and another officer should follow in a patrol unit.

If officers transport the arrestee, a description of how the restrained subject is to be transported, the number of officers required for performing the transport, monitoring procedures to be used during transport, method of restraint, direction for considering transporting to a hospital, directions for transporting physically or mentally impaired persons, and instructions on how to radio ahead to the hospital or detention center should be described. Special transport situations should also be included.

Officers should be trained in the proper methods and vehicles for transporting arrestees and detainees. Since some sudden custodial deaths have occurred during transport, appropriate training should be designed to address this issue.

This area contains numerous variables to consider, and training should encompass the contents of the transportation policy, including the type of transportation, the number of officers required for transport, the transport location, the use of seatbelts, the special needs of arrestees, and the type of vehicle used.

Training that addresses emergency medical personnel and transport should also be performed.

Reporting use of force

This section explains the minimum details that responding officers should include when submitting a report detailing their involvement in the incident.

a. A description of the nature of the incident.
b. An assessment and observation of the officers, including all behaviors, verbalizations, and types of resistance the subject displayed.
c. A description of any weapons used by the subject.
d. Officer actions in the confrontation, including the number of officers who responded, calling for back-up/ supervisors, verbal instructions, physical control methods attempted/used, intermediate weapons attempted/used, and lethal force measures used (if any).
e. The type of restraints used and how they were applied
f. Condition of the subject after restraint and monitoring procedures are used
g. First aid/ life-saving techniques used by officers.
h. Summoning of emergency medical care personnel and their arrival.
i. Decontamination procedures used (if any).
j. Transportation procedures used.

Investigation of force incidents

This section outlines incidents that may trigger investigations and outlines the responsibilities of officers. The suggested policy should include these minimum sections, with administrators also reviewing relevant standards, policies, case law, legal input, training materials, literature on the use of force, and research on custodial deaths. Consult risk managers and the legal department.

Other Considerations

Critical Incident Interrogation

An incident interrogation involving officers should be conducted as early as possible by a team of trained professionals. Agency administrators should not be involved in this process for unbiased results.

The objective is to provide a systematic debriefing for accused officers to discuss their feelings and emotions.

Final Incident Review

Administrators should conduct a final incident review and appraisal once the investigation is finished. The purpose of the meeting is not to engage in fault-finding but to constructively assess the incident and response so that they work towards reducing the possibility of such incidents in the future. Officers, investigators, supervisors, trainers, medical personnel, and other relevant personnel should be included in the assessment review process. Recommendations should be clearly defined and documented, and efforts should be made to make the necessary changes.

Untapped potential for privatization/ outsourcing of police services

Is there an untapped potential for the privatization/ outsourcing of police services in AP?

The various Police Commissions at the national and state levels do not recognize the potential of outsourcing police services or consider it necessary. Even civilianization is not recognized as an alternative to large-scale police recruitment in situations of financial constraints.

Experiments with volunteers have been sporadic and limited in scope. In A P, the Home Guards serve as an adjunct to the regular police force in times of special need, such as civil unrest or natural disasters. No doubt, in AP, human (e.g., experts) and non-material (such as vehicles and photocopiers) resources have been outsourced, but not on a planned or large scale.

Forensic science services are provided by civilians within the government system. The possibility of encouraging the private sector to provide these security services has yet to be explored. In other countries (e.g., Australia), sometimes a conscious decision is made to outsource certain functions to boost the regional economy, especially by encouraging new investment and creating new employment potential.

At the same time, and very rightly, there is a growing concern, as well as within the police system, that police forces are increasingly diverting their resources to non-core functions while failing to meet the public's expectations regarding their core responsibilities.

Experience shows that police jurisdiction in AP (and the country) has followed the contours of an ever-widening circle. The AP Police Commission pointed out in 1984 that the police functioned under at least 124 Acts, many of which were long outdated.

Even now, they are said to be acting under at least a hundred central and state enactments about both original and concurrent legislation. The burden of much of the social legislation dealing with offenses against the scheduled castes, dowry deaths, etc., has fallen on the police.

Matters that should be dealt with by other authorities (including social scientists and civil society), such as copying in examinations and anti-ragging measures, have begun to take up the limited resources of the police. Even leaving aside the Acts, the police have traditionally been intervening in issues related to drugs, civil property, marriage, etc. They have been involved in the work of other government departments, including excise, transport, forests, and electricity. A colonial Act designed to maintain peace in predominantly rural India has remained in effect for nearly 150 years.

There is thus a clear need to limit and redefine the role and responsibilities of the police. For this, it may be necessary to carry out amendments to the Police Act and the Criminal Procedure Code. Recognizing that police reform is long overdue, yet also acknowledging that some of the recommendations from the Police Commissions/Committees may be too radical for political compliance, it seems desirable to assess what can be done to improve matters, even within the constraints of the existing system.

Some possibilities appear to be:

1. Support services—such as driving and maintaining police vehicles, operating police wireless communications, managing police computer systems, and conducting forensic examinations of cases and evidence—can be carried out by non-uniformed personnel, under their respective pay scales.
2. Similar to practices in countries like Singapore, traffic regulatory personnel operating in public spaces—such as supermarkets, railway stations, and airports—can be designated as "policemen" for the limited purpose of regulating parking and traffic and imposing and collecting fines. This designation could be implemented under the existing legal framework.

3. Instead of setting up and training separate police forces such as the SPF (Special Protection Force) (e.g.) to guard power stations, the Secretariat, etc., non-police personnel (with only the top brass remaining police officers) could be trained for security duties and paid for by the client organization.
4. Retired police or defense personnel could be specially trained and issued a certificate of competence. Based on this certification, they could be employed for security duties—after proper vetting by the police—and authorized to carry arms while on duty. This would help free regular police personnel to focus on more pressing and "core" responsibilities.
5. A similar system could be implemented for general traffic patrol, traffic control, and other related functions. Such personnel could be designated as "special" police officers.
6. There is no need for personal security officers to be police officers. Security duty is a specialized one. In the US, the Executive Protection Wing comprises specially recruited and trained sharpshooters. Along the same lines, security guards can be specially recruited and trained to provide security to executive personnel, thereby amending the law to authorize them to carry weapons and to withdraw police from such non-core duties.
7. As in most of the world, airport security can be left to specialized private agencies.
8. The provision and monitoring of CCTVs and alarms (wherever these are installed), along with modern communication equipment, can generally be left to specialized private agencies.

9. There are new areas for the use of civilian personnel within the police force, such as prisoner processing, completing various forms, and other administrative tasks, as well as staffing control rooms. Prisoner escort services, among other tasks, can and should be handled by non-police personnel.

Quality Management Issues in Police Organizations

Quality management is a neglected area in India. Any quality improvement project requires the measurement of key performance indicators, but we do not see such a rigorous quantitative approach here. Some countries, like Japan, have been fortunate to have had legendary leaders, such as Edward Deming, leading the quality movement.

Apart from Six Sigma, the Capability Maturity Model (CMM) has been widely adopted in the Indian IT industry (Gallagher, 2002). Indian police could formally adopt either of the two approaches and train hundreds of police officials to be the champions for quality in police work.

The Capability Maturity Model (CMM) for Police organizations has been designed and summarized in Table 4.2. A key Supreme Court judgment held that involuntarily subjecting an accused, suspect, or witness to narco-analysis, brain-mapping, or polygraph tests violates Article 20(3) of the Constitution, which protects against self-incrimination. Even when the subject has given consent to undergo any of these tests, the test results by themselves cannot be admitted as evidence because the subject does not exercise conscious control over the responses during the administration of the test.

However, any information or material subsequently discovered with the help of voluntarily administered test results can be admitted, under Section 27 of the Evidence Act, 1872.

Polygraph	Narco Analysis	Brain Mapping
Interrogating while measuring physiological changes	Drug-induced method	Non-intrusive
Interrogating with a Standardized Questionnaire	Medical intrusion needed	Brainwave graphs provide information about the brain
BP, Pulse, EEG, GSR, VSA analyzed	The subject was made to speak in a trance	Confirms if specific information is available in the brain
Physiological changes of involuntary processes measured	Age, Sex, and health of the subject determine the drug dose	Does not confirm how information is stored in the brain
Least reliable in deception detection	Age, Sex, and health of the subject determine the drug dose	Most reliable in deception detection

Table 4.2: Capability Maturity Model (CMM) for Police

Source: Proposed Model

None of the top executive/police officials will accept implementing torture. It is observed that generally, it is the subordinate staff who are tasked with implementing the process. For the country's security, someone can be authorized by law to sign a warrant of interrogation to have a suspect tortured to extract information. He has to justify this warrant before the court.

The country's security was linked to the ticking bomb theory for interrogation, e.g., the USA.

The Supreme Court of India issued strict guidelines and amended the police's power regarding arrests.

It became mandatory to maintain transparency in arrests, inform the public, and keep records for each detention. However, in 1977, there were 80 deaths, whereas in 2007, 118 deaths took place, which shows an increase instead of a decrease.

International conventions do not become law in a country even if that country has ratified them. Legislation has to frame laws to bring them into force precisely. A convention is based on mutual consent and willingness, and can be withdrawn or modified as needed. Each generation has the right to determine the law under which it lives; the earth belongs to the living, and the dead have neither powers nor rights.

Predicting the potential risk

The study observes that problems related to individual, institutional, and legal aspects contribute to custodial deaths. Hence, a method to minimize lapses and reduce custodial deaths in Andhra Pradesh is needed. The method so developed will also help improve the standards and performance of police stations through self-evaluation.

All Universities worldwide, as well as many schools in the United States and Europe, are accredited based on performance indicators. In India, the National Assessment and Accreditation Council (NAAC), an autonomous body under UGC, provides ratings for all higher educational institutions.

Such ratings for police stations will help improve their conditions by implementing best practices.

They facilitate self-evaluation and accountability. Every police station will strive to improve its ratings through healthy competition. This also allows the Police Department to make policy decisions and allocate funding accordingly.

There must be an autonomous organization to evaluate the performance of police stations and individual officers periodically on various parameters.

Such an organization is responsible for evaluating, assessing, and accrediting every police station and individual officer under its control. The rating must be given according to criteria based on well-defined indicators. These ratings can be used to determine whether the victim should be handed over to the custody of a specific police officer at a particular police station.

Parameter	Name of the country									
	Norway	**Ghana**	**Sweden**	**U.K.**	**Croatia**	**Philippines**	**Denmark**	**USA**	**Russia**	**Slovenia**
Name of the Police Officer interviewed	Rolf Anton Groos	Felix	Ralph Gloven	Nick Robertson	Ms. Cornelia	Fitz Macariola	Frank Denz	John Heidke	Viktor Kostenko	Broajnik Matej
Rank	Inspector	Inspector	Sr. Inspector	Inspector	Inspector	Sub Inspector	Sub Inspector	Spl Agent FBI	SP	Inspector
Whether there is occurrence of custodial death in the country or not.	Yes, Few	Yes, 2 to 3 per year	Yes	Yes. Few	No	Yes	No	Yes	Yes, Few	No
Cause of death	Suicide	Torture Suicide Severe beating to death by police	Hanging in custody Drugs Alcoholic	Suicide and medical	Mental depression–suicide	Torture and medical	Suicide	Medical/ Suicide/Firing	Torture and medical	Medical
Whether Use of force applied during interrogation	No Interrogation–talking only	Yes, in some cases. Murderer, Armed robberer.	No	No interrogation except in very specific case	Minimal force	No	Minimal force	Not allowed	Yes	Minimal force
Type of record of interrogation, ifany	Audio/Video	Written	Audio/Video	Audio/Video	Audio/Video	Written	Audio/Video	Written and Audio/Video	Written and Audio/Video	Written
Whether interview room available ornot	Yes	No	Yes	Yes	Yes	No	Yes	FBI-Yes, Others-No	Yes	No
Action againsterring officers	Internal investigation ordered Criminal common case	Internal investigation, prosecuted criminally also	Investigator prosecuted Internal investigation	Internal affairs criminality case	Criminal cases Internal investigation	Criminal Case, Internal Investigation	Criminal Case, Internal Investigation	Suspension / Criminal Investigation / internal investigation	Internal investigation ordered Criminal common case	Disciplinary/ criminal
Whether property offences are there or not	Yes	Yes, common	Yes	Yes	Yes	Yes	Yes	Yes	Yes	Yes
What is the percentage of detection	40%	50%	60%	47 %	50%	50%	50%	40%	20%	40%

What is the percentage of recovery	30%	45%	20 %	40%	35%	50%	30%	50%	50%	40%
Senior officers pressure	No	Yes	No	Yes	No	Yes	No	No		Yes
Role of the prosecutor in CJS	Decides to prosecute the accused	Presents the case in court	Head of the case Presents case in the court	Whether to prosecute ornot. No permissionto arrest	Guides, whether to charge or not	Gives legal opinion	Charge or not	Works and present	Gives legal opinion	Decide whether to charge based onevidence
Qualification for a policeman (Constable)	Higher secondary	Secondary School, 18 years	9 yrs schooling/ 20yrs age 13 yrs of school/ 25 yage 1 yr. military service compulsory for males	Higher secondary	High School, 4years Academy	Secondary	Higher secondary	Higher secondary	20 Yrs & High School	Higher secondary
Performance appraised	No	Yes	No	No	Yes	Yes	Yes	Yes	Yes	Yes
Period of detention	48 hrs.	48 hrs.	4 days	24 hrs.	24 hrs.	24 hrs.	24 hrs.	48 hrs.	24 hrs.	24 hrs.
Duty hrs. to the police	8 Hrs. only / 2 days C.L.	24 hrs. on duty	8 Hrs.	8 Hrs.	8 hrs. / 5-day week	24 hrs.	8 Hrs.	40 hrs. per week	24 hrs.	40 hrs. per week
Stress recovery	No	Yes	No	No	Yes	Yes	Yes	Yes	Yes	Yes
Whether leaves are available or not	Yes	Yes	Yes	Yes	Yes	Yes	Yes	Yes	Yes	Yes
Whether permission of prosecutor is necessary to cause arrest ?	Yes	No	No	No	No	No	Yes	Yes	Yes	No.
Whether Social security scheme available or not	Available	Not well developed, infant stage	Available	Available	Available	Yes, partly	Available	Available	Yes	Available
Type of criminal justice system	Favours victim	Favours culprit	Favours victim	Favours victim	Favours victim	Favours culprit	Favours victim	Favours victim	Favours victim	Favours Victim

Table 4.3: Narratives of foreign police officers for a global picture

Source: Primary Data

Narratives of Foreign Police Officers For a Global Pictur

The author conducted video-recorded interviews and administered questionnaires to elicit responses from the ten foreign peacekeepers, who were spread across the globe while working on a United Nations Peacekeeping Mission. From the above interviews and subsequent data tabulation, as shown in Table 4.3, it is observed that deaths in police custody are rare in Europe and Scandinavian countries. If at all it happens, it is either a suicide or medical death due to pre-existing illness like drugs/ Alcohol/ depression, etc. In Africa and Asia, it has been observed from the interviews that torture and custodial deaths are prevalent and are due to torture/beating to detect property offenses or to extract a confession. In many countries, interviews and confessions are audio- or video-recorded and produced in a court of law.

In Europe and America, property insurance plays a vital role in preventing custodial interrogation. The insurance industry handles property loss. Hence, there is no pressure on the police to recover the stolen property. In most countries, the permitted detention/ custody period after arrest is 24 hours. In Sweden, it is 96 hours. It is also noted that in developed countries such as Scandinavia, the U.S., the U.K., and Denmark, the social security scheme is robust, and therefore, property offenses are less prevalent. Consequently, custodial torture or violence by police is also less common. Moreover, the insurance industry also covers the cost of property loss. The working hours are high, i.e., 24 hours in Ghana, Russia, the Philippines, and India. Hence, the stress on police officers and their resultant intolerant behavior results in custodial torture/violence. In many countries, the police operate under the close supervision of prosecutors, which influences their behavior toward suspects.

Technological remedies

Implementing emerging technologies will have a profound impact on prisons and lockups. Technologies such as the Internet of Things (IoT), artificial intelligence, facial recognition, and innovative layouts can all contribute to this.

Monitor, map, and manage custody. Therefore, technological remedies are proposed based on my 28 years of experience in various administrative roles as an Indian Police Service Officer to prevent such possible deaths and illicit activities in judicial and police custody.

5

SUMMARY OF FINDINGS

"Injustice anywhere is a threat to justice everywhere."

— Martin Luther King,

African-American civil rights activist

Verification of Objective -1

To examine the personality and behavioral dimensions of police personnel concerning custodial deaths and to evaluate their awareness levels towards the medico-legal aspects of custodial deaths.

Personality and Behavioral Aspects of the Respondents and Risk Factors that Contribute to Custodial Deaths

1. 60% of the accused (sample) belong to the age range between 35 and 44 years, and 40% belong to the age range between 20 and 35 years. Young adults and middle–aged police personnel with considerable experience in dealing with police interrogation have committed custodial death.

2. The majority (65%) of accused in custodial deaths were police constables, and sub-inspectors constituted 15% of the total sample.
3. The study reveals that the majority of respondents are males, and the majority of respondents are from the Kadiri Town Police Station.
4. The study shows that respondents with Impulsive behavior are more involved in custodial deaths when compared to respondents with reflective behavior.
5. The results show that 97% of the sample respondents exhibit intolerance of ambiguity. They tend to react with high anxiety, reflected as impatience and anger, leading to custodial deaths.
6. The result shows that the majority of the respondents possess the dimensions of tension and shrewdness, which may result in high involvement in custodial deaths of inmates.

Verification of Objective-2

To identify the causes of custodial deaths in Andhra Pradesh and analyze the organizational, psychological, and medical factors that contribute to custodial deaths.

Organizational Factors that Contribute to Custodial Deaths

1. The result shows that the majority (73%) of the respondents possess high and moderate frustration, which could be attributed to involvement in custodial deaths.
2. The study shows that 57.5% of the sample respondents perceive their work environment as non-conducive and unfriendly.

Psychological Factors that Contribute to Custodial Deaths

1. The result shows that 97.5% of the respondents have non-tolerant behavior (Test of Anxiety).
2. The result shows that 60% of the respondents have a reflective nature.
3. The result shows that most respondents have hypertension and frustration disorders.
4. The result shows that Tests of anxiety (intolerance) among the police personnel do have a significant effect on custodial death.
5. The result shows that Cognitive style (impulsive behavior) among police personnel does have a significant effect on custodial death.
6. The result shows that Police Personnel with diabetic problems do not tend to be more likely to be involved in custodial deaths.
7. The result shows that Police Personnel with peptic ulcers tend to be more likely to experience custodial death.
8. The result shows that Police Personnel with family problems tend to be more likely to be involved in custodial deaths.

Medical Factors Involved in Custodial Deaths

1. The result shows that 50% of the respondents were addicted to alcohol, and 27.5% of the respondents were addicted to the use of Tobacco.
2. It can be inferred that there is no significant difference in the evidence adduced from postmortem and inquest reports concerning injuries to the deceased persons in the custodial deaths.

3. It can be inferred that there is a significant difference in the evidence adduced from postmortem and inquest reports about the cause of death in the cases of custodial death.
4. It can be inferred that there is a significant difference among the statements given by different witnesses concerning postmortem reports in the cases of custodial death.

Verification of Objective-3

To assess the extent of applicability of D K Basu guidelines and other legal provisions about the arrest procedures, and to evaluate the issues of human rights sensitivity and ethical sensitivity of the police force at all levels involved in custodial deaths.

Compliance with Legal Provisions and D K Basu Guidelines about Custodial Deaths

1. The study reveals no compliance with the DK Basu guidelines in cases of arrest.
2. It is evident from the study that most of the victims in the custodial deaths belong to socially backward classes, and unemployed youth are more prone to the carnage compared to the other classes in society.
3. The study shows that out of the 30 victims, 54% of the deceased had no criminal history or bad antecedents.
4. The study shows that the cause of death, as declared by the police, significantly differs from the established cause.
5. The study shows that, whatever the cause of death, many of the deceased had injuries. Irrespective of the cause of death, many of the deceased had injuries.

6. The study shows that the average time for final judgment was approximately one year. Only 1/3rd of the deceased (from a sample) had received the compensation.

Verification of Objective -4

To assess the magnitude of risk to derive the vulnerability index and Custody Quotient about police officers and police stations involved in custodial deaths.

The Magnitude of Risk (Sign of Risk or Vulnerability)

1. The most affected age group of the deceased is 31 to 40 years (36.7%). About 70% of the deceased are above 30 years of age.
2. The study shows that more accused (20%) than deceased (3.3%) in the OC category, in contrast to the SC category, where there are more deceased (33.3%) than accused (7.5%).
3. It can be inferred that there is a significant difference between the police justification and the established cause of death in custody.
4. It can be inferred that there is no significant difference in the pattern of injuries and the cause of death shown in the police justification.
5. It can be inferred that there is a significant effect of organizational, psychological, medical, and legal factors in assessing risk factors for custodial deaths.
6. It can be inferred that there is no significant difference among the designations of the police personnel concerning the risk factor percentage in custodial deaths.

Vulnerability Scores, Vulnerability Index, and Custody Quotient of Custodial Deaths

The scores of vulnerability are calculated for Individual (health and psychological) (5 factors), Legal (11 factors), and Organizational (8 factors) using the following formula. The maximum value is calculated as 1.00, indicating 100% compliance. A Vulnerability index of 1.000 means the highest risk. There are more lapses in organizational and legal aspects than in individuals. Before handing over a victim for custody, the risk factor should be assessed. If the risk is found to be less than a threshold value, only custody should be given to a particular officer or the police station.

Verification of Objective -5

1. To develop a proposed Police Management Model for preventing custodial deaths.
2. A police management model was proposed, along with suggested strategies and measures to prevent custodial deaths, in an elaborate manner, under Chapter 5 of the present study. The broad headings of the proposed police management model by the author are as follows:
3. Application of Technology in the Prevention of Custodial Deaths with the Participation of the Public.
4. Prevention of death in police remand, transit, and escape.

Organogram - Police Management - Remedies:

1. Training activities for the Staff Members.
2. Psychological assumption
3. Proposed model lock-up with a toilet attached.
4. Risk minimization management strategies.

5. Administrative implications.
6. Adopting a risk management approach to reduce custodial deaths.
7. Graded Approach to Interrogation Procedures.
8. Shared leadership and police.
9. Controlling police discretion.
10. Policy development recommendations.
11. Considerations on sudden custodial death investigation.
12. Checklist for investigators on custodial deaths.
13. Other Considerations.
14. Untapped potential for privatization/ outsourcing of police services.
15. Quality Management Issues in Police Organizations.
16. Capability Maturity Model (CMM) for Police.
17. Predicting the potential risk.
18. Narratives of foreign police Officers for a global picture.
19. Technological Remedies.

Implementing emerging technologies will enhance the impeccable observation of prisons and lock-ups. Technologies such as the Internet of Things (IoT), artificial intelligence, facial recognition, and innovative prison layouts can help monitor, map, and manage prisons.

Therefore, technological remedies are proposed based on experience over 25 years of service at various administrative levels as an Indian Police Service Officer, for avoiding such possible deaths and illicit activities in judicial and police custody.

Verification Of Hypotheses

Null Hypothesis No.	Test Applied	Result
Ho1Tested through six sub-Hypothesis	Chi-Square Test	Rejected
Ho2	ANOVA	Accepted
Ho3	ANOVA	Rejected
Ho4	ANOVA	Rejected
Ho5	Chi-Square Test	Rejected
Ho6	Chi-Square Test	Accepted
Ho7	ANOVA	Rejected
Ho8	T-test	Accepted
Ho9	ANOVA	Accepted

6

SUGGESTIONS

The Police Management Model was proposed to prevent custodial deaths. Elaborate suggestions and strategies were provided and explained in the previous chapter under the heading 'Proposed Police Management Model.' However, in light of the present research findings, particular policy suggestions were given for the effective prevention of custodial deaths in the state of Andhra Pradesh. They are as follows:

Stern implementation of existing laws and guidelines

1. The existing legal provisions and legislations regarding criminal investigation procedures are sufficient, with only certain modifications needed for the current laws. Specific provisions of the Indian Evidence Act require amendments, particularly concerning the burden of proof. Presently, the burden of proof remains on the plaintiff, and this should be reversed.
2. There should exist a comprehensive law on torture.

3. The guidelines laid down by the Hon'ble Supreme Court of India in the cases of Joginder Kumar Vs State of U.P. and D.K. Basu Vs State of West Bengal are to be strictly implemented in the manner in which the Apex Court has prescribed them.
4. The guidelines specified by the Apex Court in these cases comprise rules and regulations relating to arrests, detention, and the rights of the person. It also includes provisions for CCTV in police stations and prisons, and involves the establishment of the state's Human Rights Commission, which will oversee trials and prisoners. Implementation and monitoring of all these aspects by an independent agency should be done at each level under the guidance of the court. These steps contribute a lot to the prevention of custodial torture and custodial deaths.

Policy reforms in the Police administration

1. Necessary amendments are to be made to the existing Police Act of 1861.
2. The Supreme Court, in the case of Prakash Singh v. Union of India, directed the Central and State Governments to address the existing problems in the Police law and make the necessary changes to the Police Act of 1861. But action has yet to be taken by the National Police Commission in this regard.
3. There is abundant power given to the police force, but more responsible use of great power is required.
4. The concept of vicarious liability (law of torts) applies to senior officials, wherein the superior officers are held responsible for the acts committed by their subordinate

officers. This will help project some accountability that is currently lacking in the police administration.

5. The practice of posting, promotion, and transfers across departmental divisions should be stopped. The duties of security work are assigned to a specific division within the police department, while crime and criminal investigation work are assigned to another specific division. This will prevent confusion and anxiety among the police personnel. This practice will indirectly help the particular divisions in the police department to hone their skills and approaches toward the work assigned to them.
6. The application of science and the use of the mind are to be promoted among the police department's human resources. Our Nation still needs to catch up in the application of forensic science for solving crimes. The advancements and developments of forensic science and technology will undoubtedly help the police to crack criminal cases without applying torture.
7. Mind Intelligence shall be used to manipulate the minds of accused persons, and intelligence can be applied to collect evidence and proof. The application of science can validate that evidence.
8. Counseling sessions are to be provided for the police personnel, creating a system that deals with mental health and increases the work efficiency of the police personnel.

Technological developments and innovative management policies.

1. Implementing emerging technologies will have a profound impact on prisons and lock-ups. Technologies such as the

Internet of Things (IoT), artificial intelligence, facial recognition, and innovative prison layouts can help monitor, map, and manage prisons.

2. All police vehicles are equipped with GIS/GPS/IoT-enabled audio/video recording cameras featuring tamper-proof hard disc casings, which should be enabled by legislation.
3. Thus, all the prisoners' escort vehicles, which transport prisoners to and from jails, courts, and police stations, can be safe and productive.
4. The postmortem in custodial deaths gives a big room for speculation of police managing the forensic pathologist. To make the medico-legal autopsy more objective, meaningful, documentable, reproducible, and transparent, the technology of non-invasive autopsy, including whole-body scanning, generation of 3D digital visualization with an audit trail, and radio imaging, should be utilized.
5. Thus, 75% of the autopsies can be performed without opening up the body, and the remaining 25% can be opened, which warrants an open postmortem.
6. Histopathological examination of the tissues can be performed to determine whether injuries occurred antemortem or postmortem. Judges will gain a better understanding of the visuals and scene reconstruction, as well as postmortem visuals from all angles.
7. Any arrest, regardless of location, must be documented with GIS/GPS evidence-based photographs or videos that cover 360 degrees of the scene, including the public present at the scene, who can be contacted later for evidence.
8. Audio-video links between courts, jails, and police stations

should be made mandatory to save petrol, diesel, and person-hours, among other resources, through legislation.

9. A centralized lock-up monitoring system for a cluster of police stations is made with proper audio-video recording to avoid habeas corpus petitions in the High Courts. Software for custody management and interrogation is to be prepared.

Thorough investigation and a greater degree of punishment in the cases of custodial torture.

1. There should exist an independent inquiry concerning every case of custodial deaths under the supervision of a judicial magistrate. In current circumstances, either suspension or termination is the formal mode of punishment in the cases of custodial torture. A greater degree of punishment is to be awarded to the accused persons who were found guilty in the cases of custodial torture and custodial deaths.

Amendments in Bureaucratic policies

1. Bureaucratic policies require some amendments, and the attitudes of governments regarding responsible policing need to change.

Unwarranted pressure from the government, Senior officials, and the Public

1. A massive amount of unwarranted pressure is being created on police officers working at lower levels by senior officers and the government to solve cases. This unwarranted pressure makes officers use torture to extract the truth or

confession. This pressure is one of the reasons for custodial torture. The Supreme Court had directed the central and state governments to ensure that no unwarranted pressure is created on the police. Hence, steps are to be taken in these directions to regulate the exertion of force from various sources. Vengeance is not an option in a democratic country.

The Mindset of People and the Role of Media

1. The media plays a significant role in changing the mindset of the people. The media must understand their responsibility, as it affects a person's thinking. The media often portrays an accused person as a criminal even before the judgment is released. The media's role in many cases has been questioned by the people of the legal fraternity and even by the courts. This will also help in keeping a check on police administration.

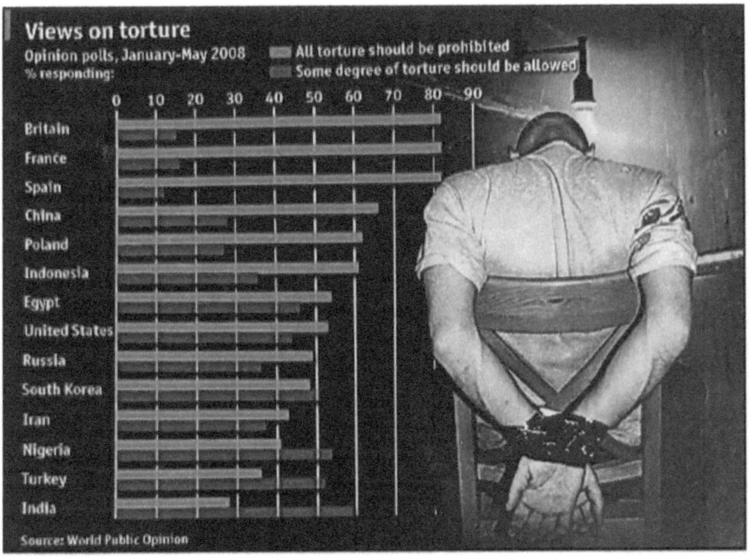
Views on torture
Opinion polls, January-May 2008
% responding:
All torture should be prohibited
Some degree of torture should be allowed
0 10 20 30 40 50 60 70 80 90
Britain
France
Spain
China
Poland
Indonesia
Egypt
United States
Russia
South Korea
Iran
Nigeria
Turkey
India
Source: World Public Opinion

CONCLUSION

Custodial deaths have become a serious concern in our society. A sudden custodial death involves an environment of complex factors. As members of society continue to lead criminal lives, the likelihood that custodial deaths may occur and pose problems for police, medical, and legal professions, over and above society in general. Therefore, administrators, police officers, healthcare personnel, and trainers are motivated to be prepared for these situations by conducting thorough investigations. The evaluated data obtained from authentic sources showed 183 custodial deaths.

A significant difference exists between the deaths of detainees in prison and of those in police custody. Remedial and preventive steps are highly recommended in the present investigation. As per the obligatory directives of the Supreme Court of India, the following risk management measures are recommended: a graded approach to interrogation and organizational police management involving training and psychological assessments.

Further, a model lock-up design based on emerging technologies such as IoT is recommended. These remedial measures will help prevent illicit, aggressive, and suicidal activities and improve the lifestyle of detainees. The recommendations suggested in this research could assist in minimizing future incidents of custodial deaths. It is the moral responsibility of the police department to maintain order, and a fundamental right of a person being detained or arrested. Police Officers should uphold fundamental rights. We are not a banana republic or a police state.

Police are our protectors, and they should act like it. The existing laws are not used properly.

The author made a lot of effort to arrive at logical and meaningful conclusions. Based on this, he gave appropriate suggestions to police management to prevent or minimize custodial problems leading to the deaths of the accused. The study's findings are beneficial to police personnel at various levels in dealing with accused individuals while they are in custody in a refined manner.

LIST OF ABBREVIATIONS

AIR	All India Reporter
ADG	Additional Director General of Police
(HR)	(Human Rights)
ADM	Additional District Magistrate
ANOVA	Analysis of Variants
APLJR	Andhra Pradesh Law Journal Report
A/V	Audio/Video
BPRD	Bureau of Police Research and Development
CBCID	Criminal Branch Crime Investigation Department
CD	Case Diary
CID	Criminal Investigation Department
CMO	Chief Medical Officer
CMS	Chief Medical Superintendent
CO	Circle Officer
CrPC	Criminal Procedure Code, 1973
CWJC	Civil Writ Jurisdiction
DCRB	District Crime Records Bureau
DIG	Deputy Inspector General of Police
DM	District Magistrate
DSP	Deputy Superintendent of Police
ENT	Ear, Nose and Throat
FIR	First Information Report
GD	General Diary

GPS	Global Positioning System
HC	Head Constable
IACP	International Association of Chiefs of Police
IEA	Indian Evidence Act, 1872
IGP	Inspector General of Police
IPC	Indian Penal Code, 1861
LRC	Law Reports of Commonwealth
MIR	Magisterial Inquiry Report
NCRB	National Crime Records Bureau
NDPS	Narcotic Drugs Psychotropic Substances
NHRC	National Human Rights Commission
PO	Probation Officer
POTA	Prevention of Terrorist Activities Act, 2002
SCC	Supreme Court Cases
SCJL	Supreme Court Judges Library
SDM	Sub District Magistrate
SHO	Station House Officer
SIS	Special Investigation Squads
SI	Sub Inspector
SP	Superintendent of Police
SPO	Senior Probation Officer
SSP	Senior Superintendent of Police

BIBLIOGRAPHY

1. Alison L, Sarangi S, Wright, A. Human rights is not enough: The need for demonstrating efficacy of an ethical approach to interviewing in India. Legal and Criminological Psychology, 2008;13(1):89-106.
2. Amnesty International Annual Report 1992, p. 34-35.
3. Amnesty International Annual Report 2008.
4. Amnesty International India – Torture, Rape and Deaths in Custody. New York: Amnesty International Publications, 1992, p. 85.
5. Andersen JP, Dorai, M, Papazoglou K, Arnetz BB. Diurnal and reactivity measures of cortisol in response to intensive resilience and tactical training among Special Forces police. Journal of Occupational and Environmental Medicine, 2016;58:e242-e248.
6. Andersen JP, Papazoglou K, Koskelainen M, Nyman M. Knowledge and training regarding the link between trauma and health: A national survey of Finnish police officers. SAGE Open, 2015;5:2158244015580380.
7. Andersen JP, Papazoglou K. Compassion fatigue and compassion satisfaction among police officers: An understudied topic. International Journal of Emergency Mental Health and Human Resilience, 2015;17:661-663.
8. APA Amicus Briefs by Issue https://www.apa.org/about/offices/ogc/ amicus/index-issues (Accessed on October 18, 2020).
9. Bandura, A. Influence of models' reinforcement contingencies on the acquisition of imitative responses. Journal of Personality and Social Psychology. 1965;1(6):589-595.
10. Bansal YS, Murali G, Singh D. Custodial deaths – an overview of the prevailing healthcare scenario. J Indian Acad Forensic Med. 2010;32:315-315.
11. Bardale RV, Dixit PG. Suicide behind bars: A 10-year retrospective study. Indian J Psychiatry. 2015;57(1): 81-84.
12. Baron RA and Byrne D. Social Psychology, understanding Human Interaction, 5th Ed, London: Prentice – Hall International Inc, 1998, p.307.
13. Bartol CR, A Psychological Approach -5thed, New Jersy: Prentice Hall Inc, 1999.
14. Basu DK Vs State of West Bengal 1997 Cri.LJ 743 (750) (para-22).
15. Basu DK vs. State of West Bengal, AIR 1997 SC 610, at 615.
16. Basu DK, Ashok K. Johri vs State of West Bengal,1997
17. Basu DK, Ashok K. Johri vs State Of U.P on 18 December, 1996.
18. Baxi PM. Public Interest Litigation 18, Second Edition, New Delhi: Asoka Law House, 2006, p. 22.

19. Beck AJ, Maruschak LM. Mental health treatment in state prisons, 2000.U.S. Department of Justice, Washington, DC: Bureau of Justice Statistics, 2001.
20. Berkowitz L. Simple views of Aggression; An essay review; Contemporary Issues in Social Psychology, 2nd Ed, California: Brooks/Cole Publishing Company, 1973, p.194:201.
21. Berkowitz L. The Concept of Aggressive Drive: Some Additional Considerations. Advances in Experimental Social Psychology, 1965;2:301- 329.
22. Bernstein JM Political Concepts: Torture:http://www.politicalconcepts.org/torture-j-m-bernstein/#fn1 (Accessed on October 18, 2020).
23. BPRD Report. Research Studies on Police and Prison Issues (1970-2016) Compendium. Bureau of Police Research & Development, Bureau of Police Research & Development, New Delhi: Ministry of Home Affairs, 2017.
24. Budner SN. Intolerance of ambiguity as a personality variable. Journal of Personality, 1962;30(1):29-50.
25. Bulman P. Using technology to make prisons and jails safer, NIJ Journal, 2009; 262:38-41.
26. Bureau of Justice Assistance. http://www.bja.gov/Publications/IACP-Wrongful_Convictions_Summit_Report.pdf (Accessed on October 18, 2020).
27. Carver CS, Glass DC. Coronary-prone behavior pattern and interpersonal aggression. Journal of Personality and Social Psychology, 1978;36:361-366.
28. CCTNS. Crime and Criminal Tracking Network & Systems.
29. Chahal PS, Aggarwal A, Singh SP, Kakkar GS, Kumar D. Custodial deaths: An unaddressed issue. J Forens Med Toxicol [Internet]. 2020;37(2):52-4. Available from: http://dx.doi.org/10.5958/0974-4568.2020.00030.7
30. Chattopadhyay S, Agarwal KG. Class, culture and organisation, New Delhi: National Labor Institute, 1976.
31. Cicero. On the Republic on the Laws, London: Loeb Classic Library, 1989, p. 467.
32. Cole DA, Ciesla J, Dallaire DH, Jacquez FM, Pineda A, LaGrange B, et al. Emergence of attributional style and its relation to depressive symptoms. Journal of Abnormal Psychology. 2008;117:16–31
33. Cole DA, Jacquez FM, LaGrange B, et al. A longitudinal study of cognitive risks for depressive symptoms in children and young adolescents. J Early Adolesc. 2011;31(6):782-816.
34. Compact Oxford Dictionary, New Delhi: Oxford University Press, 2001.
35. Conrad and S Dinitz (eds), In fear of each other, Lexington, MA: Lanham, USA. Lexington Books.
36. Cope S, Leishman F, Starie P. Globalization, new public management and the enabling state. Futures of police management. International Journal of Public Sector Management 1977;10:444-460.
37. Crime in India, Statistics, NCRB, National Crime Records Bureau, New Delhi: Ministry of Home Affairs. 2016.
38. Custodial deaths: A ten years experience from central Maharashtra. J Indian Acad Forensic Med [Internet] 2016;38(3):299.
39. Daniel A. Giffiula G. Criminal Behavior. University of Utah & George S. Everly Jr. Loyola College of Maryland, 1977, p. 177.
40. Das S. Analysis of Custodial Deaths in India: an infringement of human rights. Journal of Law Students and Researchers. 2020.
41. DK Basu Vs State of W.B. Cri.LJ 743 (750) (para-22), 1977.
42. Dollard J, Miller NE, Doob LW, Mowrer OH, Sears R R. (1939). Frustration and Aggression. New Haven, US: Yale University Press, 1939.

43. Eagly AH, Steffen VJ. Gender and aggressive behavior: A meta-analytic review of the social psychological literature. Psychological Bulletin, 1986;100(3):309–330.
44. Furnham A, Alison L. Theories of Crime, Attitudes to Punishment and Juror Bias Amongst Police, Offenders and the General Public. Personality and Individual Differences, 1994;17(1):35-48.
45. Gallagher, B. 2002.Integrating capability maturity model integration (CMMI) for operational organizations. Carnegie Mellon University.
46. Geller WA, Toch H. And justice for all: understanding and controlling police abuse of force. Washington, DC: Police Executive Research Forum, 1995.
47. Girdano DA, Everly GS Jr, Dusek DE. Controlling Stress and Tension, 8th Edition, New York: Pearson Publishers, 2009.
48. Glan DC. Behavior Patterns Stress and Coronary Disease. Hillsdale, NJ: Erlbaum, 1977.
49. Goldman H.The limits of Clockwork. The Neurobiology of Violent Behavior. In J.P Conrad and S Dinitz (eds), In fear of each other, Lexington, MA: Lexington Books, 1977.
50. Gottschalk P. Stages of knowledge management systems in police investigations. Knowledge-Based Systems, 2006;19(6):381-387.
51. Gottschalk, P. Knowledge Management Systems in Law Enforcement: Technologies and Techniques. Idea Group Publishing, 2006.
52. http://www.iapdeathsincustody.independent.gov.uk (Accessed on 06 May , 2026).
53. Hartley TA, Burchfiel CM, Fekedulegn D, Andrew ME, Violanti, JM. Health disparities in police officers: Comparisons to the U.S. general populations—International Journal of Emergency Mental Health, 2011;13:211-220.
54. Hiss J, Kahana T. Medico legal investigation of death in custody: A postmortem procedure for detection of blunt force injuries. Am J Forensic Med Pathol 1996;17:312-14.
55. Hollin C. Psychology and crime: An introduction to criminological psychology. London: Routledge, 1989.
56. Human Rights Watch report (2016).
57. International Association of Police chiefs (IACP) Report
58. Jhamad AR, Sikary AK, Millo T. Analysis of Custodial Deaths in New Delhi: A 13 Years Study. J Indian Acad Forensic Med. 2014;36(1):19-22.
59. Joginder Kumar v. State of Uttar Pradesh, (1994) 4 SCC 260.
60. Johan M.G. van der Dennen (orig. 1980) Problems in the Concepts and Definitions of Aggression, Violence, and Some Related Terms.
61. Jonathan Law, A Dictionary of Law (8 ed.), London: Oxford University Press 2015.
62. Joseph, P. N., Violanti, J. M., Donahue, R., Andrew, M. E., Trevisan, M., Burchfiel, C. M., Dorn, J. (2009).Police work and subclinical atherosclerosis.
63. Judgments Information system. Judgments of the Supreme court of India and several High Courts.
64. Kappeler V, Vaughn M, del Carmen RV. Death in detention: An analysis of police liability for negligent failure to prevent suicide. Journal of Criminal Justice -1991;19:381-393.
65. Krosch C, Binkard V, Blackbourne B. Final report of the custody death task force. San Diego, California Police Department, San Diego, 1992.
66. Kuchewar SV, Bhosle SH, Shrigiriwar MB, Padole TO. Custody-related deaths in Maharashtra state of India – Analysis of autopsies performed at a medical Teaching Institute during the period 2000-2018. J Forensic Leg Med [Internet].
67. Kulik J A, Brown R. (1979). Frustration, attribution of blame, and aggression. Journal of Experimental Social Psychology, 1979;15(2):183-194.
68. Kumar K. Custodial deaths in India, Journal of Gujarat Research Society, 2020; 22: 644-648.

69. Lawrence C. Investigator protocol: Sudden in-custody death. Police Chief 2004;1:25-31.
70. LeBlanc M M, Barling J. Understanding the Many Faces of Workplace Violence. In S. Fox & P. E. Spector (Eds.), Counterproductive work behavior: Investigations of actors and targets. American Psychological Association. 2005;30:41-63.
71. Levine, J M and Moreland RL. Small Groups. In D TGilbert, S T Fiske and G Lindzey (eds); Handbook of Social Psychology, Boston: McGraw Hill, 1998;2:414-469.
72. Lobnikar B, Pagon M. The prevalence and the nature of police cynicism in Slovenia. Document No.: 207979, December 2004. https://www.ncjrs.gov-
73. pdffiles1/nij/mesko/207979.pdf (Accessed on October 18, 2020).
74. Lorenz K, Wilson MK, Huxley J.On Aggression .Routledge, New York: Psychology Press. 2002, p. 61.
75. Lorenz, K. (1963). Das Sogenannte Böse, Wien: Borotha Schoeler Verlag; translated as On Aggression, London: Methuen 1967.
76. Lorenz, K. (1963). Das Sogenannte Böse, Wien: Borotha Schoeler Verlag; translated as On Aggression, London: Methuen 1967.
77. Mandar RS, Kailash UZ, Anand BM, Pradeep KM, Sujata PL. Custodial Deaths: A Ten Years of Experience from Central Maharashtra. Journal of Indian Academy of Forensic Medicine. 2016 ;38(3):299-302.
78. Mark F. The Ambiguity of Accountability: Deaths in Custody, and the Regulation of Police Power. Current Issues in Criminal Justice. 1994;6(2):234-251.
79. Mark K, Laurence A, Emily H (2008) Sex offenders' perceptions of the effectiveness and fairness of humanity, dominance, and displaying an understanding of cognitive distortions in police interviews: A vignette study, Psychology, Crime & Law, 14:5, 435-449, DOI: 10.1080/10683160801950523
80. Mathias CW, Marsh-Richard DM, Dougherty DM. Behavioral Measures of Impulsivity and the Law. Behav Sci Law. 2008;26(6):691–707.
81. Mayer KE. The Physiology of Aggression, New York: Harper & Row, 1976.
82. McCreary DR, Thompson MM. Development of two reliable and valid measures of stressors in policing: The Operational and Organizational Police Stress Questionnaires. International Journal of Stress Management 2006;13:494-518.
83. Mirkov A, Gelles M. The future of policing. The policing innovations shaping the future of law enforcement.
84. Morris D. The Naked Ape: A Zoologist's Study of the Human Animal. New York: Vintage Penguin, 1994.
85. Moyer KE. Kinds of aggression and their physiological basis. Communications in Behavioral Biology, 1968;2:65-87.
86. Naik R, Shaha KK, Chaudhari VA. Are prisons safe? Death due to depression while in custody: a case report. Int J Res Med Sci. 2016;4(4):1304-1306.
87. National Summit on Wrongful Convictions: Building a Systemic Approach to Prevent Wrongful Convictions Report from the International Association of Chiefs of Police/U.S. Department of Justice, Office of Justice Programs Wrongful Convictions Summit August 2013
88. NHRC Human right case statistics, 2020
89. NHRC, National Human Rights Commission Annual report 2002- 2003.
90. National Police Commission ; fourth report (June 1980, at 27 26) cited in Amnesty International, p. 34

91. OHCHR 1996-2020, International Human Rights Law https://www.ohchr.org/EN/ProfessionalInterest/Pages/InternationalLaw.aspx(Accessed on October 18, 2020).
92. Ozdemir F, Oner-Ozkan B. The nature of crime: Different approaches toward the causes of the criminal act. Nesne Psikol Derg [Internet] 2017;5(11). Available from http://dx.doi.org/10.7816/nesne-05-11-01
93. PACE Code G 2012.Revised code of practice for the statutory power of arrest by police officers. Government of United Kingdom.
94. Parameswaran EG, Beena C. An Invitation to Psychology, Tata McGraw-Hill, New Delhi, 1988.
95. Parker AL, Mohr PB, Wilson C. Attitudinal and personality predictors of diversionary behavior by police. Policing [Internet] 2004;27(1):9-21, Available from http://dx.doi.org/10.1108/13639510410519886
96. Patnaik AK. Model protocol for autopsies in custodial deaths. Indian Journal of Medical Ethics 1999;7(2):48-49.
97. Police Standing Order 456-1, Andhra Pradesh Police Manual (Investigation), Part-I Vol. II A. Government of Andhra Pradesh Police Department, Amaravati. 2017, 860-861.
98. Abu Ghraib: A Global Family Portrait, The Believer, 3/2 (March 2005).
99. Reay DT, Eisele JW. Death from law enforcement neck holds. Am J Forens Med Path. 1982;3:253-258.
100. Rebecca Gonsalvez , Vijay Hiremath. Ignoring Custodial Deaths in India. Economic and Political Weekly 2013;48(19).
101. Reiss AJ Jr. Consequences of Compliance and Deterrence Models of Law Enforcement for the Exercise of Police Discretion. Discretion in Law Enforcement 1984;47(4):83-122.
102. Ross DL, Chan TC. Forensic Science and Medicine: Sudden Deaths in Custody, Totowa, NJ: Humana Press Inc., 2006.
103. Ross DL. A content analysis of the emerging trends in the use of non-lethal force research in policing. Law Enforcement Executive Forum 2005;5:121- 148.
104. Ross DL. Civil Liability in Criminal Justice (3rd ed.), Cincinnati: Anderson Publishing, 2003.
105. Roy Roberg, Jack Kunythendell, Kenneth Novak, Police Nabagenbt, 3rd ed, California: Roxbury Publishing Company, 2002.
106. Ruiz G, Wangmo T, Mutzenberg P, Sinclair J, Elger BS. Understanding death in custody: a case for a comprehensive definition. J Bioeth Inq. 2014;11(3):387-398.
107. Saggi D. Custodial Deaths and Role of Judiciary: A Critical Analysis. Published on 25 Jul 2020.
108. Saini RS. Custodial Torture in Law and Practice with Reference to India 36 JILI (1994) at 166.
109. Sane MR, Zine KU, Mugadlimath AB, Mishra PK, Sujata PL.
110. Sarah VH. Making Prisons Safer Through Technology. Corrections Today, 2003, 65(2), https://www.ncjrs.gov/pdffiles1/nij/04_03.pdf (Accessed on October 18, 2020).
111. Sarangi, IPS Director General (Investigation) at NHRC, Human rights is not enough: The need for demonstrating efficacy of an ethical approach to interviewing in India; Centre for Investigative Psychology.
112. Section 164 CrPC cases data.
113. Section 176 CrPC cases data.
114. Selye H. A syndrome produced by diverse noxious agents. Nature, London 1936;138:32.

115. Selye H. The physiology and pathology of exposure to stress. In: A Treatise Based on the Concepts of the General Adaptation Syndrome and the Diseases of Adaptation. Montreal: Acta Inc. 1950.
116. Shakya NK, Siddiqui MN, Shakya P, Singh NB, Gupta OP, Ahmad N. Custodial deaths- a retrospective study. Indian Journal of Applied Research 2018;8(5):67-69.
117. Siddle BK. Defensive tactics instructor manual. Pressure Point Control Tactics, Bellville, IL: Management Systems, 1996.
118. Social Science Statistics https://www.socscistatistics.com/tests(Accessed on October 18, 2020).
119. Soyemi SS, Faduyile AF, Sanni AD, Mgbehoma AI, Obafunwa JO. Custodial deaths seen in the Office of the Chief Medical Examiner, Lagos, Nigeria: An 11-year autopsy study. Med Sci Law [Internet]. 2021;61 (4); 286-91.
120. Stepka E, Basinska M. (2014).Chronic fatigue and strategies of coping with occupational stress in police officers. Medycyna Pracy, 2014;65:229-238.
121. Stoner J. Risky and Cautious Shifts in Group decisions. Journal of Experimental Social Psycholoigy. 1968;4:442-459.
122. Storr A. Human Aggression, New York: Atheneum, 1968.
123. Taylor SE, Peplan LA, O Sears AD, Social Psychology; ed 12th, New Delhi: Pearson Education Inc, 2006.
124. Tedeschi LG. Methodology in the forensic sciences. Documents of human right abuses. Am J Forensic Med Pathol. 1984;5:301-303.
125. The Hindu. News Paper Clipping, Custodial death. Published on 10-05- 2003.(Accessed on October 18, 2020).
126. Todd PM. Heuristics for Decision and Choice. International Encyclopedia of the Social & Behavioral Sciences, New York: Elsevier, 2001, 6676-6679.
127. Universal Declaration of Human Rights. https://www.ohchr.org/EN/UDHR/Documents/UDHR_Translations/eng.pdf
128. Violanti JM, Burchfiel CM, Hartley TA, Mnatsakanova A, Fekedulegn D, Andrew ME, Vila BJ. A typical work hours and metabolic syndrome among police officers. Archives of Environmental & Occupational Health, 2009;64:194-201.
129. Vipra J. Police custody death in Indian jails statistics released by NCRB. The Hans India News Paper. Published on 18thJune, 2016. https://www.thehansindia.com/posts/index/National/2016-06-18/Police-custody-death-in-Indian-jails-Statistics-released-by-NCRB/236074 Accessed on October 18, 2020.
130. Virkkunen M, Goldman D, Nielsen DA, Linnoila M. Low brain serotonin turnover rate (low CSF 5-HIAA) and impulsive violence. Journal of Psychiatry and Neuroscience. 1995;20:271-275.
131. Walsh K J, Henry VE. Compstat, OODA loops and police performance management – policing. Journal of Policy and Practice. 2008;2(3)
132. Wirth MD, Burch J, Shivappa N, Violanti JM, Burchfiel CM, Fekedulegn D, Charles LE, Steck SE, Hurley TG, Vena JE, Hébert JR. Association of a dietary inflammatory index with inflammatory indices and metabolic syndrome among police officers. J Occup Environ Med. 2014;56(9):986-989.
133. Worchel S. The effect of three types of arbitrary thwarting on the instigation to aggression. Journal of Personality. 1974;42(2):300-318.
134. Wuestewald T, Chief of Police, Broken Arrow, Oklahoma, and Steinheider B, Shared Leadership: Can Empowerment Work in Police Organizations? 2006.

135. Zhao J, He N, Lovrich N. Predicting five dimensions of police officer stress: Looking more deeply into organizational settings for sources of police stress. Police Quarterly, 2002;5:43-62.
136. Zillmann D. Transfer of excitation in emotional behavior. In J. T. Cacioppo & Petty RE (Eds.), Social psychophysiology: A sourcebook. New York: Guilford Press, 1983, p. 215-240.
137. 2020;70(101915):101915

ABOUT THE AUTHOR

Dr. A. Ravi Shankar, IPS is a distinguished Indian Police Service officer currently serving as the **Director General of Police (DGP), Crime Investigation Department (CID), Andhra Pradesh**.

Born on **20 October 1968** at the Air Force Station in Chakeri, Kanpur, he comes from a family with a strong service background — his father served as a Flight Engineer in the Indian Air Force with over 10,500 flying hours.

Dr. Ravi Shankar's educational background is diverse and impressive. He earned his **MBBS degree from JIPMER (Pondicherry Central University)** in 1991 and subsequently attained a **PG Diploma in Hospital and Health Care Management** from Symbiosis University and a **Master's Degree in Police Management** from Osmania University. In 2023, he completed his **Ph.D. in Management Studies** from Acharya Nagarjuna University, Guntur.

Before joining the police service, he worked as an emergency medical officer and performed more than 250 medico-legal autopsies, presenting evidence in courts as a certified forensic pathologist.

Over a career spanning nearly three decades, Dr. Ravi Shankar has held key positions across India, including leadership roles in anti-Maoist operations with Greyhounds, superintendent of police in various districts, and senior posts in the **National Investigation Agency (NIA)** where he led investigations into terror networks and major blast cases.

He has also overseen law and order, anti-corruption work, drug control administration, and served as CEO of the Arogyasri Health Assurance Scheme, which later contributed to the national Ayushman Bharat programme.

Dr. Ravi Shankar's contributions have earned him numerous honors, including the **President's Police Medal for Gallantry**, **Distinguished Service Awards**, national innovation awards, and recognition for election management excellence.

A committed public servant, he continues to shape policing and public safety in Andhra Pradesh with a focus on technology, community engagement, and investigative excellence.

www.ingramcontent.com/pod-product-compliance
Lightning Source LLC
Chambersburg PA
CBHW031320230926
51848CB00001B/22